Genisis

The author is well versed in the subject which is loosely termed sacred geometry. As he was trained in military survey techniques and owned a reprographic company he could produce fugitive maps at the scale he required and then apply a technique used in World War II, or an adaptation of it, to provide high-speed mapping from aerial photographs.

Although it has never been fully understood why, the pentagram (a five-pointed star) has always been at the root of matters esoteric. With this in mind templets were prepared based upon 36° radials and when applied to the valley of mystery – Rennes-le-Château – they produced unbelievable correspondences between churches and châteaux which dated between the 11th and 12th century AD. Even more remarkable, if not unbelievable, was the fact that the pentagonal geometry was interlaced with the Paris meridian, which was supposedly not established until the 1600's. We are here immediately confronted with a chronological impossibility, but only the first of many.

The pentagram, generated by what is now referred to as the circle of churches, is in itself indicative of a sophisticated mathematical intelligence. In order to construct it the circle, contrary to normal practice, is divided into fifteen portions and not five as is the case in a regular pentagram. It was at this point that the author recognised the geometry was a symbolical representation of an Egyptian legend; the story of Isis and Osiris. Osiris's body was dismembered by his brother god Set, who was husband of Nephthys and who lusted after Isis, wife of Osiris. Here then are the gods who provided the geometric and mathematical solution of the temple at Rennes-le-Château – significantly their initials spell the name of the enigmatic organisation, the Priory of Sion, which claims to be the custodian of the greatest secret of mankind. Furthermore, the numbers attributed to these gods and confirmed in the *Pyramid Texts* total 58, the previously unexplained number of the Priory of Sion. This number was that which appeared on a skull revered by the Knights Templar. The identity of this famous skull of Baphomet is revealed.

Having once recognised the source of the numerical keys implicit in the geometry, the author sought and found others with which to continue the solution of the geometry. He then identified famous works of art which were related to the mystery. Then followed a remarkable chain of events which culminated in the recognition of a vast temple plan marked on the ground. At first sight it seemed there were small errors in what had previously appeared to be a perfect symbolic temple covering some forty square miles of landscape. Detailed examination of these errors showed them to be intentional. What would have been a symbolic circle of 360,000 inches in diameter had been enlarged to 372,564 inches. Twice the speed of light!

Any attempt to date the design failed, its origin was lost in

---

LARGE SCALE MAP OF THE SOLUTION (24″ × 30″)

For those who want to check more carefully and for those who want to carry on the Mathematical Research, large scale (approximately 1:25,000)) copies of the map printed in grey, with the geometry overprinted in distinctive colours, are available from the publisher.

To: Baton Press Limited, 44 Holden Park Road, Southborough, Tunbridge Wells, Kent TN4 0ER

From:

Please supply ..... copies of the map of the solution to the Rennes Valley.

I enclose a cheque/P.O. for

Send this coupon with £6.50 plus £1.00 p&p

Subsequent copies £12.50

the mists of antiquity. Naturally it was of prime importance to establish whether the speed of light factor was coincidental or intentional. The continuing search left no doubt, for the number was further demonstrated in the geometry and confirmed in the measurements of the tomb illustrated in Poussin's *Les Bergers D'Arcadie*. Little wonder that Louis XIV went to considerable lengths to obtain the painting. A new meaning is also now apparent in the mysterious letter received by the King's Superintendent of Finances, Nicolas Fouquet. Fouquet's brother had met Poussin in Rome and wrote as follows:– 'He and I discussed certain things, which I shall with ease be able to explain to you in detail – things which will give you, through Monsieur Poussin, advantages which even kings would have great pains to draw from him and which, according to him, it is possible that nobody else will ever rediscover in the centuries to come. And what is more, these are things so difficult to discover that nothing now on this earth can prove of better fortune nor be their equal.'

Further implications of the geometry and the secret doctrine contained in it left the author in no doubt of the validity of that letter. In one respect, however, it was wrong – it *has* been discovered! This discovery has opened a door resulting in a solution which leads us through the massacre of the Cathars to the Arthurian legends. It reveals the previously unpublished secrets of the Grail, the Rose Cross, the Crucifixion and the building of the Temple of Solomon. Furthermore it discloses the secret of that most enigmatic artefact of them all, the Ark of the Covenant.

At this point one would imagine that historical revelation must cease, but for those who can read the secrets of the Temple of Rennes-le-Château this is only the beginning.

We are then taken to the very origin of history, to Pre-Dynastic Egypt and even beyond that time when man first emerged as a thinking creature. There are the legends of creation, cherished by the Ancient Egyptians and they form the symbolism of the ground feature of the temple at Rennes-le-Château and it was in those that the author discovered the language of the Gods. He found a series of numerical identities representing forces of science and attributed to the gods. So axiomatic is the mathematical language that it is indestructible. It could not be mistranslated or misunderstood, because by the very process of achieving intelligence the primitive mind would discover the relationship between geometric figures. These would in turn reveal the numbers and the identity of those who were responsible for the origin of Man..

So why was this remote mountain area chosen as the place to record the story of the origin of Man – if not the creation of the Universe itself? The answer was not difficult to find for there in the dialogue of Plato was the allegorical description of one of the most powerful mysteries of mankind – Atlantis. The geometry of Atlantis responds precisely to the same codes which solved Rennes-le-Château. Codes which originated in the *Pyramid Texts* and which were perpetuated by secret organisations in their rituals, subsequently the meaning they contained was forgotten. But who could have created a design which although constructed of seemingly simple geometric shapes had interwoven them in such a way as to *demonstrate*, and *inescapably prove*, they were in possession of the very forces of creation itself?

GENISIS

The First Book of Revelations

David Wood

The Baton Press

First published in 1985 by
THE BATON PRESS,
44 Holden Park Road, Southborough,
Tunbridge Wells, Kent TN4 0ER

ISBN 0 85936 180 2

Wood, D.
   Genisis : the First Book of Revelations.
   1. Curiosities and wonders   2. Rennes-le-Château
   (France)
   I. Title
   001.9'4'094487   DC801.R4/

   ISBN 0-85936-180-2

Produced for the publisher by
Chambers Green Ltd, Tunbridge Wells, Kent

Colour reproduction by
Fleet Litho (Kent) Ltd., Tunbridge Wells, Kent

Printed in Germany

Contents

Foreword
by Henry Lincoln

Amazement! Over more than fifteen years of my research into the Rennes-le-Château mystery, the word has become a part of my internal vocabulary. 'Amazement'. No other word describes so well my reaction to the crucial discoveries which have been made since I set out to unravel the 'little local puzzle' of what a nineteenth-century priest found in a tiny, lost, mountain village in the foothills of the Pyrenees.

One of the most naggingly persistent questions which I have struggled with was: 'Why did this story, which seemed to range so far through both time and space, keep returning to this seemingly insignificant place? Why Rennes-le-Château?' It was the question to which, slowly, I had begun to perceive the shadowy form of an answer.

And in the geometric and mathematical evidence which he has presented in this book, David Wood has brought a substance to that shadow.

I must stress that in this statement – indeed in all that I have to say about this book – I am concerned only with the demonstrable geometry, mathematics and measure which the author sets out. Of his conclusions and his interpretation of his evidence I have nothing to say. They lie beyond my competence.

The 'structured layout' of the Rennes valley, as demonstrated in this book is startling. But, unlike most writers who 'jump' to such conclusions, David Wood has a basis in geometry and measure on which to found his statements. I see no wishful thinking in this aspect of his work. The conclusions have not been 'jumped to', but reasoned towards.

David Wood's point of departure was the pentagonal geometry which I had demonstrated in my BBC Chronicle films. And for me, the pentacle has, since I discovered it, been the most amazing piece of the Rennes-le-Château puzzle. I was certain of its significance when, in 1970, I first found it incorporated with a superb logic into one of the famous parchments allegedly discovered by Saunière in 1891. I have seen many published attempts at describing the geometry of this parchment, all of them based on little more than guesswork. I knew that the pentagonal geometry I had found was significant because it is totally provable. It

demonstrates its own internal logic with its own confirming proofs. And so, when Professor Christopher Cornford demonstrated that the geometry I had stumbled upon in Poussin's *Les Bergers d'Arcadie* was also pentagonal, I was amazed – though not surprised.

It was as if I had found a key, and Christopher Cornford had identified the door into whose lock it fitted. In 1979, when I wrote *Shadow of the Templars*, I was able to push that door slightly open. However, for its usual fathomless reasons, the BBC allocated only sixty minutes to the ninety minute film which I had written and shot, and so the extraodinary pentacle of mountains which I had discovered at Rennes-le-Château was only partially explored. But enough remained to convince David Wood of the direction he had to follow.

I have received innumerable letters from people who claim to have solved – definitively – the Rennes-le-Château mystery. Every 'solution' is, to a greater or lesser extent, based in whole or in part on guesswork, wishful thinking, or a purely subjective interpretation of one or other fragment of the evidence. As I was constrained to say in a letter which was circulated to the 'solvers of the riddle': 'No-one has the monopoly of credibility, the mere statement of your certainty cannot convince us of anything. Demonstrable proof must be the sole arbiter . . .'

In relation to Rennes-le-Château, evidence – demonstrable and provable – was my prime goal. The pentacle which I had found in the parchment and in the landscape – the pentacle which Professor Cornford had found in *Les Bergers d'Arcadie* – these were my criteria. They were demonstrable and provable. Nothing sent to me by the growing band of 'solvers' could stand thus solidly against argument.

When David Wood first contacted me, he, too, was set against my yard-stick of objective proof. And, for the first time, here was unarguable evidence. His measurements were accurate, his geometry was meaningful. And again – amazing!

I have learned from the reaction to my own work that there are many people who react 'emotionally' to such startling evidence. They are disinclined to believe it and so they dismiss it out of hand. I would remind such 'critics' that to say 'I don't believe it' is as much an act of faith as to say 'I do believe it'!

I will not make an act of faith of this sort. And I implore the reader to be equally cautious. Let him check the geometry. Let him measure the angles and the lengths of lines. Let him confirm the astonishing circle of churches. Let him neither believe nor disbelieve . . . but check and verify. If he finds errors, he may then dismiss David Wood's geometry. But, unless those errors be found, only a fool will dismiss out of hand the phenomenon of Rennes-le-Château.

I have checked. I have measured. To the extent of my limited competence, I can find no errors in David Wood's calculations. They may be there. Let those with the expertise find them . . . if they exist.

To those who would claim that such a precise and meaningful pattern can be produced on any map of any area, I would say: 'Show it to me.' To those who would say that it is all a meaningless coincidence, I would say: 'It is your privilege so to believe. You are – again – making an act of faith.' And I still find such a 'coincidence' amazing and worthy of careful investigation. I must remind the reader too, that such an attitude would not have been shared by those who may have recognised that coincidence in the past.

For myself, in the face of David Wood's geometry, whether it be proved right or wrong, I am bound to say: 'Amazing! Amazing!!'

© Henry Lincoln
1st March 1985

Foreword
by Geoffrey Smith

For many centuries, man has attempted to lift the 'veil' of Isis. Throughout the ages, successive groups of men have struggled to reveal the symbology of the Secret Doctrine. We name the Knights Templar, the Brothers of the Rose Cross, Freemasons of High Degree and Occultists of every persuasion.

With the work of David Wood, the hitherto esoteric Wisdom teachings achieve a new twist of the spiral. *Genisis* marks the true beginning of scientific spirituality – the first massively detailed breakdown of arcane wisdom into mathematically acceptable and provable formulas.

Genisis is truly a new beginning. Its import is epoch making. Quite simply, there has been nothing like it in the religious history of mankind.

Many teachers have sought to awaken man to the quest for the famed 'philosopher's stone'. Centuries later, their names are themselves symbols of the increasing initiation of humanity into the Greater Mysteries.

Although he does not acknowledge it himself, David Wood will become a name as illustrious and revered as that of any secret society's Grand Master. Only this time, there will be a difference! The previously occult knowledge is not only being made public and this for the man in the street, but many existing 'underground' Orders will ALSO now be enabled to make a guaranteed leap into the future.

Never before has mankind been presented with a text which provides such a secure foundation – a veritable Corner Stone – for those who will henceforth build anew the Temple of Light. To date, and no doubt of necessity, the Wisdom has been couched in a labyrinthine welter of ciphers and symbols which have only been half-broken after decades of intensive research.

To those who approach the portals of the Temple for the very first time, I say: You are privileged people. Never before have such erudite subjects been subjected to such an honest, sober and respectable study as that inaugurated by David Wood. Never before have the alleged myths and legends been presented in such a self-evidently lucid and plausible format.

Ask David Wood how he did it and he will display the astonishingly self-effacing modesty of all true 'Initiates'. He sees himself as the privileged custodian of knowledge not of his own manufacture and he humbly and openly acknowledges the fact.

Many solutions have already been proposed to the mystery of Rennes. In David Wood's analysis, an epic step forward has been taken. All can now see how the mystery is no mere local affair but a magnet of urgent world-wide importance.

For many years, David Wood has carried the burden of the knowledge he has won through to on his own. And he knows only too well that all major prophets of the past have initially been reviled and ridiculed. There is still no reason to believe that it will be otherwise in our twentieth-century. Nevertheless, the cubic stone has now been pin-pointed.

It is up to all mankind to complete the SPIRITUAL Great Work in which it will find its true niche in Cosmos.

Geoffrey Basil Smith
Grand Master, M.A.A.T. Lodge (Egyptian)

This book is dedicated to those who gave their lives to preserve the truth, and to those who live and 'have the understanding'.

1. The author surveying with a theodolite on the escarpment at the northern apex of the pentagram.

Introduction

Ah Love! could thou and I with Fate conspire
To grasp this sorry Scheme of Things entire,
    Would not we shatter it to bits – and then
    Remould it nearer to the Heart's Desire!*

This book is the story of several years of research into the
mystery of Rennes-le-Château, and its eventual solution in
1984.

I am greatly indebted to the innumerable authors who have
provided the material out of which I have pieced together what can
only be described as a gigantic jigsaw puzzle. Some parts of it were
obvious, but for others I had to interpret veiled references in old
paintings, engravings, myths and legends. It may be that the
publication of this information will be considered by some to be
offensive to their beliefs and I would hasten to say that no offence
is intended. My standpoint is that a belief, like a theory or a
hypothesis, is but a temporary bridge, spanning a gap in our
knowledge. We should always be ready and willing to replace it
later with proven fact. Science and truth do not need faith to
support them. They are demonstrable, and so is this solution.

When I decided to attempt to unravel the mystery I had very
little idea of where the trail would lead. I had long been interested
in ancient geometry, and in the BBC Chronicle film *The Priest, the
Painter and the Devil*, first broadcast in about 1974, Henry Lincoln
had made a reference to 'pentagonal geometry' existing in the area
of Rennes-le-Château. But this was not all. The story he related
told of fabulous treasures which might be buried in the area,
possibly even including the long-lost artifacts from Solomon's
Temple. He spoke of secret societies and violent death, of
memorable periods of the past, the Visigoths, the Cathars and the
Knights Templar. I felt I had to learn more about the subjects and
the events in the film.

No one could fail to be impressed by the possible treasures
surrounding the mystery. But although an impressive array of
wealth was implied, it was not this which intrigued me. I was fully
aware of the French laws governing 'treasure trove' and realized
there would be little profit in pursuing the mystery with hopes of
benefiting by finding lost gold. It struck me that the area had too

*The verses used at the head of each chapter are from the *Rubáyát of Omar Khayyám* much history for where it was, too much mystery for what it was – almost as if it attracted gold and events totally disproportionate to its size and importance.

I began to recognize – or sometimes merely to sense – a background pattern which pervaded the whole subject regardless of the historical periods which highlighted the locality. It furthermore appeared that such periods as were historically important were always those which were controversial.

I wondered whether all this could be attributable to buried treasure or might there be something else?

Much of the history of the Church of Rome is concerned with religious persecution, and the Languedoc received more than its fair share of it. I was intrigued by what it could be which was so important that it warranted such intense suppression. I began to wonder whether the valley may contain something which, in the opinion of Rome, we were not meant to find. Could it be – as was also implied – that the valley held a much greater secret than treasure, buried or otherwise?

Was there something which could survive this passage of time and was still there, waiting to be found?

For centuries Rome considered the pursuit of scientific knowledge to be evil, and I wondered if the valley held something of this nature. Alternatively, could it be historical or religious knowledge potentially damaging to the infrastructure of the Roman Catholic Church?

In 1828 the Abbé Gregoire stated, and others have agreed with him, that Christ delivered to St. John the Evangelist a secret doctrine which was in time in the keeping of the Cathars and the Templars. Could this be why these two organizations were persecuted and why so much attention was given to the Languedoc?

Could there be great secrets from the past, which Rome had decided would be better kept from general knowledge?

Did something exist there which could expose this organization as being far less than it claimed to be? I considered all these questions, and I concluded that if anything had to be hidden, it would need to be done using a formula which was unlikely to be known by the Vatican.

One of the symbols most detested by the church is the pentagram, which it considers to be the sign of the devil. This, coupled with Henry Lincoln's references to it, made me decide to examine the possibility of pentagonal geometry at Rennes-le-Château. Equally important were the references to the Ark of the Covenant and, by association, this directed me to the ground plan of the Temple of Solomon.

We know that in the construction of ancient temples the orientation, the adornments, the configuration and the measurements were strictly controlled. It is sometimes possible to analyse these and, where historical records have been lost or falsified, to discover a great deal about the people who constructed them. Concealed in these structures we can recognize the superstitions and the beliefs of these ancient cultures. Certain shapes and numbers were apparently of great significance and the reverence shown to them appears to contradict the intelligence of the designers. It might appear incongruous to find a highly developed culture obsessed with a desire to perpetuate a few simple numbers or a geometric figure – but they did. Could these ancient people, or the 'initiated' among them, have been far more advanced than we have given them credit for?

In the early history of mankind detail is sparse and we have lost so much that it is impossible to reconstruct an accurate picture. However, it is my firm belief we may have underrated the intelligence of the people of the past, particularly those of the ancient or pre-historical periods. I believe we have lost an essential link with those ancient times. It is possible the recent resurgent interest in magic and mystery is a deep-rooted desire to recall that lost past. In recent years an ever-increasing number of authors have produced a welter of books which could almost qualify as 'science fiction' and yet they have been based upon enigmas in the development of mankind which cannot seemingly be answered by the accepted disciplines of theology, archaeology or anthropology. Not so very long ago there were those who were considered mentally unbalanced for believing that the earth had been impacted by another celestial body. I even recall being scolded as a child for suggesting that South America looked as though it had been broken off from the African continent. I wonder how my tutor feels now?

Any logical mind can invent a plausible scenario to bridge this gap with little fear of contradiction. Such stories that have come to us across this void have been classified as myth and legend rather than a record of events stated to the best of the ability of the authors. But the picture, of thousands of hours being spent chiselling a 'pack of lies' into rock, hardly rings true to me.

The more we try to analyse this gap in our knowledge, the more it appears to be of our own doing. But who so effectively created this vacuum which lies between archaeology and history? As I studied the evidence I became convinced that it was largely the work of one agency. It was the wholesale intentional destruction of past records by the Church of Rome. It seems to me the major part of the work of the early Christian monasteries was to collect evidence, apply censorship to it and then to issue an amended copy as if it were a facsimile of the original. Where the original was so explicit that its meaning could not be successfully perverted, it was destroyed!

My reasoning, however, was that an intelligent early civilization, would leave signs or 'markers' of a far more permanent nature than the written or spoken word. I hoped that sufficient of it had not been recognizable to the Church and had therefore escaped censorship. One thing which would meet these requirements would be sacred geometry.

Thus it was I set out on an intensive geometrical analysis of the area of Rennes-le-Château. This book is the story of my search and how I found the Temple of Rennes, but even as I saw the temple layout unfolding before me – I saw something else. An astonishing secret which has lain hidden for thousands of years. This was the answer not to one mystery, but to *all* of them. And behind them I glimpsed a shadowy awesome truth.

The result of this work was initially the recognition and identification of an immense geometrical figure, indelibly marked on the ground, which I have called the Temple of Rennes. It is designed in a manner so perfect and so logical that it is undeniable; a deliberate and verifiable construction, so brilliant and on such a vast scale that it staggers the imagination.

When it was conceived, which advanced intelligence built it, and for what reason, are the questions this book attempts to answer.

It covers an area of over 40 square miles, and every part is marked by a mountain top, a church, an outstanding rock feature or some intersection of carefully designed geometry. It is the largest such 'temple' ever discovered. It incorporates such detail as to obviate totally any possibility of the design being coincidental. Apart from the temple layout, shapes are generated which at first appear contrary to those commonly associated with a 'holy' place. But as I researched further into the mystery, these initial contradictions dissolved and I was left with the firm conviction that I was in the presence of something awesome in its power and majesty – a presence I hope the reader will be able to share with me. These claims may be seen to be exaggerated, but I assure you they are not. It would be impossible in a single book to demonstrate completely the ingenuity of the authors of this incredible achievement; a great deal more research must be done before we fully appreciate the significance of the discovery.

For students who may be interested in the *modus operandi* I adopted, I will provide an outline of the method which I developed and which could conceivably be used to research other ancient sites in the future.

It is a photogrammetric system generally referred to as 'radial control' and requires no special equipment. It was widely used in World War II for the compilation of maps in areas where insufficient ground control existed to employ standard methods. In this system matrices are made from aerial photographs on which a central point or nadir is selected together with a number of secondary control points. The nadir is then punched as a hole and the secondaries cut as slots radiating from it – hence its name 'Slotted Templet Method'. These templets are buttoned together with pins and the result becomes a self-adjusting overall 'mosaic'.

My method was to employ the corollary of this technique. I took several large sheets of astrofoil, punched a control hole and, because I was searching for pentagrams, cut nine slots at 36 degrees. I pinned the nadirs to positions on the map known, or likely, to be associated with the mystery. It was then possible to slide metal studs along the slots and, by so doing, determine other positions on the map which correlated to both angular and ground position disciplines.

In this manner I searched for, and finally found, the 'key'. Once I was in possession of it, the 'doors' through which I then passed were so perfectly in sequence, that if every calculation, map and drawing I have produced during the past five years were to be taken from me, I could reconstruct the entire solution and identify every location, known and secret, within an hour.

I have been advised not to make apologies, but nevertheless it should be understood that I am a reader, a researcher, and not a writer. The time involved in recording this information I can ill afford and if at any time the reader should be intolerant of the style or quality of the grammar, I beg him to remember this is knowledge of a calibre far removed from that which we have come to expect: it is an opportunity to open our minds to 'the mysteries'.

Let me close this introduction by quoting Alfred Lord Tennyson's famous poem *The Holy Grail*. I realize now that I had seen the knowledge of the 'secret doctrine' displayed often in literature, but the true meaning has been too 'veiled' to be recognized. This will be more easily understood by the end of this book, but for now read in innocence. Later, return and read it again. Not one word will have changed, but judge for yourself how different your 'understanding' has become.

> At once I saw him far on the great sea,
> In silver-shining armour starry-clear;
> And o'er his head the holy vessel hung
> Clothed in white samite or a luminous cloud.
> And with exceeding swiftness ran the boat
> If boat it were – I saw not whence it came.
> And when the heavens open'd and blazed again
> roaring, I saw him like a silver star –
> And had he set the sail, or had the boat
> Become a living creature clad with wings?
> And o'er his head the holy vessel hung
> Redder than any rose, a joy to me,
> For now I knew the veil had been withdrawn.
> Then in a moment when they blazed again
> Opening, I saw the least of little stars
> Down on the waste and straight beyond the star
> I saw the spiritual city and all her spires
> And gateways in a glory like one pearl –
> No larger, tho' the goal of all the saints –
> Strike from the sea; and from the star there
> shot a rose-red sparkle to the city, and there
> Dwelt, and I knew it was the Holy Grail,
> which never eyes on earth again shall see.
> Then fell the floods of heaven drowning the deep.

D.W.
January 17th 1985

1

Revelation

And those who husbanded the Golden Grain,
And those who flung it to the Winds like Rain,
Alike to no such aureate Earth are turn'd
As, buried once, Men want dug up again.

A mad, mid-summer dash – background and motives – the need to confirm – locating the site – a painful scramble – the discovery, and confirmation, made – return to base, and basics

Where can I say the start of my involvement in this story really lies? I had been interested in it, or at least its associated themes, for as long as I can remember – and in all probability before that.

I have always been attracted by mysteries – not in the sense of idle curiosity, but rather that to me the word says 'not explained as yet'. Given sufficient data, scientific technology – at present an infant – will encompass all our 'local' mysteries. I believe the word will then achieve its true meaning, specifically – beyond the comprehension of man.

The greatest current mystery is probably the UFO phenomenon, but the story of Rennes-le-Château seems to run it a close second. I certainly have strong opinions on the first subject but its intermittent character prevents me from testing my theory. In the case of Rennes-le-Château there seemed to me enough data for a serious study. This, coupled with expressions such as 'it will never be solved', 'we will never know for sure' and worst of all 'very likely there is no solution', goaded me into action. Over the years I was described as 'possessed', 'obsessed', and no doubt a good deal more. But obsession is not the usual word that is applied to someone who achieves a solution, and this I have done.

This book is not a summary of questions leaving the reader more confused than at the outset – it is answers. Where the true beginning lies I cannot tell – only that it is beyond recorded history. When it ends 'God only knows' – and I do not use the expression lightly.

This book is the key which fits many doors and with it the reader may continue the search at many different levels. For the active, there is a great deal of searching left to do – for others, a simple calculator, the Bible and patience will open new doors. An immense task lies ahead, and the more who take part in it the quicker it will be completed.

2. The small mountain village of Coustaussa showing the ruined château. In the distance can be seen Rennes-le-Château.

I am advised that the person described by the media as the 'man in the street', who by all accounts seems to them to do everything but think, requires something to be found, something for him to see. Whenever I question who this 'man' is, I receive a description of someone who appears to have lived a hundred years ago when a sharp distinction existed between the educated classes and those less fortunate who were concerned with little other than keeping themselves and their families fed. Having come from that environment, I know who that 'man' was and I am equally aware there are very few of them still around. Today people *do* think. However, although I do not consider it the most important part of the discovery, I will begin at the point where 'something' was found. The picture will then dissolve as I take you back, far back, to times, places and events so distant and so misty, you may well believe they were never there and never happened.

Dawn had not yet broken when we left very early on Friday the 6th July, during the summer drought of 1984, to drive to a remote and fairly inaccessible location in southern France. It was in this particular valley that there nestled a hamlet by the name of Rennes-le-Château. I had made the journey many times in the months and years preceding. The last time had been over Easter in the same year when, as usual, I had travelled down with my team in two vehicles piled high with camping and surveying equipment. But this time it was different. Now there was only

myself and two others – Norman Latter and Fred Palmer in one vehicle – an American-built four-wheel drive, and our equipment was minimal. Just enough for a quick, single-purpose sortie. The purpose was to confirm the final plot of a location disclosed by the incredible solution I had discovered.

Ever since 1979 I had worked with all-consuming drive to track down, identify and solve the mystery. This mystery, involving secret societies, lost or 'heretical' knowledge, fabulous treasure and violent death, has been made universally known by the British author Henry Lincoln through a series of BBC films and the 1982 best-selling book *The Holy Blood and The Holy Grail*, written with Richard Leigh and Michael Baigent. The hypothesis put forward was that Jesus was married to Mary Magdalene and that they produced offspring and eventually settled in France where he founded the Merovingian dynasty of Jewish kings. Apart from following the mystery and tracing its elements, Lincoln and his partners had not, so far, managed to solve the central riddle or to locate the lost sites. Both of these things I was determined to do.

If the reader were to have asked me why, I am sure I could not have given him a simple answer. I could only say I felt compelled to do it – like climbing Mount Everest, simply because 'it is there'; but in my case I was not even sure it was there.

From the outset I had decided not to treat the problem as a historical mystery. I am no historian, and those much better qualified in this field than I had failed to produce a

3. Château d'Hautpoul in the village of Rennes-le-Château. The d'Hautpoul family were supposedly one-time custodians of the secrets.

solution in spite of years of work. I was, however, convinced there must be other paths to the truth, as there usually are. The one that seemed not only appealing, but most likely, was that which had been suggested previously and never fully explored – a mathematical or geometric one. I had therefore decided to attempt a solution to the Rennes mystery by the rational application of both disciplines on to a ground plan of the whole area. In other words, by a close and detailed study of precision maps with precision equipment.

Here, I was on altogether surer ground. I had qualified as a surveyor and cartographer which, together with the advantage of owning a small reprographic company, placed me in the invaluable position of being able to reproduce accurate maps to scales suitable for the investigation. Month after month I worked on these maps of the Rennes valley, drawing, redrawing, measuring, remeasuring. I lost count of the number I threw away in frustration. Nevertheless, it served me well, for long before I had set foot in the area it had become as familiar to me as if I had lived there all my life. My training permitted me to 'read' a map as if I was there on the ground and it also alerted me to other factors which I will refer to later. Finally came success, slowly at first and then at breathtaking speed, breakthrough followed breakthrough in spiralling succession until I could hardly believe what was being shown to me.

During the winter of 1983–84 I completed the compilation of a series of some dozen large-scale maps of the Rennes valley on which I plotted the sequence of precisely interconnected geometric patterns. It was dazzling, not only in its arrangement and correspondence, but also in its explicit implications and the conclusions this evidence forced on an incredulous mind.

The purpose of the Easter visit had been to confirm all the geometry executed during the previous winter. This was achieved by precision – checking the ground measurements and angles with a theodolite. By the end of June, with all the geometry verified and the minor errors resolved, I was in a position to confirm my conclusions – shattering though they were. Fundamental to these had been the accurate plotting of a particular location. I believed it held tangible proof and probably the key to the entire mystery. I had not seen it, had never visited the site and had absolutely no evidence there was anything there – yet the geometry, and all my reading and understanding of the subject said it had to be; the pointers were inescapable, the geometry too perfect. I did not know what would be there, but I was sure some recognizable marker would have to be. At the same time I knew I could not take the evidence on trust. There are too many doubters and too many interests, official as well as unofficial, which might not want it to see the light of day. I knew I would have to see the evidence for myself and confirm with my own eyes its existence on the ground.

Thus it was I set out with my two colleagues that Friday

morning. Our mission: to make a single 'hit'. To find, measure
and photograph whatever lay at the spot. To confirm – or not –
whether actual locations were involved in addition to the
revelations of the geometry.

Driving non-stop round the clock, taking turns at the wheel,
we arrived among the mountains in the centre of the Rennes
valley in the early hours of Saturday morning. After a brief sleep,
we were up, we breakfasted at dawn and headed straight for the
location a few miles south of the little town of Rennes-les-Bains.
The area was as familiar to us as our home territory and we knew
exactly where we were going and what we had to do. Even so, an
anticipation hung in the air. By mid-morning, with the sun high
in a clear blue sky and the day already stiflingly hot, we had
parked and begun the long arduous climb through dense
undergrowth to the spot we had marked on the map. The trees
and foliage prevented us from making an accurate 'fix', so I
established boundaries and marked out an area for us to search.
If my calculations were correct, whatever we were to find had to
be within a circle of 50 yards radius. With a perimeter
established, we spread out in a line one hundred yards wide. We
could not see each other but maintained voice contact and moved
slowly forward in an initial sweep over the area. I was at one end
of the line, Fred at the other and Norman in the middle. When I
emerged, scratched and battered at the limit of the marked area,
I found Fred already there, but there was no sign of Norman. We
walked towards each other and waited a while. It is no joke
climbing in that area; it takes fitness, dedication or just plain
stupidity. However, hearing nothing from Norman, we edged
back into the undergrowth to look for him; we called out and
Norman answered, his voice pregnant with meaning: 'You had
better come and have a look at this,' he said. We scrambled down
to where Norman stood and there, almost invisible, in the hard,
deep shadows under the trees, covered in honeysuckle and ivy
was the clear remains of a large stone structure. In the tangled
gloom it was so densely hidden, Norman had stumbled right into
the middle of it without realizing it was there. We stared at it for
a long time. I had seen many old buildings in the Rennes area in
the years I had visited it and I believe I can recognize a
shepherd's hut when I see one. This was certainly no shepherd's
hut – it was something altogether different. The building was
perched in a ludicrous position on the side of the hill and
sufficiently intact for us to establish its dimensions – 50 feet by 30
feet. Inside there were clear indications that it had once been
divided into three rooms and had at one time undoubtedly had a
second floor. High up on one remaining wall, about thirteen feet
from the ground, was the remains of what appeared to be a
circular window almost four feet in diameter. Looked through
from the level of what would once have been the second floor, it
acted like a gun-sight to provide a perfect central view of one of
the most prominent physical features in the area: Pech Cardou.

It was more than we had dared to hope for. I would have been happy with a marked stone, but here we had something akin to a 'keep'. It was certainly much more than a simple shepherd's hut. I wondered if it had once been a Templar construction which had been maintained to guard the entrance to some underground tunnel or cave. At the back of ruins, inside and against the solid rock face of the hill on to which it had apparently been so carefully moulded, there were signs that this could be so. But if that is what it was, it had long since been filled in and covered by rubble from the collapsed building. We had vowed if we found anything we would leave it undisturbed, and this we did. For a while we busied ourselves with taking detailed measurements and making a pictorial record, including a video film. Then, as quickly and quietly as we had come, we departed leaving everything exactly as it was – not a stone disturbed. Within twelve hours of our arrival in the valley we were on our way back, reaching our base in Kent at 11 o'clock on the morning of Sunday July 8th – a round trip of little over 48 hours. We were tired and dazed but we knew we were right. It was more than geometry, something had been hidden!

What follows is the account of what led to that location – and of the full, awesome implications of the geometry which demonstrated it. Inevitably, it is an account that must begin with the tiny village of Rennes-le-Château.

2

The Local Mystery

There was a Door to which I found no Key;
There was a Veil past which I could not see:
Some little Talk awhile of ME and THEE
There seemed – and then no more of THEE and ME.

Route to, and description of, Rennes valley – its violent history – the arrival of a poor parish priest – mysterious discoveries, events and a death – Celtic connections and ancient geometry – investigations begin – early success, and disappointment – a meeting with Henry Lincoln and encouragement – collection of data – occult knowledge and the need to diversify – the importance of the pentagram.

If you travel south in France on the Route du Soleil, then branch right on La Languedocienne you come to Narbonne. There you take the Autoroute des Deux Mers to Carcassonne. Some forty kilometres south of Carcassonne you find the tiny village of Rennes-le-Château. Once it was the city of Rhedae, in an area now known as the Razès. Then it boasted a population of 30,000, but today this tumbledown hamlet houses no more than a couple of hundred people. History has passed it by – but still a great mystery remains there.

Movement in the area is difficult. The only roads follow the river valleys of the Aude, the Sals, the Rialsesse and the Blanque. Between these valleys, the ground rises sharply to hill and mountain-tops of two thousand feet or more. Time has clothed the mountains with dense pine forests, which to some degree camouflage the rugged terrain. But huge rock outcrops serve unmistakably to identify each particular location. As you travel through the area, tricks of light and shade allow you to imagine that the rock features could represent almost anything.

The French forestry workers have cut fire-breaks on the mountainsides as well as tracks through the forest. These provide limited access to positions from which one is confronted with unexpected and breathtaking panoramas. Any deviation from these forest routes can be dangerous. As one would expect, the villages, with the exception of Rennes-le-Château, are confined to the lower slopes of the valleys.

Long ago, certain positions on high ground were chosen as sites for fortified châteaux. These were to become of considerable significance as my enquiries progressed.

The area has a colourful and violent history. Romans, Visigoths, Knights Templar, all contribute to its intriguing past. The violence is the exclusive property of the Vatican, for it was these valleys which formed part of the setting for one of the most savage acts of butchery the Church of Rome ever committed: the Albigensian Crusade.

From 1209 for forty years, on the express orders of Pope Innocent III, an 'extermination occurred on so vast, so terrible a scale, it may well constitute the first case of genocide in modern European history'.* The agents of the massacre were an army of some 30,000 knights and foot-soldiers from Northern Europe. Their victims: almost the entire 'Cathari' or Albigensian population of the Languedoc region of what is today southern France. At that time it was a peaceful and cultivated population of independent people whose only crime seems to have been that it followed a religious way of life contrary to the one decreed by Rome.

The Cathari, or Cathars as they are more popularly known, were Gnostics. To Rome they were infected, and therefore infectious. 'By the time the Crusade was over, the Languedoc had been utterly transformed, plunged back into the barbarity which characterized the rest of Europe.' With that transformation came anonymity. And so it remained for 600 years – until the end of the nineteenth century.

Here our mystery begins. The story has already been extensively told elsewhere, notably in the best-selling *The Holy Blood and The Holy Grail*, but its essential elements bear repeating.

In 1885 a certain priest, Bérenger Saunière, was appointed to the church of Rennes-le-Château. At that time the eight-hundred-year old building was badly in need of extensive restoration. The impoverished priest was, however, without funds to achieve this. Eventually, in 1891, a small loan was arranged and during the subsequent process of restoration one of the supporting stones of the altar was moved. It proved to be hollow. Inside were found documents, genealogical charts and Latin texts of such complex codes that it is perhaps surprising they were ever deciphered. The key to their solution was however eventually found on a gravestone in the churchyard of Rennes-le-Château. When the decoding was completed the solution, although in plain language, was apparently meaningless.

It reads:

4. Emma Calvé – famous opera singer and close friend of Saunière.

5. Bérenger Saunière curé of the church of Rennes-le-Château.

BERGERE PAS DE TENTATION QUE POUSSIN TENIERS GARDENT LA CLEF PAX DCLXXXI PAR LA CROIX ET CE CHEVAL DE DIEU J'ACHEVE CE DAEMON DE GARDIEN A MIDI POMMES BLEUES.

[SHEPHERDESS, NO TEMPTATION, THAT POUSSIN, TENIERS, HOLD THE KEY, PEACE 681. BY THE CROSS AND THIS HORSE OF GOD, I COMPLETE – or DESTROY – THIS DAEMON OF THE GUARDIAN AT NOON. BLUE APPLES.]

The Holy Blood and the Holy Grail, (Jonathan Cape: London) 1982, p27.

And another extract, possibly more direct in its meaning, proclaimed:

A DAGOBERT II ROI ET A SION EST CE TRESOR ET IL EST LA MORT.

(TO DAGOBERT II, KING, AND TO SION BELONGS THIS TREASURE AND HE IS THERE DEAD).

6. The coded manuscript which provided the second cipher. (Note the emphasis on SION and the persistence of SI or IS which occurs 14 times.)

Such apparently, was the importance of the discoveries that Saunière was sent to Paris with the blessing of the Bishop of Carcassone, in whom he had confided. The precise purpose of this mission remains undiscovered, but another who would almost certainly have been aware of these events would have been Saunière's close friend Henri Boudet, curé of the sister church of Rennes-les-Bains.

Saunière had been told previously whom he should contact in Paris. All were people of considerable eminence: actors, authors and artists. One, in particular, is worthy of closer examination. Emma Calvé was to become a close associate of Saunière in the years that followed.

At this time in Paris there was, in successful and educated circles, a strong revival of what may be loosely called 'the Magic Arts', but is more correctly termed hermeticism or gnosticism, largely inspired by the celebrated occultist Eliphas Lévi (Alphonse Louis Constant) who had died in 1875. It had been suggested that Emma Calvé was a prominent figure in the many occult societies then flourishing as a result, one of which was known as the Temple of Isis.

In Paris, Saunière visited the Louvre, where he bought copies of three paintings. The significance of at least two of these will become clear later. But what is immediately, and mysteriously, clear is that on his return to Rennes-le-Château Saunière became fabulously rich. He lived a life of opulence and spent a large sum of money on the restoration of the church. In doing so he filled it with controversial imagery, seemingly designed to desecrate the very faith which he represented.

Told in this fashion, as it usually is, the story suggests that Saunière chanced upon a treasure which gave him sufficient power to adopt an impertinent attitude to his ecclesiastical superiors who had relegated him to this inferior post. Even at this early stage, I began to doubt the simplicity of the story. As I collected more data on the subject, the romantic idea of a penniless priest stumbling on a hidden fortune and then becoming the champion of the local peasantry began to fade.

It transpired it had been common knowledge in the district that a secret of great importance was in the hands of a family called d'Hautpoul de Blanchefort. The last surviving member of the family, Marie de Négri d'Ablès, had passed its secret to the curé of Rennes-le-Château in 1781. The curé was one Antoine Bigou and it would appear that he decided to record their secret in a more material form. He was the author of the coded Latin text which provided the strange message found a century later by Saunière and it was Bigou, too, who was responsible for the strangely engraved headstone that provided the key to the cipher which Saunière promptly obliterated when he returned from Paris.

At about the same time, Saunière's close friend from Rennes-les-Bains, Henri Boudet, had given him a book, published in 1886. Written by Boudet himself, it was called *La Vraie Langue celtique et le Cromleck de Rennes-les-Bains* (The True Celtic Language and the Stone Circle of Rennes-les-Bains). In this book Boudet demonstrates the amazing similarities between English and the dialect of the Languedoc, a dialect still largely unintelligible to the French.

Some 2,500 years earlier, the area of the Languedoc was an important Celtic settlement and the present city of Narbonne is on the site of their capital, Narbo. The Celtic link was familiar to me. I had made a long-term study of stone circles and ancient geometry. The exciting possibility therefore occurred to me there may be a geometric solution to the secret of the Rennes valley.

In the summer of 1978 I obtained some maps of the area and scanned them casually. Place names at once began to seem odd: Valdieu (Valley of God), L'Homme Morte (the Dead Man), Fauteuil du Diable (Seat of the Devil), Le Cercle (the Circle), Arques (Arc or Arch), La Serpent (the Serpent), Roque Nègre (Black Rock), Blanchefort (White Fort?). Esoteric names everywhere. But why? I began experimenting with geometric patterns based on the pentagram that Henry Lincoln had used in his films.

At this stage there was no particular rhyme or reason to my method. In fact I was mostly preoccupied with running my business. After several months I realized I could not leave the mystery alone. My mind kept returning to some aspect of it at every unguarded moment. A strange pattern of numbers would appear as I tried to identify the angles surrounding the historic sites . . . then it would be lost again and I would be left with a meaningless jumble of lines.

Gradually, I began to form a very definite attitude towards the subject. I supposed that everything I had noticed, which suggested that this area could have some unique property, must have been equally obvious to the local inhabitants. I began to take a sceptical view of the original story. In fact I felt I could take nothing at face value. The more I looked at the available evidence, the more I became convinced Henri Boudet had known that something of great value existed in the church of Rennes-le-Château or if not that he would find the clue to its whereabouts there. I suspected Boudet might even have 'jockeyed' Saunière into the position of curé for the express purpose of searching the building.

One such curious anomaly, for example, was that before Saunière travelled to Paris he was visited by no less an eminence than the Archduke of Hapsburg, cousin of the Emperor of Austria. The Archduke appears to have made financial contributions to Saunière, before the priest visited Paris. What, I wondered, could possibly have attracted a man of his standing to visit the likes of Saunière if it was not important? I was also suspicious enough to consider that the loan to renovate the church was obviously inadequate. I suspected it was nothing more than an excuse by the two priests to close the doors and carry out a more thorough search, involving structural demolition. I believe they were convinced that a key to a great secret was concealed somewhere in the building. Undoubtedly their assessment was correct, and I am sure it was not only Saunière who benefited from the discovery.

On the 17th January 1917, at the age of 65, Bérenger Saunière, although still a healthy man, suffered a sudden and fatal stroke. After his death it was discovered that his housekeeper Marie Denarnaud had ordered his coffin ten days previously – when he had appeared to be in the best of health! What happened?

It may be that Saunière's flamboyance, at first amusing, was for a time tolerated but finally became unbearable to the occult society into which he had probably been initiated. Wealth was there in abundance. But were there also other secrets, greater and more dangerous secrets, which Saunière hoped would be made public in his lifetime? He may have decided that time was running out and have intended to make disclosures. Others who shared in the secret, however, may have considered that the time was not right.

All this was, nevertheless, conjecture and I needed evidence for a starting point.

I began assembling as much information on the subject as was publicly available: video tapes of the BBC films made by Henry Lincoln for the 'Chronicle' series, *The Priest, the Painter and the*

Devil and *The Shadow of the Templars*; copies of paintings
which Saunière had acquired from the Louvre during his stay in
Paris; and most important, the largest-scale maps of the district I
could obtain. I was fortunate to have already a collection of books
on myths, legends and occult geometry. Even so, it took me a
year to collect everything I felt I needed. Eventually I was ready,
and in September 1982 I set out for the Rennes Valley on what
was to prove the first of many fact-finding visits.

Today the area is as familiar to me as my own garden. But then
it was an exciting and mysterious world. The atmosphere hit me
forcibly, tangibly, the moment I first drove into the valley from
the town of Couiza.

Even now I feel reluctant to speak of it bluntly. It was an
unmistakable sensation of entering a vast and familiar building –
although I had never been there in my life before. My first call
was, of course, Rennes-le-Château where I visited the church and
took a number of photographs of Saunière's bizarre adornments
and many other interesting features of the area.

7. *La Peste d'Azoth* by Nicolas Poussin. (*The Plague of Azoth.* Azoth is
the alchemical name for Mercury.) This work contains a great
number of confirmations of the secret doctrine concealed in its
imagery.

One of the three paintings that curé Saunière had brought back to Rennes-le-Château from Paris in 1891 was Nicolas Poussin's famous *Les Bergers d'Arcadie* (The Shepherds of Arcadia), painted around 1640 (see illus 8). The attention already focused on this painting by Lincoln's films made me decide to make it my starting point. Back in England, I began work on an extensive analysis of it. I could scarcely have guessed how quickly – and spectacularly – success was to follow.

Within a few weeks I was back in France to check my findings. I had recognized some geometric coincidences pointing quite definitely to a position on the eastern slopes of one of the highest mountains in the area – Pech Cardou. It seemed an unlikely position as that part of the mountain was featureless but, after only a few moments searching, one of my colleagues discovered a small hole about six inches in diameter. We passed a stick into the hole and it disappeared with a clatter. We stared at each other in disbelief.

We began enlarging the hole and to our amazement discovered it was an entrance to a cave which had been walled up. But by

8. *Les Bergers d'Arcadie* (*The Shepherds of Arcadia*) by Nicolas Poussin, featuring the famous Poussin tomb which provided both geometric and numerical clues.

whom and when? About ten feet into the cave was a vertical shaft, approximately eight feet deep, which led to a chamber. But our excitement soon turned to disappointment. The roof had collapsed and it was impossible without tools to proceed any further. With mixed feeling we returned to England.

In fact the journey had been far from wasted. Not only had we found a cave, but we had found that climbing the mountains in that area was a nasty, painful business. Another fairly important discovery was that I was considerably overweight and I would have to lose a couple of stone at least if I was going to be equal to the task which confronted me! At this moment of taking stock, I decided to report our findings to Henry Lincoln.

By this time, Henry Lincoln, Richard Leigh and Michael Baigent had published the *The Holy Blood and the Holy Grail* – a work which I consider to be a milestone on the road to opening the mind of man to the greater mysteries. In my opinion the authors showed admirable courage in not shying away from the controversial parts of the enigma.

Henry Lincoln agreed to meet me, in spite of the pressure of work he was under at the time. It was my intention to tell him not only of the cave but of my startling sensation of familiarity as I had entered the area of the Rennes valley. In the event I decided to leave it unsaid. Lincoln did, however, agree there could be value in my pursuing the geometric search since he had himself already established a clear link with the pentagram and its associated geometry in the Rennes valley. I returned to my labours, reassured that my geometric approach was a valid one.

Several times during the next two years I returned to the valley to make observations and I was thankful for my survey training. During these visits I added to my collection of books by obtaining an archaeological study of the ancient buildings of the area.

It is essential at this point for the reader to understand my belief, contradicted in some academic quarters, but commonly held to be true nevertheless, that geometry and numerical values appear, sometimes obviously and sometimes concealed, in ancient myths and legends. So important were they once considered that temples and many other buildings incorporated the sacred shapes and numbers in their dimensions. The Pyramids and the Temple of Solomon are prime examples. The mathematics involved in these figures, and the symbols they demonstrate, are sometimes so simple that modern science dismisses them as nothing more than the product of an elementary mind, displaying no more than a rudimentary knowledge of mathematical relationships. Fortunately, there have always been those who will not run with the pack, and in recent years several authors have emerged who are willing to re-examine the knowledge of the past with more open minds.

The studies they have produced have proved conclusively, to my satisfaction at least, that our ancestors were far from the primitive savages we are led to believe. They have also led to a number of startling revelations when read in the light of recent advances in science, medicine and technology. Myths and legends clearly seem to carry within them a seed of truth which multiplies as examination of them is intensified. A considerable amount of this information was once thought of as 'magic' – and still is by many. Much of it was labelled 'pagan' by the Vatican and anyone showing interest in these ideas stood a reasonable chance of being burned as a heretic. As a good deal of this information is connected with astronomy, mathematics, chemistry and medicine we can realize why little progress was made in these subjects for so long.

Of all the symbols contained in early science the one most reviled by the Christian Church is the pentagram. This five-pointed star is held to represent all that is evil, particularly in its inverted mode. The church considers this sign to represent the devil (even though the devil is a purely Christian creation!). The pentagram was revered for thousands of years before the conception of the famous 'Goat of Mendes', with the familiar horns and cloven hoofs.

The French occultist Eliphas Lévi, in his *Transcendental Magic*, stated that the pentagram signifies the dominance of the mind over the elements and that the demons of the earth, the air and water are enchained by it. Elsewhere he claims that the pentagram is dangerous in the hands of the uninitiated. He likens the temptations of Saint Anthony to the confusion between direct and reflected 'astral light' (inner wisdom) resulting from the misuse of this knowledge. *The Temptation of Saint Anthony* by Teniers was the second of the paintings which Saunière had brought back with him from the Louvre. Again I remembered the coded message found in the church at Rennes-le-Château: 'Poussin, Teniers hold the key'.

'The Pentagram,' continues Lévi, 'profaned by men, burns ever unclouded in the right hand of the Word of Truth and those who set at naught the Sign of the Cross, tremble before the Star of the Microcosm.' The pentagram was, in fact, the secret sign of the initiated Pythagorean – initiated, that is, into the hermetic secrets of Trismegistus or Thoth, the Egyptian god of magic. To reveal its meaning to the uninitiated was punishable by death. Any school-boy will associate Pythagoras with the right-angled triangle, where the sum of the squares on the sides enclosing the right angle is equal to the square on the hypotenuse. But this was a mere fragment of the sacred geometry of the ancients acquired by Pythagoras during his service as a priest in the temples of Egypt. There he was instructed in the wisdom of Thoth, Lord of the Measures, God of Right and Truth. How many schoolchildren realize when they learn geometry that they are actually being instructed in magic?

Thoth is identified with the Roman god Mercury, and I next recalled that the alchemical name for Mercury was Azoth. In the Louvre in Paris is another painting by Poussin called *La Peste d'Azoth*. It shows people dying in the streets of an ancient city. But there is something else in the picture, I noticed, relevant to my investigation. The 'Ark of the Covenant' is clearly depicted, balanced precariously on a stone plinth – not where one would expect to find it, in the 'Holy of Holies', but exposed (see illus 7). Furthermore, the Ark is positioned between the pillars at the entrance to the temple. I was amazed to find that the side of the pillar divides the carrying staff of the Ark precisely in half. This 'half-staff' feature is in the *Shepherds of Arcadia*, where the arms and the bodies of the shepherds also divide the staffs exactly, was demonstrated in Lincoln's film.

With the Ark of the Covenant, and the Temple of Solomon in which it was kept, I was at once aware I was seeing a link with Freemasonry, membership of which is referred to as being 'on the square' (Pythagoras again!). The rituals of the Brotherhood of Freemasonry are largely concerned with the building of the Temple of Solomon and with its architect Hiram Abiff.

My examination of the pentagram had alerted me not only to its geometrical significance but to its numerical values and factors. These, I found, also occurred in subjects associated with the Rennes mystery. In gathering and reading material on both the Templars and the Rosicrucians, for example, I had been intrigued by the apparent importance of the number 9. In the 'Ancient and Mystical Order of the Rosae Crucis' (A.M.O.R.C.) the ninth is the last degree of ritual in which the student can be instructed on the material plane. After this he passes into the stage of the Illuminati. From the Illuminati we are one small step from the alchemists and thence to the Brothers of the Rose Cross. As is clearly demonstrated in the *The Holy Blood and the Holy Grail*, the Brothers automatically link with the mysterious Priory of Sion, the innermost 'cell' of the Templars, who worshipped the Egyptian goddess Isis and had vowed to rebuild the Temple of Solomon. The links were multiplying and the circle closing.

It was now, however, very clear to me that it would be necessary to possess a ground knowledge in many subjects in order to pursue the mystery successfully. As I progressed through the solution I found I had to equip myself with the elements of several subjects to appreciate fully what was being shown to me – and as I did so I became aware of the brilliance of the minds of those behind it, those who presumably also conceived it. Eventually I am sure specialists in many subjects will recognize far more than is apparent to my eyes, but for present purposes I will provide readers with sufficient for them to share with me in realizing the awesome magnitude of what lies ahead.

My continuing investigations of all the subjects connected with Rennes-le-Château – and particularly my initial success on Pech Cardou – had convinced me of the importance of mathematics, geometry and, in particular, of the pentagram. For my next step I therefore decided to clarify that enigmatic figure in my mind.

3

The Pentagram and
the Serpent

O Thou, who Man of baser Earth didst make,
And who with Eden didst devise the Snake;
For all the Sin wherewith the Face of Man
Is blacken'd, Man's Forgiveness give – and take!

Relationship to the circle – the first numbers – the serpent as wisdom – the caduceus –
serpent mounds – the Peyrolles serpent – biblical connections – Eve's sin – Isis appears.

With the benefit of hindsight I now know the pentagram, the five-pointed star beloved of occultism, to be fundamental to the solution and proper interpretation of the Rennes mystery. But at the start of my inquiry I had no such insight. I merely set out, during the winter of 1978-79, to discover all I could about the precise mathematics and geometry of the famous figure. Since the importance of these details will quickly become apparent as the mystery unfolds, I make no apology for stating what may well seem to be the obvious. Indeed it is vital that I do, for unless the reader continually keeps the details in mind much of what follows is likely to be unintelligible.

The pentagram is a five-pointed star formed by dividing the circumference of a circle into five equal arcs and then joining the points of division by a unicursal line (see illus 9).

Lines drawn from the centre of the circle to the points of the star bisects the angles thereby forming angles of eighteen degrees (**18°**). Therefore, if one examines the diagram, our complete list of angles is: **18°**, **36°** and **72°** which when multiplied by five (**5**) equal **90°**, **180°** and **360°**. The right angle, the straight line, and the circle.

The angles at the intersection of the arms are shown as **72°** and **108°**.

One should also notice that all these numbers reduce to nine: **1+0+8 = 9. 3+6 = 9, 7+2 = 9** etc.

It is essential for the reader to realize a unique relationship exists between the pentagram and the circle. Much of the secret doctrine will be misinterpreted unless this is continually kept in mind and for that reason I cannot over-emphasize this factor. The star-points of the pentagram are formed with an angle of **36°** and a circle is **360°**. The circle is the ultimate symbol of femininity and this in turn stamps the pentagram with the same gender.

By referring to the diagram it may be seen that the bisection of the **36°** star-points produces the five axes which intersect at the

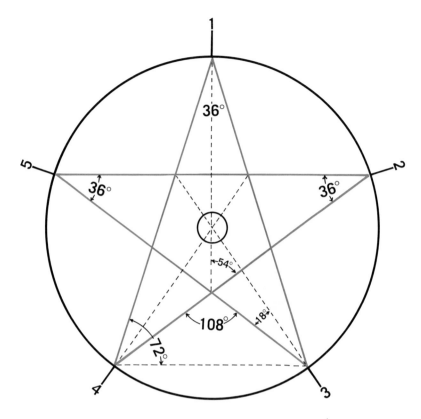

9. The regular pentagram, displaying some of the 'holy' numbers.

centre of the circle. They then proceed to the division of the 'legs' opposite them. The division of the **36°** angle to **18°** is thereby making **18** a significant factor.

Here I was at a great advantage, for in my previous studies of the Egyptian goddess Isis, I had noticed that she was related in some way to the numbers one (**1**) and eight (**8**) and her identity was undoubtedly eight (**8**). This will become increasingly clear to the reader as we progress.

I examined all the possible combinations that could have been of significance to the people of the past. The sum of the numbers from one (**1**) to eight (**8**) is thirty-six (**36**). As **9** represented death or pregnancy (not yet born) this would render **36** as the sum total of living functions.

Considering the importance of the pentagram to the Greek mathematician Pythagoras led me to another important 'link' in the mystery: in ancient Greece the three most venerated symbols of their mysteries were the phallus, the egg and the serpent.

A curious affinity has always existed between the pentagram and the serpent, and this will be examined in considerable detail later. I became aware that both of these items were related in some way to Rennes, and during my travels in the vicinity I noticed a village called 'La Serpent'. I thought it curious that the feminine gender was incorrect. Then I noticed something even

10. The mystical pentagram. (Note the central motif of the caduceus and the symbol unifying the sexes.)

more peculiar. Nearby on the map (see illus 11) was a ground feature which was unmistakably in the shape of a serpent. I was reminded of my meeting with Henry Lincoln, during which he had suggested that I should examine a somewhat recondite publication called the *Le Serpent Rouge* (The Red Serpent) a small booklet which we will deal with later and which was to provide me with many clues.

The serpent shape turned out to be a perfectly natural topographical feature, but it is well known that serpent features of this kind were of great importance in past religions. The Greeks, Egyptians, Celts, Phoenicians all revered the serpent; in India it is found associated with the oldest traces of Buddhism. In certain respects, it is synonymous with the circle, where the serpent is illustrated swallowing its own tail (see illus 13). Mysterious serpent mounds may be seen in widely separated locations. At Glen Feochan, Argyllshire one such shape has been found and the famous serpent of Adams County, Ohio (see illus 12) is well known. It has been assumed this particular serpent is in the act of swallowing an egg and the bulbous head of the serpent, near the village of Peyrolles, gives a similar impression.

It is worth noting that these serpent mounds are clearly discernible only from the air, and I had identified the Peyrolles serpent from a map. So obvious did the feature appear to me, I was amazed that I could fined no record of it being publicly identified previously. Nevertheless I had little doubt it was the one referred to in 'The Red Serpent'. The rock face forming the spine is certainly red. Its length at 2340 yards makes it the largest of these symbols as yet identified.

Not only did the serpent manifest itself in the history of every religion but the further one probes back, the more significant it becomes. Christianity ensures that it makes an early appearance where, in the Old Testament, it tempts Eve and it appears later as a feature of demonstrable magic. Snake-charmers were known to have the ability to cause a snake to become as rigid as a staff, and it is obvious from Exodus that Moses and Aaron were well versed in this art:

> And Moses and Aaron went in unto Pharaoh and they did as the Lord commanded and Aaron cast down his rod before Pharaoh and before his servants, and it became a serpent. (Illus 14)
>
> *Exodus VII*, 10

Moses had previously been witness to the phenomenon of the burning bush and, when he expressed doubt in his ability to confront the Pharaoh, the Lord had asked him what he held in his hand. Moses replied that it was a rod:

> And the Lord said unto him, Cast it on the ground. And he cast it on the ground and it became a serpent: and Moses fled from it. (Illus 15)
>
> *Exodus IV*, 3

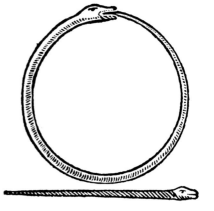

13. The rigid and the tail-swallowing snake.

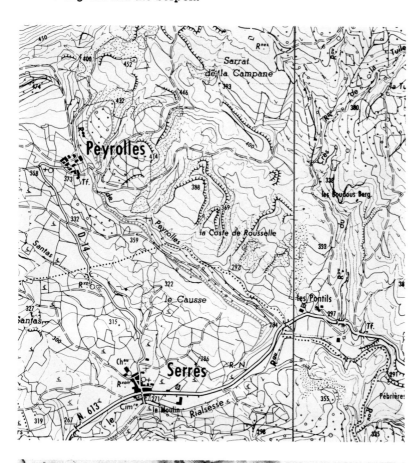

11. The ground feature of the serpent at Peyrolles near to the tomb of Poussin's painting.

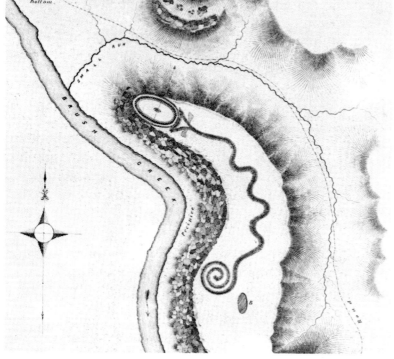

12. The great serpent of Adams County Ohio.

14. Aaron's rod changed into a serpent before the Pharaoh.

One can now easily recognize the significance of the symbols. The serpent in its rigid form represents the phallus. In its circular form it becomes the female generative organ. Hence, the significance of the number **10**, which some suggest represents

15. Moses's rod becomes a serpent at the burning bush.

mathematical perfection or God. It has the power to multiply without changing form: a female function. And Io was the Greek name for Isis!

Another important symbol of the ancient doctrine is the caduceus, a symbol formed by two snakes or serpents entwined round a central staff – a geometric figure referred to as a lemniscate (illus 16). Viewed from the side it appears to be a figure **8** divided by the vertical staff (illus 17) – but it also implies that **8** should be combined with the vertical staff which represents a 'one' giving us **18** – an obvious icon for the Goddess Isis.

This symbol occurs in other places in the Old Testament, for example when Moses was leading his people through the desert and many of them died from serpent bites:

> And the Lord said unto Moses, Make thee a fiery serpent and set it upon a pole: and it shall come to pass that everyone that is bitten, when he looketh upon it shall live. (See illus 18)
>
> *Numbers XXI*, 8

18. The raising of the Brazen Serpent by Moses.

Here it would appear that the role of the serpent has altered
somewhat from when it first appeared in *Genesis*. There it was
considered to have been a symbol of evil, beguiling Eve to taste
the forbidden fruit. But did not the Lord predict that eating the
fruit would cause Adam and Eve to die? In this case the serpent
was obviously more knowing, for they surely did not die.

Although Christianity casts the serpent in an evil role, in all
other religions the serpent is admired. It signifies wisdom, and
one is forced to admit that wisdom was also shown by the serpent
in the Garden of Eden. It would also seem that if Eve had not
been so beguiled, and had she not committed this so-called 'sin',
we should not be here at all!

The allegory of the Garden would be easier to understand if we
moved away from the sexual inference and the partisan story of
Genesis to another possibility: suppose for example the sin was
merely the acquisition of knowledge or wisdom. With this
interpretation there would be no contradiction between the
beliefs. The Vatican made no secret of the fact that it condemned
the pursuit of scientific knowledge. Therefore with the serpent
representing this knowledge it follows it would be considered
evil. One facet of knowledge which could be considered the curse
of mankind is the certainty that death is inescapable, and in
knowing this man is unique in the animal kingdom. What greater
curse could one suffer than to know that at the end of life was
perpetual darkness? Most religions compensate us with promises
of a hereafter or reincarnation, subject of course to our
conforming to a particular set of rules laid down by the 'club
chairman'. One pays one's 'dues' in some form or the other
during one's natural life, hoping to qualify for the hereafter.
Those who manipulate this psychology have little fear of any
unhappy customers returning with complaints.

Some suggest that the sin of Eve was of a sexual nature,
but we could hardly blame her if it were. She was given the
organ to unite with man and thereby achieve creation. Other
doctrines suggest an extraordinary union which Eve had prior
to the one with Adam, and if Cain was the result of that
first union, the division between Cain and Abel is quite
understandable.

The identity of Eve and her previous consort, together with and
the far-reaching consequences of it, I will come to later.

We could not leave this subject without mentioning the
Ophites, in whose doctrine the serpent played a vital role.

The primary belief of any of the Ophite sects was of a triad
consisting of a union of intellect (primal man) with the spirit,
which is the female generative principle and the result of that
union which is second Man.

From the female principle, the Christ or third man is
generated and in his ascent, a ray of light fell upon the waters.
The light was Sophia, the wisdom – and this union of light and
water gave birth to the 'demiurge' (Ialdabaoth), who in turn

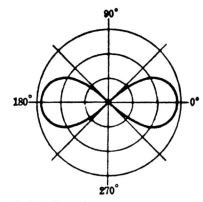

16. The Lemniscate.

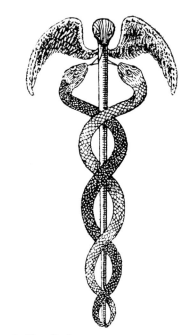

17. The Caduceus.

produced the six powers and from matter he created the serpent.

As we proceed with the investigation of Rennes-le-Château, the significance of the wisdom of the Sophia temple and the serpent will become more apparent; but one other link with the serpent is worthy of note at this stage.

You will recall that the priest, Bérenger Saunière, showed interest in the artist Poussin, and so I decided to examine the rest of Poussin's works to see if any other clues were apparent. Poussin had produced four paintings illustrating the seasons of man. *Spring* was a landscape depicting Adam and Eve in the Garden of Eden. *Winter* also referred to as *The Deluge* (see illus 19 & 20) shows the Ark of Noah, over which is a full moon divided on the horizontal axis by a line of stratus cloud. In the foreground is a very obvious serpent – so obvious that it must have been put there for a reason. The moon is a female love symbol, and it will become clear later that the horizontal line and the Ark are in the same symbolic category.

My working knowledge of the legends of Isis and the imagery associated with her placed me in the advantageous position of recognizing certain connections with the mystery which might otherwise have escaped my notice.

I will now acquaint the reader with the essentials of those legends in order that the solution will follow a logical path.

19. *L'Hiver* from Les Quatre *saisons* by Poussin.

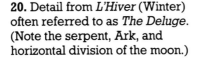

20. Detail from *L'Hiver* (Winter) often referred to as *The Deluge*. (Note the serpent, Ark, and horizontal division of the moon.)

4

The Legends

For in and out, above, about, below,
'Tis nothing but a Magic Shadow-show,
Play'd in a Box whose Candle is the Sun,
Round which we Phantom Figures come and go.

The gods of the Egyptians – the creation – the year of 360 days – the murder of Osiris – the parts of the body – more numbers – the 'seat' of Isis.

Isis was the most famous of all the Egyptian goddesses. She was supreme in magical power, which was taught to her by Thoth, Lord of the Measures, god of science and knowledge. Although she was born as flesh, her powers rivalled those of the gods of spirit. She personified feminine creative power, and although she was the beneficent mother of mankind she was worshipped as a virgin for 'no mortal man had ever her unveiled'. She was the faithful and loving wife of Osiris – first king of Egypt and the teacher of men, who raised mankind from savagery. Set, the brother of Osiris, desired Isis and was jealous of the popularity of Osiris so he murdered him. Nephthys was the sister of Isis and although she was the wife of Set, she always remained faithful to her. These gods of great antiquity – Set, Isis, Osiris and Nephthys – form an important part in our inquiries, and I spent a considerable amount of time examining the iconography associated with them.

An example of this may be seen in illus 21, which is one of the innumerable examples of Egyptian art I examined. It is the *Papyrus of Ani* (British Museum No. 10470 Sheet 3 and 4) and it depicts very clearly some of the values I sought.

In this plate Osiris is shown enthroned in a shrine; behind him we find Nephthys (partly obscured) and Isis; before him the children of Horus stand on a lotus blossom. The fringe passing behind Osiris is a line of **35** serpents, each surmounted by a globe and, counting from right to left, it may be seen that the globe which is interrupted by the head-dress of Osiris, is the fourteenth, (**14**). The head of Isis carries her symbol – a 'seat' or throne – and it clearly points to the eighth globe (**8**). Not only, therefore, do we confirm the presence of Isis as **8**, but we are shown that Osiris in the underworld is represented by **14**. Later it will be shown that Osiris was **15**, but his body was dismembered and only **14** parts were found.

According to the Egyptian legend, Nut, goddess of the heavens

21. From the *Papyrus of Ani* (British Museum No. 10470, Sheets 3 and 4) Osiris attended by Isis and Nephthys. This is one of the best examples of the numerical identities of the gods.

and Mother of the gods, angered Ra, the sun-god, by secretly consorting with her brother the earth-god Geb, the Great Cackler, and they laid horizontally together. So incensed was Ra by this incestuous act that he sent Shu, great god of the Pillars of Light and the father of Geb and Nut, to separate his children. Shu commanded them to part, which they did – to perform the first act of creation. Nut's star-spangled body remained forever separated from her brother, arched from horizon to horizon, so dividing the earth and the sky (illus 22 & 23). However, the union had already taken place and Nut was pregnant. Knowing this, Ra forbade Nut to shed her offspring on any day of his year. Now the orbit of the earth was such that at this time the year consisted of **360** days; which one may consider is good reason why the circle is divided into **360°**.

Thoth, Lord of the Measures, who controlled the movement of the stars, took pity on Nut and came to her assistance. He played the moon at chequers (draughts) and won from her a seventy-second (pentagonal) part of her light, whereby (**360 ÷ 72 = 5**) five intercalated days were added to the year. With these additional days, Nut was now able to give birth and this she did (5 again is pentagonal). The names of the gods born out of Nut were Set, Isis, Osiris and Nephthys. It is coincidental that the initials of these spell S.I.O.N. (reminding us of the famous Priory of SION).

These four gods of Nut were born on separate days, and in one version of the story it was said Isis and Osiris had consorted while

22. The arched body of Nut – the sky goddess separated from Geb – the earth god or 'Great Cackler' (*Papyrus of Tameniu*, British Museum).

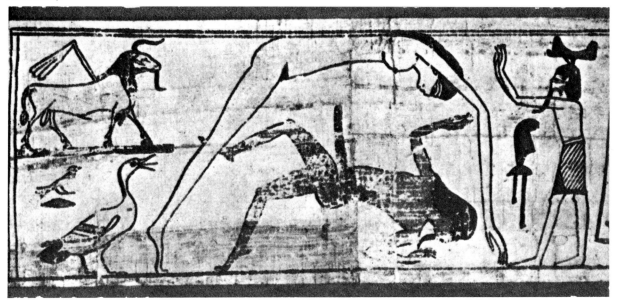

23. The creation myth, showing Shu supporting the body of Nut. Geb, the earth god, lies at his feet.

still in the womb whereby Isis gave birth to Horus, who was then born on the fifth day. This part of the story is contradictary to other texts, which clearly indicate that at the time of her husband's demise Isis was without child. However, the legend is clear on one point – the year was thereby changed to **365** days and we will discuss later the probability that these myths carry in them a record of actual celestial movements. One of the Egyptian temples used as an observatory was the Temple of Dendera which, although dedicated to Hathor, was supposedly the birthplace of Isis. The Temple of Dendera had in one room a magnificent Zodiac carved in the roof and it is of interest to us that its axis was at approximately **18°** (pentagonal) to the walls of the temple (see illus 25).

Isis was queen to Osiris, and it was he who was responsible for the transformation of men from barbarity and cannibalism into civilized creatures. Osiris moved around the world introducing to them agriculture and science. During his absence Isis ruled over Egypt and was greatly revered. Set, brother of Osiris, became jealous of the power, popularity and success of Osiris. So he devised a plot to murder him.

I would remind the reader at this stage that these five gods of the Osirian pantheon – although born from a mother of pure spirit – were creatures of flesh, and as such could be killed. On the other hand, so perfectly were they created that unless their lives were terminated by violent means they would live for a

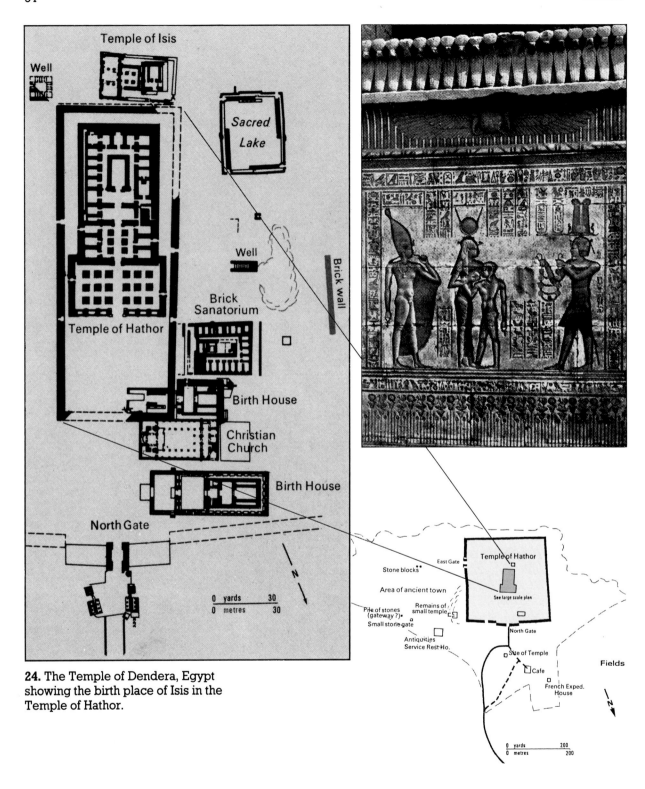

24. The Temple of Dendera, Egypt showing the birth place of Isis in the Temple of Hathor.

thousand years or more and it is significant that nowhere in the *Pyramid Texts* is there any record of the death of Isis or Set.

The plan of Set was to construct a chest of exceptional beauty, shaped in such a manner as to fit precisely the body of Osiris. Then he and **72** accomplices (note the pentagonal number) would invite Osiris to a banquet. Each of them would lie in the chest on the understanding that the one who it fitted best would take it for his own. The plan succeeded. When Osiris climbed into the chest they quickly sealed the lid and threw the chest into the Nile. On hearing this, Isis was grief-stricken and went in search of her husband's body.

Isis had the power to resurrect the dead and, having eventually recovered the body, Set knew that Osiris would live again. Determined not to be outdone, he cut the body into fifteen (**15**) pieces and scattered it far and wide. The lamentations of Isis are well known. She gained great respect from her subjects, when they saw the way she would not rest until she had recovered all the parts of her husband's body. Nephthys, her sister, assisted her in the search. Despite being the wife of Set, she did not approve of his actions and was always ready to assist Isis in times of need.

Eventually, all the parts of Osiris's body were recovered except one – the phallus – and it is important for the reader to remember this critical number. The male body consists of fifteen (**15**) parts. Fourteen (**14**) were found, one was lost, thereby explaining the apparent contradiction concerning the number of Osiris. You will recall that the number representing Osiris was **14**, but this signifies a female body, or alternatively a male body with the phallus removed. The complete body of Osiris is indicated by the number **15**.

The illustration (21) from the *Papyrus of Ani* now becomes intelligible. At the head of the plate we find two groups of six serpents (**6** × **6** = **36**, pentagonal and female), but the line of serpents was only **35**, clearly showing us that one part, the serpent or phallic emblem, is missing.

The pentagonal influence appears throughout the plate, but nowhere more obviously than in the four (**4**) children of Horus standing on a lotus of six (**6**) petals and three (**3**) leaves.

$$4 \times 6 \times 3 = 72 \text{ (the base angle of a pentagram)}$$

Returning to the legend, we find Isis with the body of her husband resurrected but without the essential phallus. Thoth took pity on Isis and permitted her to conceive another child from the dead body of Osiris, using a wooden phallus as a substitute. This she did, and there is some confusion as to whether the child was Horus or another who was premature and born crippled. His name was Harpocrates in Greek or Heru-P-Khart 'who came into the world before his time, and lame in his lower limbs.'[1]

25. The zodiac from the ceiling of the observatory at the Temple of
Dendera. It represents 36 periods of 10 days. The outer figures are
the 12 months.

Perhaps the statue which Bérenger Saunière placed inside the door of the Church at Rennes-le-Château is Harpocrates (see illus 26). This statue can be seen to represent someone who is lame, dark-skinned and horned; born of the Black Madonna, by necrophilia of the deceased body of Osiris, who was by then Lord of the Underworld.

These events all appear to have been related to numerical processes and, as we progress, I hope to be able to accustom the mind of the reader to the methods which were used. By way of introduction to this system, let us consider the time when the year was **360** days. It was composed of **12** months of **30** days, or as the Zodiac of Dendera indicates **36** decans which are ten-day weeks. The month was thereby composed of three weeks, an understandable division which is feminine and pre-dated the division of four – a male number. The symbolic period of a woman's pregnancy was nine months and therefore **270** days. Later, it will be clear that Isis was the superior female creation adapted to this planet and was, therefore, the first female generative principle – born in flesh out of the gods. She has the number eighteen, (**18**) and **270** divided by **18** is **15**, which is the number of parts of the male body or Osiris prior to losing his phallus (see illus 27). The numerical reciprocal of **15** is **666** which will associate man with the number of the beast and it is a useful connection that the sum of the numbers from one to thirty-six (pentagonal) is **666**.

We must now look in more detail at the creation symbol, and in particular at the implication of the circular inference of the body of Nut being arched over the earth. Her back, you will notice, serves as the support for the boat of Ra which traverses the heavens on its daily course.

I knew that the number of Isis was **18** but I needed a position at Rennes-le-Château, or nearby as a starting point. In the *The Hidden God* by that eminent scholar of the occult, Kenneth Grant, I thought I may have found it. He states that there is a legend, known to initiates, concerning the secret abode of the goddess Isis. It says:

The Spirit of Nodens – God of the Great Deep – flashed forth as lightning from the depths and formed a throne in celestial realms – a seat of stone – whereon the Goddess was established. She ruled from the throne of stone which Nodens had fashioned, and about her the temple of Nu-Isis grew into being. This also was of stone, hollowed out, and of the lightning. And this Seat of Stone whirled forth in the heavens – the vehicle of Nodens' fire – veiled from mortal eyes by a vitreous curtain of deep unyielding ocean.

1. *Gods of the Egyptians*. Vol. II p.194 (Dover: New York)
2. *The Hidden God*, 1973, p.148 (Frederick Muller: London)

26. The demonic statue erected by Saunière which stands in the doorway of the church at Rennes-le-Château.

27. The fifteen parts of the male body.

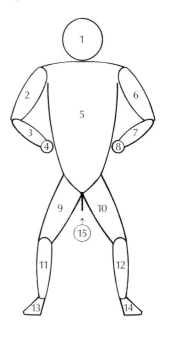

He goes on to say that the name Isis literally means a stone seat. E. A. Wallis Budge, one-time Keeper of Egyptian Antiquities at the British Museum, confirms this but he admits there is no rational explanation for it.

Encyclopedia Britannica describes Isis as the most famous of the Egyptian goddesses. She was of human form. Large temples were dedicated to her worship. She was of great importance in mythology and religion, and she was supreme in magic and knowledge. If this were her description, it seemed to me the title – Stone Seat – was, to say the least, inappropriate. But I was elated when I recalled something I had visited near Rennes-les-Bains called locally *Le Fauteuil du Diable* – The Armchair of the Devil – (see illustration and map insert 29). It was certainly a stone seat. Furthermore, it was of such antiquity that, nothing could be suggested as to its origin. I was told, however, a local priest interested in the archeology of the district had found parts of a stone statue nearby, which suggested the existence of a pre-Christian temple.

28. The boat of Ra traversing the back of the goddess Nut.

I remembered reading that a few miles away at Alet-le-Bain, the remains of another temple dedicated to Isis had been identified. I felt sure if I were to ever find the hidden temple, this position would be near to the centre of the mystery.

There is another legend involving the goddess Isis and Ra the sun-god and knowledge of it is essential to the solution, but before dealing with this we will examine a strange little leaflet called *Le Serpent Rouge* (Secrétariat aux Recherches et Études Spéciales), Véritas Anciennes.

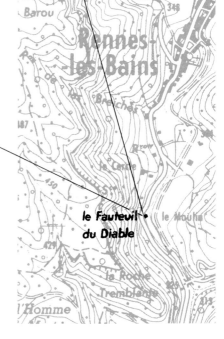

29. Le Fauteuil du Diable (the armchair of the devil) and its position near Rennes-les-Bains.

5

Le Serpent Rouge

The secrets of the world, as we
Succinctly on our tablets write,
Are not expedient to recite:
A plague to heart and head they be.

A fateful discovery – contents of a vital clue – the path of Ophiuchus – poet pointers everywhere – ancient astronomy and further Egyptian legends – the Black Madonna – Isis and the church of Rennes-le-Château – the Priory of Sion – a starting point at last.

In the autumn of 1982 I had purchased an expensive theodolite and decided to make yet another trip south to Rennes. I wanted to check a number of sightings and angles, inter-visibility to use the jargon. I was thankful for my military training in this field. While there I also wanted to make another visit to the church at Rennes-le-Château. Something – and I cannot now be clearer than that – told me I should go there again.

Ever since my meeting with Henry Lincoln I had been trying to track down a copy of a book called *Le Serpent Rouge.* Lincoln had suggested I should acquire a copy as I might find it 'interesting'. But try as I might I could find no trace of the publication. Even an enquiry at the British Museum met without success. Then, on a sunny Sunday in October 1982, as I and the small group accompanying me strolled round the tiny church building at Rennes-le-Château, something quite odd happened.

As I turned to walk out of the church I noticed on a table right in front of me a battered copy of a small book – booklet rather than book in fact. I turned the booklet over – and nearly dropped it in shock.

It was *Le Serpent Rouge.* I paid for it at the little bookshop in the church, though I do not even know if it was properly for sale, and walked away. I was bewildered by this strange turn of fate, not just for the shock revealed in the book's preface but (and more important to me at the time) for the positive panorama of clues which now revealed themselves to me. To friends and colleagues to whom I showed them, they were, and probably remain, unfathomable mysteries – but to me, who had by this stage become so steeped in the lore of the legends and mysteries it was overflowing from me, every line, every word, was a revelation, an instant enlightenment.

The three authors died under strange circumstances. Let the facts speak for themselves:

Louis St. Maxent deceased Monday the 6th March 1967 at 7 a.m.
Gaston De Koker deceased Monday the 6th March 1967 at 9 a.m.
Pierre Feugere deceased Tuesday the 7th March 1967 at 6.20 a.m.

If these reports are true, it is quite obvious that someone is passionately opposed to investigations in the Rennes area. The deaths occurred within a 24-hour period, which in itself would seem to warrant a major inquiry; but it appears this did not happen. Significantly all the deaths of the authors were by hanging. An associate of theirs, Janjua Fakhar-ul-Islam also died in strange circumstances – he was found dead on the railway track at Melun on 19 February 1967.

However, despite these macabre circumstances, part of it had been published, and I had a copy. I have never been totally convinced of the purpose of this publication. Initially I thought it may contain the complete solution, but as the mystery deepened I realized that it fell far short of it. It appears to have been the work of someone who had far more information than was publicly available and yet could not find the complete answer to the riddle. It was certainly composed during or after Saunière's time, as it refers to things which did not exist prior to his period. In my opinion, the only reason for having produced it was to put the 'hounds' on the right scent and then to obtain benefit – not necessarily materially – from being present at the 'kill'. I settled down to reading 'between the lines' to see if it would help me in my search.

I found it to contain a geneological chart, a plan of the Chapel of Saint Sulpice in Paris and a map of France showing boundaries at the time of the Visigoths. The area of Rennes-le-Château was contained in the province of Septimanie. The maps were dated AD 511 and AD 620.

The bulk of the publication, however, was thirteen verses, each attributed to a house of the Zodiac, which are reproduced in their entirety in the Appendices. The additional sign was that of Ophiuchus, Keeper of the Serpent. The astronomical name of this constellation is Aesculapius and it lies between Scorpio and Sagittarius in an area rich in nebulae.

In *Arachne Rising*, James Vogh points out that, considering its size and position, it is surprising it is not included in the normal zodiac.

Aesculapius was the Greek god of Medicine (see illus 30) associated with healing by medicinal springs or spas, and often revealing himself as a snake or serpent, which is why snakes were kept in his temples, particularly at Cos. This was the birthplace of Hippocrates, the ancient Greek father of medicine, who bequeathed us the Hippocratic Oath and the Caduceus – the famous symbol of the medical profession. Medicinal spring water

30. Aesculapius – the Greek God of Medicine.

brings us back to Rennes-les-Bains, which is a well-known hydropathic station. The Caduceus and serpents remind us of the link with Isis mentioned previously.

If one traces the thread which separates the two houses of Sagittarius and Scorpio – the line of the Ophiuchus – back through the centre of the circle of the Zodiac, it passes directly into the Gemini-Taurus division. I saw here a further coincidence, for another Greek legend tells of Theseus penetrating the Labyrinth in order to destroy the Minotaur – a mythical creature, half-man and half-bull. The hybrid beast-man connection is one which will constantly appear throughout our inquiries. It was Ariadne who assisted Theseus in the execution of his task. She gave him a clew of yarn in order that he could use the thread to retrace his steps and avoid being lost in the Labyrinth.

James Vogh asks us to examine the name MINOTAUR and suggests that it is a compound of the latter part of GEMINI and the beginning of TAURUS.

31. The line of Ophiuchus – the serpent holder.

$$\text{geMINi} + \text{TAURUS} = \text{MIN(O)TAUR}$$

A combination of the human and the bull. He also suggests the line which separates them is the thread of Ariadne. Thread, clew, yarn, these are items of spinning or weaving and their connection with Rennes-le-Château was clearly detectable in *Le Serpent Rouge*.

Under Aries we find:

> . . . Desperate to find the way I was aided by the parchments of my friend, they were for me like the thread of ARIADNE.

The French Ariane, is very similar to *araignée*, the spider, which also spins. And when we eventually see the diagram of the solution of the mystery of Rennes-le-Château, the reader will need little persuasion to recognize its remarkable similarity to a spider's web. It will eventually be shown, this web is merely an allegory of a sophisticated geometric pattern – the labyrinth.

The labyrinth, therefore suggests an inter-breeding between man and beast – or alternatively between beast and something else, with man as the resultant offspring. Legends are full of such suggestions and it is quite probable the famous Sphinx is indicating this. It will be shown that its location on the planet is not a thing of chance and neither is the position of the Temple at Rennes which also carries evidence of inter-breeding between man and beast.

We may now begin to appreciate why certain religious factions would have been inclined to suppress this symbolism together with the inevitable conclusions which the position of the serpent in the zodiac would bring us to.

Let us look again at *Le Serpent Rouge*, under Aries:

> In my arduous search, I was trying to hack a way with my sword through the dense vegetation of the woods. I wanted to reach the place of the 'Sleeping BEAUTY' in which some poets can see the QUEEN of a lost kingdom. Desperate to find the way I was aided by the parchments of my friend, they were for me like the thread of ARIADNE.

The 'parchments of my friend' were also to be of great assistance to me when I began the geometric analysis, but for the moment we should consider the well-known fairytale referred to in the text.

In essence the story is that of a beautiful princess who was cursed by a wicked fairy: if ever she should prick her finger on a spindle she would die. Another fairy, a little more benign, was able to modify the spell to some degree. She decreed that in the event of the princess pricking her finger she would simply sleep for one hundred years. The king and queen, determined to avoid this, ensured that no spinning-wheel or any associated items were ever kept in the palace. For a while all was well and the princess grew into a young maiden. However, one day she was exploring the palace and came across a serving woman in her room – spinning. The princess, never having seen a spinning-wheel, was intrigued. Inevitably she pricked her finger – and fell into a deep sleep for a hundred years. Another kind fairy, realizing that when she awoke she would need her servants, caused everyone in the palace to fall into a deep sleep with her. The palace was sealed and in the passage of a hundred years became overgrown and lost in the surrounding forest. The princess was eventually discovered by a prince, who cut his way through the dense vegetation and woke her up.

The spindle alerted me – it was a symbol associated with one of the most ancient of Egyptian goddesses, Neith, which many experts consider to be an early name for Isis, and Neith is depicted with a shuttle on her head. Furthermore, the essence of the story implies something 'frozen in time' – a strange echo of the allegorical *Chemical Wedding* by Christian Rosenkreuz which will also figure in our inquiries.

Returning to the text under, Capricorn we find the author of the famous fairy-tale *Sleeping Beauty*:

> My emotions are elated, DELIVER ME OUT OF THE MIRE, immediately I woke up, my dream is over, I meant to tell you that it was a dream I had on the 17th JANUARY, the day of St. SULPICE, but the nightmare persisted. On reflection I wish I had told it to you as a fairytale by PERRAULT. In this story, my friend, you have followed the most strange and mysterious story in the world.

The French pronunciation of 'Perrault' is very similar to PEYROLLES and that is the name of the small village at the throat of the serpent (see illus 32) could 'by Perrault' also mean 'near to Peyrolles'? Was this a starting point?

January 17th is mentioned, and it also has some enigmatic connections. On January 17th, 1917 Saunière had a stroke and he died a few days later.

January 17th AD 681 was the date Sigisbert IV was reputed to have arrived at Rennes-le-Château. He is the mysterious link in the Merovingian line who, as son of Dagobert II, would have been his heir. As his life was in danger he was apparently concealed and from him came a line of kings who have never ruled.★

January 17th is also the day that the Marquise d'Hautpoul de Blanchefort died. And on the gravestone of Jean Vie, the abbé of Rennes-les-Bains before Henri Boudet, appears the number 17.

Personally I have nothing against people dying on the 17th, but I would not like to think it is an inevitable consequence of pursuing the mystery of Rennes.

I assumed there must be some significance in the number. I noticed almost immediately that 1 and 7 added up to 8, but I do not consider this to be one of my most inspired calculations! Nevertheless the number did seem to ring a distant bell and eventually I recalled it.

I have never seen a copy of Whiston's *Theory of the Earth*. But Higgins quotes it at considerable length in the *Anacalypsis* and I in turn will quote him:

> Since neither the year of 360 days, nor the month of 30 days, is agreeable to any of the celestial motions, it must be granted that the Postdiluvians were not the first framers of this year; and, therefore, that it was used before the deluge also. This farther appears by the most ancient and most valuable testimony of Moses, whereby we understand, that from the 17th day of the second month, when the flood began, till the 17th day of the 7th month, when the Ark rested, were just 150 days, or just 30 days for every intervening month. The words are these: 'In the 600th year of the Noah's life, the second month, the 17th day of the month, the same day were all the fountains of the great deep broken up, and the windows of heaven were opened. And the waters prevailed upon the earth 150 days. And after the end of 150 days the waters were abated; and the ark rested in the 7th month, on the 17th day of the month, upon the mountains of Ararat.' So that hence it is evident that five months, *viz.* the 2nd, 3rd, 4th, 5th and 6th had just 30 days a-piece; and by consequence it is most probable that all the rest had so likewise, and that therefore the whole year had no more than 360 days.

There was a connection, then, between the 17th and the Ark of Noah and, furthermore, with a year of 360 days. By accepting the actual, or maybe purely symbolic, value of 360 days a relationship is established between time and the angular measure of a circle. This connection was used to form a mathematical 'bridge' between spatial and temporal numbers. Later it will be

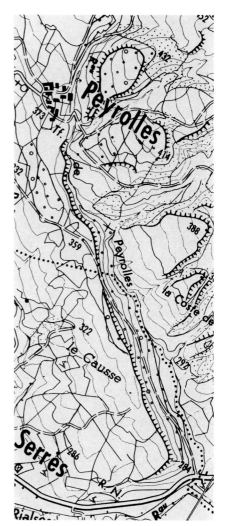

32. The serpent at Peyrolles.

★For historical details see *The Holy Blood and the Holy Grail* seen that the allegorical story of Noah's Ark will provide a 'flood' of numerical clues.

For the earth's year to have changed from 360 to 365 days implies that the planet must have changed its orbit and this was strongly suggested in the legend of the five intercalated days of the Osirian Gods. It is also an important factor in our solution.

Continuing with *Le Serpent Rouge*, under Pisces we have:

> This friend, how would you know him? His name is a mystery but his number is that of a famous seal . . .

Here we are speaking of the sun, whose name, it says, is a mystery, and this is a direct reference to a well-known Egyptian myth. Hence, we must return to Egypt – and its legend of the famous sun-god Ra and how Isis by her cunning acquired his secret name, giving her powers which equalled those of the spirit gods.

In the *Pyramid Texts* we are told a year in the life of Ra was said to be 120 of our years, or a double *hen* period (a *hen* period being 60 years,) and we also find his names are:

> Manifold and unknown even the gods know them not

The number referred to in *Le Serpent Rouge* is easily established – it is 6. And the Seal of Solomon is two equiangular triangles of 60 degrees set in a circle (see illus 33). This is generally referred to as the Star of David – a six-pointed star – symbolically male.

According to legend Isis knew that great power could be hers if she discovered the secret name. She said she could:

> . . . make myself mistress of the earth and become a goddess of like rank and power to Ra in heaven and upon earth.

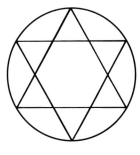

33. The Seal of Solomon – the Star of David.

At that time the legend states:

> Ra had grown old, he dribbled at the mouth and his spittle fell upon the earth.

Isis decided to take advantage of the sun-god's plight so she mixed the saliva with the earth and moulded it to create a sacred serpent (yet another serpent) and laid it in the path of Ra. The next day as he traversed the heavens, the serpent stung him:

> . . . and the cry of his Majesty reached unto heaven.

The gods descended to assist him, but the poison spread:

> . . . swiftly through his flesh just as the Nile rusheth through all his land.

The whole assembly of gods came to him, but none was able to assist him. Then Isis spoke to Ra and said she would disperse the poison if Ra divulged his secret name to her. Ra resisted her and, after extolling his virtues at some length, tried to deceive her by saying:

> I am Khepera in the morning, I am Ra at noon and I am Temu at even.

But Isis knew none of these was the secret name and she withheld her cure. The poison continued to spread.

> . . . it burned like fire and it was fiercer than the flame and the furnace.

Finally, having no alternative, Ra conceded and said:

> Isis shall search into me and my name shall pass from me into her.

Then came a period of darkness on earth, during which Isis was given the secret name of Ra. Isis then released Ra from his suffering saying:

> Depart thou poison go forth from Ra, let Ra live.

> These are the words of Isis – mighty lady – mistress of gods, who, knew Ra by his own name.

The links were joining and it was obvious that Isis was becoming the central figure.

Returning to Pisces in *Le Serpent Rouge*, we find also a reference to the pilot or custodian of the Ark of Noah, and the word used in the actual document is *le nautonnier*. This, it seems, is a direct link with the Priory of Sion, whose highest grade is Nautonnier.

In *Anacalypsis*, the eminent scholar G. Higgins considers that the Ark of Noah relates to *noe* – meaning mind or intellect.

So the Ark, in this sense would appear to be a preserver not only of life, but of intelligence. It is very important to grasp this concept, for it would have been impossible for the inundation to destroy every life form on this planet. It could however have totally destroyed man – the only creature entrusted with, or endowed with, intelligence.

My mind returned to Poussin's *Déluge* linking the Ark with the serpent which signifies intelligence. In the foreground another 'boat' can be seen acting as a 'life-saver'. The distinct shape of it reminded me that in the mythology of Egypt, Greece and Rome, a 'boat' of this design was a well-known symbol of Isis. In astronomical terms her boat was positioned in the constellation of Argo. Specifically, in Egypt this constellation was named Sothis or Soth-Isis, the Star of Isis. Furthermore, in the Egyptian legends this vessel represented the female organ of generation.

Two direct references to Isis occur in *Le Serpent Rouge* under
Virgo:

> . . . Two times I.S. embalming and embalmed. Miraculous vessel
> of the eternal White Lady of the Legends.

and under Leo:

> . . . long ago her name was ISIS, Queen of the benevolent
> springs, COME TO ME ALL YOU WHO LABOUR AND ARE
> HEAVY LADEN AND I WILL GIVE YOU REST. Others
> knew her as MAGDALENE with the celebrated vase full of
> healing balm. The initiated know her to be NOTRE DAME DES
> CROSS.

Later it will be seen that the 'vessel' referred to is a clever *triple
entendre* relating boat, chalice and the female generative organ.

The second reference blatantly discloses the equation:

ISIS = MAGDALENE = NOTRE DAME DES CROSS.

This certainly confirms the opinion of the eminent authority
Friedrich Nork who stated that the temple of Nôtre Dame in
Paris was formerly a temple of the goddess Isis. To include
Magdalene in the equation could cause some offence, but only if
we accept the opinion of the church authorities that this lady was
a prostitute. In fact there is no biblical reference to that effect,
but history has marked her a 'fallen woman' on whom Jesus took
particular pity, whereafter she was redeemed. In fact this
popular image, like so many other stories inspired by a
censorious Church, is a nonsense.

No less an authority than William Caxton, in his famous
fifteenth-century translation of the influential Genoese work
Legenda Aurea (Golden Legend) published in 1275, provides
clear evidence that Mary Magdalene, far from being a woman of
the gutter, was in actual fact a woman of the noblest birth. To
quote:

> Mary Magdalene had her surname of Magdalo, a castle, and was
> born of right noble lineage and parents, which were descended of
> the lineage of kings. And her father was named Cyrus, and her
> mother Eucharis. She with her brother Lazarus, and her sister
> Martha, possessed the castle of Magdalo, which is two miles from
> Nazareth, and Bethany, the castle which is nigh to Jerusalem, and
> also a great part of Jerusalem, which, all these things they
> departed among them. In such wise that Mary had the castle
> Magdalo whereof she had her name Magdalene.

> Then when Magdalene abounded in riches, and because delight is
> fellow to riches and abundance of things; and for so much as she
> shone in beauty greatly, and in riches, so much the more she
> submitted her body to delight, and therefore she lost her right
> name, and was called customably a sinner.

In fact, she was also high priestess of the Temple of Ishtar at Magdala, and as such she would have been the keeper of the doves. Furthermore, she was a Benjamite, the tribe which was ostracized because they were of the line of Cain. So too was Hiram Abiff, architect of the Temple of Solomon.

Henry Lincoln reminds us that the Benjamite tribe were exiled and eventually settled in Arcadia, a strong link with the 'Et in Arcadia Ego' theme of *Les Bergers d'Arcadie* by Poussin. They were the ancestors of the Merovingians – a race of kings supposedly descended from the mythical Quinotaur, a sea creature who raped the mother of Merovee. The name suggests the sea, as does Mary or Marie. We should remember that the symbol of Jesus when he was living was a fish, and that the eventual cross was not of his choosing.

In France – particularly in the south – many churches are adorned with images of a Black Madonna, and at the Cathedral at Chartres she appears in association with the Isis 'boat' symbol. There seems to be no escape from these obvious connections. We meet the same controversy in Italy. I quote G. Higgins again:

> There is scarcely an old church in Italy where some remains of the worship of the Black Virgin and Black Child are not to be met with.

Roman Catholic priests have discredited themselves by explaining this as discoloration due to the smoke from the candles. They apparently fail to notice that the eyes and teeth of the statues are not affected in the same way. In some cases the statues were painted white in an attempt to pass them off as the Virgin Mary. Despite this suppression of the Black Madonnas we need have no doubt – we are seeing here the Queen of the Heavens – ISHTAR – ASTARTE – ISIS. An image pre-dating Christianity by hundreds, if not thousands, of years.

The almost inescapable conclusion is that the Virgin Mary is a remodelled image superimposed on the cult of the Black Madonna because it was too strong to destroy. Furthermore the image of the Black Madonna has more in common with Magdalene than with the Virgin Mary. At the church of *Les Saintes Maries-de-la-Mer* near Marseilles the association of Magdalene is acknowledged and it is a matter of historical record that the three Marys fled from the Holy Land to Marseilles, which is, of course, very close to the valley at Rennes. There is sufficient imagery in the area to leave us in no doubt that the inference from Leo of *Le Serpent Rouge* is not unreasonable.

As Henry Lincoln so succinctly puts it, maternity related to the Magdalene is a somewhat different image to the one the Vatican would have us believe. Possibly, with the passage of time, the French will be proud of the association which at the moment seems to embarrass them. I sincerely hope so.

Bérenger Saunière certainly had no misgivings about this lady.

His church at Rennes-le-Château had been consecrated to the
Magdalene in 1059 and using part of his wealth he erected both
the Villa Bethania (see illus 34) and the Tour Magdala (see illus
35). The latter strongly resembles a 'castle', acting as a link with
the name Magdalo and the chesspiece. This connection will
become apparent as we move into the world of the Knights
Templar.

34. Villa Bethania built by Saunière and named after the castle of
Bethany owned by Lazarus, brother of Mary Magdalene.

Many other references in *Le Serpent Rouge* were to be valuable
confirmations as I threaded my way through the morass of
imagery surrounding the mystery. In particular it provided me
with one of the possible starting points to solve the geometry.

It was under Pisces that I read:

> . . . on his white rock looking beyond the black rock towards the
> south.

I had my starting point at last: there, near to Rennes-le-
Château, was the Château de Blanchefort (white fort?). And on
the same mountain, Roque Nègre (black rock). The line from
one to the other was southerly.

35. La Tour Magdala built by Saunière to house his library. It is situated at the left hand of the pentagram. (It is named after the castle Magdalo owned by Mary Magdalene.)

36. Statue of the Magdalene in the church of Rennes-le-Château, to whom the church was dedicated (note the skull at her feet).

6

The First Line

For 'Is' and 'Is-Not' though with Rule and Line,
And 'Up-and-Down' without, I could define,
I yet in all I only cared to know
Was never deep in anything but-Wine.

Help from the sun – a rainbow becomes a clue – white rocks and black rocks point the way – the Paris Meridian – the Poussin tomb – the English mile – the incredible circle of churches – the secret pentagram – the Meridian becomes a miracle – the Celts – or the gods?

Using the slotted-templet method described in the intro-duction, I had identified pentagonal angles between important positions in the area round Rennes-le-Château. My first impression was that I may eventually be dealing with a much larger figure than anyone had anticipated.

I had circled these positions on a large-scale map and although the pentagram evaded me I could see, or maybe sense, certain correspondences.

37. A Black Madonna, typical of those to be found throughout Europe. This one is from the Cathedral of Tarrogona in Spain.

Now with the clues from *Le Serpent Rouge*, I concentrated my attention in a specific area.

Aquarius and Pisces linked together read:

> How strange are the manuscripts of this friend, great traveller of the unknown. They come together as white light but for one who knows, separately they are the colours of the rainbow; for the artist these six colours unite like magic in his palette and form black.
>
> This friend, how would you know him? His name is a mystery but his number is that of a famous seal. How can one describe him? Maybe like the pilot of the everlasting Ark of Noah, impassive like a pillar of his white rock looking beyond the black rock towards the south.

To me there was absolutely no doubt about the interpretation. 'Great traveller of the unknown' was clearly the sun – Ra of Egyptian legend fame, and 'friend' indeed. The 'manuscripts' referred to previously under Aries as 'parchments' could only be messages of some sort, delivered in the form of sunlight which, 'coming together', appear to be white light, but this is in actual fact a composite of all the colours of the rainbow: red, orange, yellow, green, blue, indigo and violet. As painter's pigment they combine to make black. But surely here we have seven colours? For a moment I was puzzled by the reference to the figure six.

Was his name a mystery? It certainly was according to the Ra-Isis legend. I had therefore already decided that it was the sun which was being referred to; did this confirm it? Esoteric, and particularly Egyptian, doctrine states that the number of the sun is **6** – in geometric terms, the hexagram. Or the famous Seal of Solomon, (SOL-OM-ON) means sun. It was proof enough for me.

There were obvious clues in *Le Serpent Rouge* pointing to the church of Rennes-le-Château such as under Cancer:

> The Mosaic tiles of the sacred place alternate black and white and JESUS like ASMODEUS observes their alignment.

The 'chessboard' tiled floor is a well-known feature of the church, as are the two statues referred to, Jesus and Asmodeus. Asmodeus is the King of Demons, associated with Solomon. He guards the door of the church as he did the temple, but in my opinion he may also be the son of Set and Isis.

Another well-known phenomenon of the area is that when standing at the church the sun rises over Blanchefort on the 22 July – the feast day of Santa Maria Magdalena to whom the church is dedicated. It follows, therefore that from Rennes-le-Château the sun would appear like an impassive pillar on a white rock guiding, or acting as a beacon or pilot for, Noah's Ark (rainbow? white light? sunlight?).

38. The ruins of the Château-de-Blanchefort on the 'white rock' – a reference point on the 'sunrise line'.

I drew a line representing the sunrise from the church to Château Blanchefort (see illus 38) and to my amazement the continuation of it passed through the church of Arques (Ark?) and then to the gate of the cemetery of Arques.

Following the instructions in *Le Serpent Rouge*, I returned to the white rock (Blanchefort) and looked in a southerly direction for the black rock. There could be no doubting its identity, for there on the same mountain only half a mile away is Roque Nègre (black rock, see illus 39). But we are told to look *beyond* the black rock so, having drawn the line from Blanchefort to Roque Nègre I extended it. The result was little short of breathtaking. It passed precisely through the church of Rennes-les-Bains, the sister church of Rennes-le-Château. It was even more convincing when I realized the line I had just drawn was at **90°** to the line of the sunrise (see illus 41).

I looked through *Le Serpent Rouge* again for anything which might indicate direction, and under Gemini I read:

. . . find the line of the meridian in going from East to West . . .

Knowing the Greenwich meridian lay well beyond Toulouse to the west this must necessarily refer to the French meridian based on Paris which was clearly passing across my sunrise line between Blanchefort and Arques.

The Paris meridian is the original European marker of longitudinal measurement, established around 1670. It was replaced in 1884 by the British Greenwich meridian despite vehement opposition from the French, who made a strong plea that if an international meridian was to be established it should

39. The Roque Nègre – the black rock showing the way to the centre of the circle of churches.

be a line based on either the Great Pyramid of Giza or Jerusalem! Feelings ran so high that the French only finally accepted the international verdict in favour of Greenwich as late as 1978 – and to this day domestic maps of France still feature their national meridian instead of Greenwich. As it happens, the evidence this solution eventually discloses strongly favours the French line.

Two things then became significantly clear. Firstly the angle of intersection between the meridian and the sunrise was 72° – the base angle of a pentagram. Secondly, very near to this intersection was the famous tomb depicted in Poussin's painting *Les Bergers d'Arcadie* (illus 40).

What should I do next? As so often in these early stages, I turned back to Rennes-le-Château. I remembered the reference to the six colours of the rainbow under the verse for Aquarius in *Le Serpent Rouge*. Was it possible, I wondered, that 'rainbow' could in any way relate to the distance to the church of Arques (rainbow = *arc-en-ciel*)?

I decided on a simple test; I measured the line between the churches of Rennes-le-Château and Arques – the sunrise line – and divided it into six equal parts. At once I felt I had something; the second division moving west from Arques brought me exactly into the Paris meridian intesection. This was, of course, impressive enough. But what further correspondences were there?

I felt I could perceive a similarity in the distance between each sixth part and the distance between Rennes-les-Bains and Roque Nègre. Tentatively I tested it; it fitted precisely. I felt that special tingle of anticipation together with a sense of conviction; this was the right path.

With six 'manuscripts' (or components of light) identified, I examined the possibility of that measure having numerical significance. I found it was ONE ENGLISH MILE!

I scanned the area to see if there were more 'coincidences' – one was amazing. The distance between the sister churches of Rennes-le-Château and Rennes-les-Bains was exactly three miles!

I looked at the tomb again, I felt Poussin had to be important to have been mentioned in the original cipher. Then I noticed that, when extended, a line drawn from the tomb to the intersection of the meridian and the sunrise, passed through Rennes-les-Bains church. This was impressive to say the least, but at the time it did not appear to make any contribution to the solution. Extending the line further south took it close to Le Fauteuil du Diable (Seat of the Devil or Isis) and L'Homme Mort (the dead man). Could this be the 'He who is there dead' from the second cipher?

My next move was either inspired or just plain lucky. I felt sure there was something of importance on the Poussin line south of Rennes-les-Bains and, taking my proven 'one English mile', I struck off that distance to the south of the church. It seemed to be no help at all; I marked the spot and pinned the map on the wall to try to understand how the designers would have made the next move. When I viewed it from a distance something quite uncanny seemed to be happening. Could this really be so? It was 2 o'clock in the morning and I was very tired – almost too tired to believe my imagination was not playing tricks. My slotted-templet positions seemed to be ranged round the position I had just marked in a perfect circle. I hunted for the extensions for my compasses which would accommodate this massive circle. With the position near L'Homme Mort as centre, I set the radius to the church of Rennes-le-Château. I will never forget my surprise – even disbelief – as the compasses traced the circumference.

Rennes-le-Château – the church of Coustausssa precisely – Cassaignes a near miss – Château Serres – the church of Serres precisely – the strange rock feature on the side of La Berco Grando which resembled a female head – the church of Bugarach precisely – the church of Saint Just-et-le-Bézu precisely.

It must have been 3 a.m. when I discovered this circle of churches, and I refrained from waking the household, confident that by daybreak I would have a complete solution. Little did I realize it would be months before I would finally break the code of the geometry (illus 42).

Startling as it was to find the circle of churches, I had to be convinced that it was not coincidental, and the best test of that was to verify their antiquity.

Rennes-le-Château was beyond question but, nevertheless, as a reference I needed an authoritative source and I found it, together with other useful data in *Les Châteaux Cathares*.* The document which first mentioned Rennes as a chateau was dated 1002. The next position on the circle was Coustaussa. This was

*René Quechen and Dominique Dieltiens, *Les Châteaux Cathares* (René Quechen: Montesquien-Volvestre)

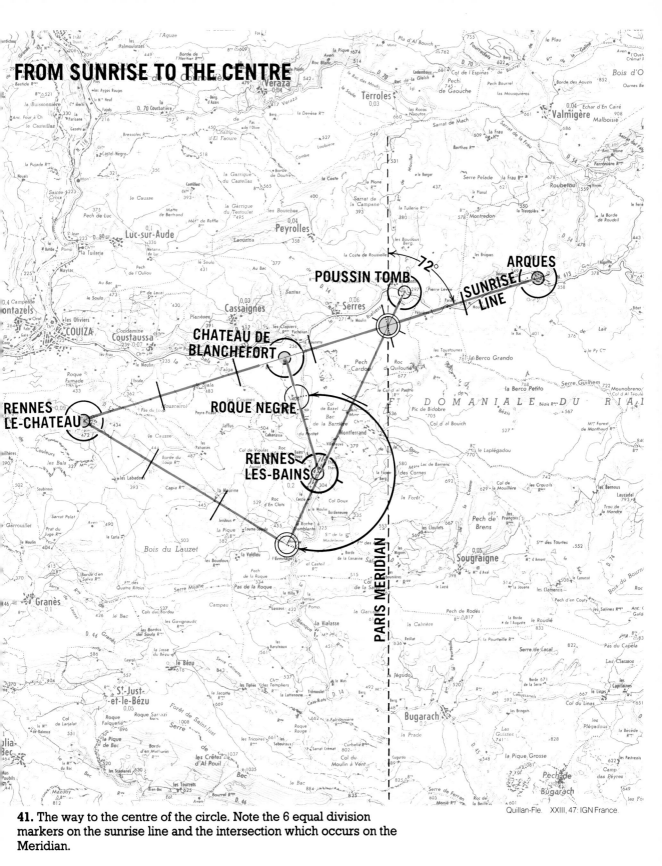

FROM SUNRISE TO THE CENTRE

41. The way to the centre of the circle. Note the 6 equal division markers on the sunrise line and the intersection which occurs on the Meridian.

Quillan-Fle. XXIII, 47: IGN France.

dated 1157. It was the fortress which was surrendered to the army of Simon de Montfort, the 'butcher' employed by Pope Innocent III in the Albigensian Crusade. Cassaignes was not mentioned in my data of the Albigensian Crusade, but the church was obviously very old. I found 17th-century references to it and as it was not precisely on my circle I was not deterred. The Château of Serres (illus 44) first appeared on a map by Roussel in 1713, but the church again obviously pre-dated it. The next position was a strange looking rock feature on the eastern slope of the Berco Grando. Together with another rock outcrop, it is referred to on the French maps as *Les Toustounes*. Our circle passed through the largest of these and by referring to the photograph we will see that it is an outstanding feature. On observing it for the first time, I was immediately struck by its similarity to Queen Victoria, it certainly appeared to me to be a stately head – and female. Its antiquity is indisputable.

The next church was Bugarach, near to the highest summit of the Corbières – the impressive Pique Grosse – Pech de Bugarach (illus 43). The church was very old and its existence had been verified as early as 1231. Some interesting graffiti were discovered on the walls, which can be seen in illus 45. The pentagram is once more evident.

Our last church is Saint Just-et-le-Bézu for which I could find no reference in the Albigensian Crusade period, but the architectural style indicates that it is of similar age to those of Coustaussa and Cassaignes.

Another remarkable coincidence became apparent when reviewing the circle of churches. The circle exactly intersects the position where the line of the 'sunrise' crosses the meridian. To my mind this was a perfect confirmation.

The next part of my task was to discover whether a pentagram or some other 'star' figure was being controlled by this circle.

Although I had rejected the idea of a regular pentagram as being too obvious to have avoided previous detection, nevertheless I knew from my previous work the angles of a pentagram – **36°** – existed in several places.

By taking a line from Rennes-le-Château to the church at Bugarach and marking off **36°** in an anticlockwise direction I found that, although there was nothing of significance on the circumference of the circle, the line passed through the ancient fortified position of Montferrand.

The position of Montferrand seemed to be confirmed by the fact that using the line from Bugarach to Rennes-le-Château and measuring **36°** clockwise, this radial also passed through it. Furthermore it passed precisely through the peak of Pech Cardou, the highest peak in the valley. By way of confirmation, it then went precisely to the Château of Serres.

My confidence grew and, reassured by Montferrand, I constructed the line **36°** anticlockwise from the arbitrary point on the circumference which Montferrand had led me to. The result

40. The tomb illustrated in the Poussin painting *Les Bergers d'Arcadie*, carrying the famous inscription 'ET IN ARCADIA EGO'.

THE CIRCLE OF CHURCHES

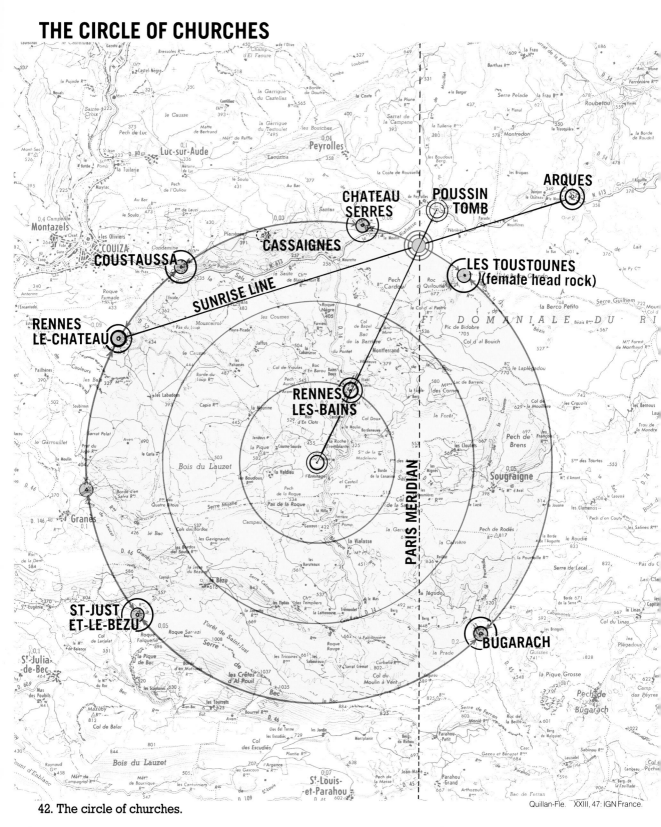

42. The circle of churches.

Quillan-Fle. XXIII, 47: IGN France.

was remarkable. It led directly to the church of Saint Just-et-le-Bézu and as further confirmation it intersected the Serres–Bugarach line at exactly the same point as did the meridian.

The next move was obvious, **36°** from this line went directly to the church of Cassaignes. Admittedly it was not on the circumference, but it was only 150 metres short of it. Was this an error on the part of those who conceived this plan? At this stage I could not be sure, so with caution I continued the line to the circumference. My pentagram did not close. I extended the truncated lines until it did. I was disappointed there was nothing

43. The church of Bugarach at the south-east point of the pentagram on the circle of churches.

44. Château Serres – built on the remains of an ancient chateau. An important intersection of the circle and the extended pentagram. It also figures in the final solution.

45. Ancient pentagonal graffiti at Bugarach.

of significance at their intersection, but the figure was truly remarkable. The angle which had been subtended outside the circle was exactly **36°**. As I considered this figure I began to realize just how unusual was the speciality of this pentagram. It was perfectly symmetrical – displayed **36° ± ½°** on all its star-points, but it extended outside the circle. What other special properties did it have? To my amazement, the axis from the north point to the centre of the circle of churches was exactly north to south!

Despite the fact the pentagram was symmetrical, it was obviously not a regular one and, as a consequence, the axis from the north point to the opposing intersection failed to go through the centre of the circle.

It is tempting, at times like these, to start 'juggling' to achieve a result. The temptation had been heightened by the fact I had also found that a line drawn from the northern point to the centre of the circle passed through the Château de Blanchefort. I refrained however, determined to allow the logic of the geometry take its true course. My honesty was later rewarded, for when I began to work with maps of a much larger scale, I could then see that although my axis had just missed the Château de Blanchefort, so had the sunrise line to Arques – but their intersection with the Rocque Nègre line was perfect (illus 41).

At this stage I had two concentric circles – that of the churches and a small one which only passed through Rennes-les-Bains. The smaller was one third of the radius of the larger. This prompted me to draw the intermediate circle. I was so engrossed in my pentagram that I was disappointed to find that this appeared to contribute nothing to it; but by now I was learning the technique. I strengthened my confirmed geometry and viewed the result from a distance. I saw something which took me completely by surprise – I wonder at it even now. I was looking at the French meridian and, as my eyes traced slowly

46. The cemetery of Bugarach with the Pique Grosse in the background.

47. La Pique, a distinctive feature near La Valdieu, used as a survey beacon and confirming the line of the pentagram from Rennes-le-Château to Bugarach.

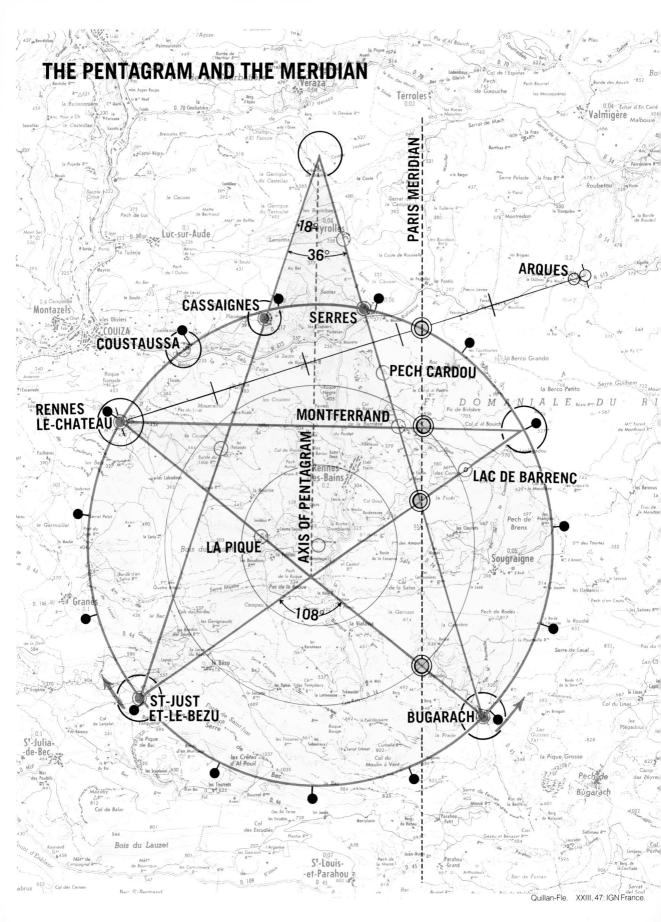

THE PENTAGRAM AND THE MERIDIAN

PARIS MERIDIAN

18°
36°

ARQUES

CASSAIGNES
SERRES
COUSTAUSSA
PECH CARDOU

RENNES
LE-CHATEAU
MONTFERRAND

LAC DE BARRENC

AXIS OF PENTAGRAM

LA PIQUE

108°

ST-JUST
ET-LE-BEZU
BUGARACH

Quillan-Fle.   XXIII, 47: IGN France.

down from north to south, I saw not only that it crossed the circle of churches at the sunrise intersection, but that a little further south it crossed the intermediate circle at the point where the upper left arm of the pentagram had intersected it. I found this incredible but there was still more. Even further south the meridian coincided with the right 'arm pit' conjunction of the pentagram. By this time I could have believed in miracles and that is precisely what I found. When the meridian crossed the intermediate circle again, it was at the same point where the inside line of the right leg of the pentagram coincided with it.

This may seem tedious to the reader, but in considering the quality of observation necessary to achieve such a figure, the mind boggles. Could there be more? In perfection anything is possible, and as the solution progresses it will be seen that the meridian still had a couple of trump cards to play.

The fact that an occult society with sufficient funds could arrange churches in the 12th and 13th centuries to form this image over such terrain was unbelievable enough – but how could they have anticipated the position of the Paris meridian, which was not established until the 1600s?

A geometric figure of these proportions threaded through mountainous terrain to coincide with a meridian to this degree of accuracy would require 'star-fixes' using sophisticated equipment. After all, meridians are not lines painted on the ground for all to see. But quite apart from this, we are confronted here with a chronological impossibility: when the churches were built the meridian was not there! Or was it? Was even this to be doubted? Had someone established a global grid reference long before we could even imagine?

Stunned by the magnitude of these discoveries, I returned to the geometry. If the layout of a temple existed here, circles and pentagonal angles would not form it, I needed right angles. As I proceeded I was pleased to find that the eastern arm of the north point of the pentagram formed a right angle with the line of the sunrise. I wondered if the walls of the temple were beginning to take shape. Try as I might I failed to find features on the ground to support that particular right angle so I next started a systematic search for anything which would form **90°** with any other arm of the pentagram; I found nothing.

48. The Pentagram in the circle of churches showing the perfection with which it was designed to coincide with the Paris Meridian. Note also the close proximity of the star-points to the 15 equal divisions of the circle which control an extended pentagram of this type. It is also coincidental that the chord of the fifteenth part is almost exactly one fifth of the distance from Rennes-le-Château to the gate of the cemetery at Arques. The head of the female pentagram removes one part of the fifteen parts leaving the 14 parts of Osiris which were found. Note also that compared to a regular pentagram where the legs would span one fifth of the circumference – these legs are opened to accommodate a quarter of it.

There was no alternative but to return to the laborious task of sifting evidence and searching for clues. I needed to recognize another ground feature, and I eventually found it in the illustrated sculpture on the face of the altar in the church at Rennes-le-Château, one of the works commissioned by Bérenger Saunière (illus 49 and 50). Many things interested me in this feature.

49. The altar design of the church at Rennes-le-Château. Magdalene kneels in a cave with the persistent skull at her knees. Outside can be seen the Berco Petito and the arch feature of a rock on Berco Grando.

50. The gold tooth surrounds of the altar design carry the significant numbers of the mystery. On the left can be seen 14, representing the body of Osiris with the phallus removed. The main design is surrounded by 35 teeth showing that one has been removed from the pentagonal 36, but the 16th one from the left or 20th from the right, is twice as large as the others. This suggests that $20 + 16 = 36$ is confirmation of our interpretation.

It may be seen in the illustration that the Magdalene kneels in a cave, with a skull at her knees. Outside we see a distinctive hill, and an even more definite shape – like a ruined arch. I had seen that shape before – but not upright. It was the shape of the rock at the summit of the Berco Grando when viewed from above (illus 51). The hill in the sculpture was recognisable as the Berco Petito. I checked my diagram and there was no doubt; the line between them, or to be more exact, between the rock outcrops on them, was tangential to the circle, and met the western arm of the north point of the pentagram at **90°**.

As I drew the line across the meridian I knew instinctively that I was about to receive another shock. On the **180°** of approach my new line generated the angles of **72°** and **108°**. Here was the number of the goddess Isis (**18**) with her mother Nut (**0**) in attendance. Dividing these two numbers by **18** analysed their 'hidden' meaning: the first became **4** indicating the square or construction, the lineage of the temple walls: the second becomes **6** the number of the sun-god Ra. The relationship between the meridian and the temple walls burst into my mind. Longitude marks time and so does the sun. The numbers disclosed by the Isis factor acting on the meridian were **4** and **6** which when multiplied give the **24** hours of the day. And Osiris was there as well, for the **360°** cycle, when divided by **24** gave his number before he was dismembered (**15**).

I drew the tangential square on the circle of churches and marked the central axes. The reason, or one of the reasons, for the extended north point of the pentagram was now clear to me – it marked the distance of the north wall. I completed the rectangle and there was the Temple of Isis inclined at **18°** to the meridian as was the temple of her birth-place at Dendera in Egypt.

51. The plan view of the altar feature of Berco Grando as marked on the 1/25,000 map of the area.

53. The old church of Cassaignes, one of the pentagonal churches.

52. Les Toustounes – a prominent feature and an essential part of the geometry. It occupies the position of the angel Sandlephon in the wings of the Ark of the Covenant and is referred to in the text as the female head rock.

It was simple logic to mark the diagonals of the square (**45°**) which at their intersection with the circle would fix the corners of the largest square which could be drawn inside the circle. How can I keep on saying amazing, incredible, miraculous? Here is perfection! The south-east corner of that square was the position where the circle was intersected by the meridian! (illus 55).

I asked my business partner to look at my work and give me an opinion; he had also qualified in large-scale mapping techniques in military survey. His answer was instantaneous – aerial survey based on known ground control positions. I reminded him that if the Cathars or the Knights Templar had possessed aircraft, it had certainly escaped the notice of the historians, and that

54. Berco Grando and Berco Petito looking south.

furthermore I was not trying to write a script for a science-fiction film. Nevertheless, as we together analysed the necessary requirements for such sophisticated work the conclusions became even more bizarre. In simple terms we decided it would be easier to say this was 'the work of the gods'. Little did I realize at that time that I was seeing only the tip of the iceberg. I forced my mind back to more rational considerations. I would have to examine more closely the paradox of the dating between the churches and the meridian.

Coincidence – it could never be! Could the dating be wrong? – Impossible! Could the meridian have been there before the churches? If this was the case, who was constructing maps on a world meridian through Paris in the 1200s. But even if this were so, how could it be in a position which so precisely conformed to the final established French meridian of the 1600s?

Or was it that the whole concept was of much greater antiquity than I was able to believe?

Were these churches built on known positions, merely reinforcing the markers laid down in the remote past – a Celtic circle of standing stones. Again, the thoughts rushed in. Narbonne was nearby and it was the site of the Celtic capital Narbo. Le cercle – a Celtic marker; Le Fauteuil du Diable – Celtic or before?

And a book that Henri Boudet had given to Saunière. *La Vraie Langue celtique et le Cromleck de Rennes-les-Bains*[*] (The True Celtic Language and the Stone Circle of Rennes-les-Bains).

The mythology of the Celts is admittedly confused, but there can be no doubting the power they once wielded in the south-west region of France. Their original beliefs were greatly influenced by the female generative principle and their major deity was Dana, the goddess of life and death, who in her vengeful mood is Black

---

[*] *La Vraie Langue celtique et le Cromleck de Rennes-les-Bains*, 1886.

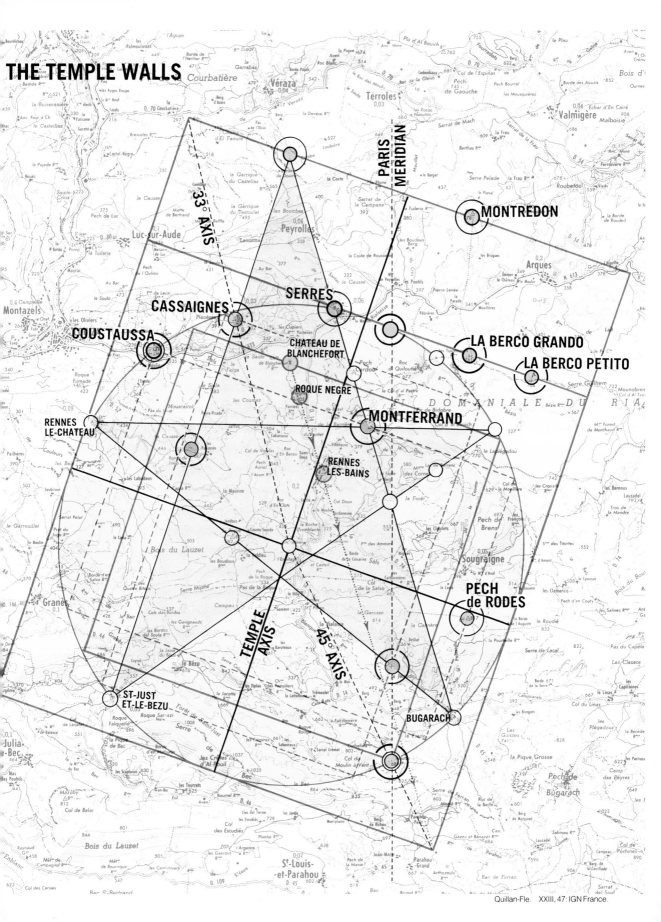

THE TEMPLE WALLS

PARIS MERIDIAN

33° AXIS

45° AXIS

TEMPLE AXIS

MONTREDON

SERRES

CASSAIGNES

COUSTAUSSA

CHATEAU DE BLANCHEFORT

ROQUE NEGRE

LA BERCO GRANDO

LA BERCO PETITO

MONTFERRAND

RENNES LE-CHATEAU

RENNES LES-BAINS

PECH de RODES

ST-JUST ET-LE-BEZU

BUGARACH

Annis. She is compared to Isis by many Celtic authorities, inasmuch as she was the conglomerate of many of the lesser deities. The origin of the Celts is a mystery, but they appear to have manifested themselves in Wales, Ireland and along the western seaboard of Europe. They failed to put their myths in writing to the extent that the Greeks did, so unfortunately a good deal has been lost. But one thing is sure – they believed in a paradise beyond the sea of the setting sun – a sea that their forefathers had rowed across in the distant past.

It is difficult to imagine this sea was the Atlantic Ocean and the land was the Americas. We could therefore, consider this to be one more shred of evidence to suggest the lost continent of Atlantis. I do not intend to assail the reader with a mass of circumstantial evidence pointing to the previous existence of an advanced civilization occupying an island continent in the Atlantic Ocean. I believe I read somewhere that more books had been written about Atlantis than about almost any other subject and I am sure that, like Troy, it will be found one day. I suppose, like millions of others, I feel a deep-seated desire for something to be found which will solve the riddle of the origin of man. However, leaving aside the romantic appeal of such an idea, I would recommend anyone to read Ignatius Donnelly's two books on the subject although they have been discredited: *Atlantis*[2] (The Antediluvian World) and *The Destruction of Atlantis*[3] (The Age of Fire and Gravel).

Recent developments in science lean toward a scenario of disrupting celestial events in which myths rest more comfortably. As far as we are concerned there are certain unavoidable connections with Rennes-le-Château. If this planet has been subjected to the destruction of its surface in comparatively recent times, evolution from ape to intelligent man would be hard to visualize. For an environment to accommodate this process, it would require millions of years of geological tranquillity.

Even at this early stage, it was evident that to have a complete understanding of the mystery at Rennes-le-Château I would need to consider every possibility. If this diagram was the work of an early intelligence – where are those beings now? Was there an event in the history of our planet which caused them to leave? Or was it us? Are we the savage remnants of a golden age?

55. The outline of the temple showing the male and female axes, with the control features marked in yellow. Note the coincidental intersection of the meridian with the south-eastern corner of the square in the circle. The reason that the church at Cassaignes is not on the circle is also apparent – it controls the 'holy' rectangles which are dealt with in 'The Chess-board'. It also fixes the 33 degree axis to the most northerly corner of the temple. It is interesting to note the most southerly corner is confirmed by the fact that a line from Château de Blanchefort through Roque Nègre and the church at Rennes-les-Bains passes through it.

2. Dover Publications, New York.
3. Multimedia Publishing Corp., New York.

7

Cosmic Interference

Awake! for Morning in the Bowl of Night
Has flung the Stone that puts the Stars to Flight:
And Lo! the Hunter of the East has caught
The Sultan's Turret in a Noose of light.

*Asteroids and comets – did Earth move? – another circle – finding the crescent of Nut –
more miracles – the abyss – the circuit of Ra – the first sexual inference.*

An age-old problem exists between those who support continuous evolution and their adversaries who believe that at
times the earth has been subjected to cataclysmic events. Wishful
thinking leads people to prefer the idea of this planet as a safe place
to live and so, until recently, the reasons given for the
disappearance of the dinosaurs at the end of the Mesozoic period
were confined to scenarios of slow change. Changes in climate over
a long period – diminishing food supplies over a long period –
excessive vegetation lowering the temperature to a point which
triggered an ice age, over a long period. The fact that all the
evidence points to a brief cataclysmic event does nothing to
dissuade those who are determined to present this planet as a safe
haven for mankind. This 'head in the sand' attitude prevailed until
quite recent times, despite the fact any reasonable pair of field-
glasses would show the observer that our close 'neighbour', the
moon, appears to have been used for target practice.

Our 'acquired twin planet' (for it is far too large to be considered
a satellite) has little romantic appeal when viewed at close range.
The surface is pock-marked and scarred to such a degree that it
suggests cosmic catastrophe on an alarming scale, and much of it
looks not so very old, in astronomical terms. Admittedly, with no
erosive processes on the moon, the evidence of any impact is
retained for a vast period, but we can still be sure the greater
number of these occurred in two specific phases.

Where was our earth when this was going on?

The academics provided answers of course. They told us that
the earth's atmospheric shield had reduced these cosmic missiles
to dust before they reached the surface and that the earth sailed on
majestically through space – protected by the grace of God, for
thereon dwelt His 'chosen ones'. However, it seems that he did get
a little cross on a couple of occasions and decided to drown
mankind; we are told he poured the oceans over us. But there
again, we must have deserved it.

Science – to the Roman Church, that wicked instrument of Satan – continued its investigations and evidence began to appear of missiles which had managed to penetrate our defensive atmosphere. Of course these were aimed specifically at the 'wicked'. But – if the statistics published by *Scientific American*[1] are accurate – there must have been a lot of wicked people living in Canada from time to time. As the caption says (illus 56a) that unfortunate area – although only one per cent of the land mass of the earth – has received about fifty per cent of the impacts. The article also points out that on a statistical basis there must have been twice as many objects falling in the water.

Most of these missiles approach the earth from the same direction, from the north-west to the south-east. The Atlantic Ocean begins to look like 'ground zero' and this suggests that the greatest percentage of impacts must have been in the ocean. One of the most favoured positions for the mythical lost city of Atlantis is just north of the Azores and, as such, it would be directly in the line of fire (see illus 56b). There is a possibility of cataclysmic impact being the reason for the disappearance of the dinosaurs and an excellent summary of the evidence is given in *Scientific American*. The article by Dale A. Russell says the evidence leans heavily towards ocean impact by an asteroid. Part of the report from the Berkeley Group (University of California) was to suggest an abrupt deposit of five hundred billion tons of extra-terrestial material on to the Earth's surface. Whether these objects are asteroids or degassed comets need not concern us for, whatever they are, as our methods of detection improve so previous thoughts as to their frequency are found to be grossly underestimated. We need not concern ourselves in this exercise with the origin of these destructive missiles, but we should give some attention to the likely results of an impact and to the revised data on the probable frequency of their occurrence.

The Cretaceous impact, previously referred to, occurred approximately sixty-three million years ago and

> no land animal weighing more that about 55lb survived.
> (*Scientific American* – Jan 82. 'The Mass Extinctions of the Late Mesozoic', Dale A. Russell.)

It is difficult to imagine a force which could achieve such wholesale destruction, and there is some excuse for past generations overlooking it. In the nuclear age we are witness to power which was incomprehensible to our grandparents. Forcibly and in terms which we can understand, Clube and Napier pointed out in *The Cosmic Serpent*[2] that although impacts of the scale to achieve annihilation of life may be rare, as we come down the scale – we are confronted with the probability of smaller impacts. These occur at far more frequent intervals and in recent times, say the last five thousand years, we are likely to have experienced some fifty impacts with an energy range of 1-100 megatons, five impacts between 100-1,000 megatons and

1 George W. Wetherill, Apollo Objects, *Scientific American*, March 1979
2 Clube & Napier, *The Cosmic Serpent* (Faber & Faber: London) 1982

possibly one from 1,000 to 10,000 megatons.

We are dealing here with a time period easily within the reach of archaeology and prehistory and I feel I can do no better than to quote from *The Cosmic Serpent:*

> Indeed it must be counted a scholarly error of extraordinary dimensions that the past history of short period comets should have been so disguised in the form of mythology, that their awesome consequences have been overlooked and have so far found no place at all in conventional prehistory. Standard interpretations of archaeological facts, for example, take no account at all of comets striking or threatening the Earth. It is, of course, possible that the omission is simply rectified without damage to our present understanding of prehistory. On the other hand it is also possible that previous interpreters have, in their ignorance, so missed the significance of certain facts that the very framework of our present knowledge is seriously undermined.

So were they really so 'disguised' in mythology? I think not. The descriptions exist in the legends of all the past cultures, but they have been largely discounted and even supressed. The public have, to a large degree, been misled into thinking that a comet is nothing other than a 'snowball'.

Mythology, on the other hand, is very clear on the matter, it speaks of 'pillars of fire' and then the earth shook and trembled, we hear of the gods battling in the skies. But, above all, we hear in every mythology of the destructive serpent. Could this be the comet? The contradiction continues – the serpent destroys, yet it represents life, intellect and the cycle of regeneration. Possibly we are speaking of two different serpents, with the earthly snake merely being the nearest image which could be found to represent both concepts.

On the one hand the connection is obvious. The comet could be related to only one creature commonly known to man – the snake or serpent. The other image as a symbol of life is equally obvious to us – it is the male sperm, but one wonders whether this connection could have been visualized before the days of the microscope. I believe that to dismiss the sexual connection as nothing more than a rigid snake representing the phallus, and in circular form representing the female organ would be an over-simplification. Recalling the serpents of Ohio and Peyrolles, it could be assumed that, far from depicting a serpent swallowing an egg, it may be carrying it. If we accept the egg as being an obvious symbol for the seed of life, the male sperm could hardly be better illustrated.

Let us recall the legend of Ra and Isis, where we are told that the sun was weakening. Certainly, the material from the tail of a comet could veil the light of the sun sufficiently to produce such an illusion. The atmosphere thus 'seeded' by a near-miss could also cause rain to fall at a time when it was not anticipated – if indeed it had ever fallen before. The sun 'dribbling' is thereby explained. Schooled as we are in the horrific aftermath of a

56. The arrows indicate the angle of approach of celestial objects entering the Earth's atmosphere.

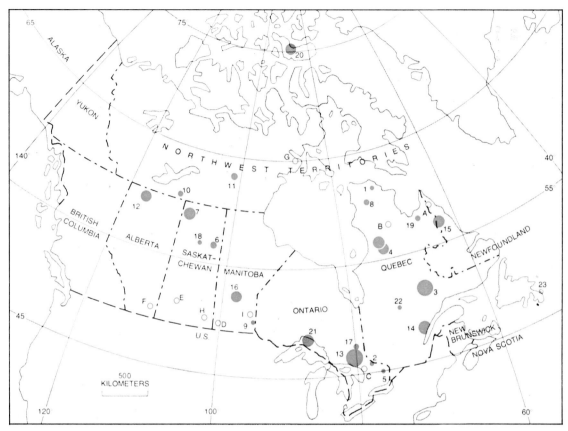

NEARLY HALF OF THE ANCIENT CRATERS that are well established have been found in central and eastern Canada, a region that represents only about 1 percent of the earth's land area. The filled circles show the location and relative size of 23 well-established impact craters, numbered in the order of their recognition; the open circles identify possible impact structures. The youngest-known crater (No. 1) is less than five million years old; the oldest-known (No. 13, near Sudbury, Ontario) is about 1.8 billion years old. The latter crater is one of only two craters that can be traced to the Precambrian era, which ended 600 million years ago. Crater No. 3 is the Manicouagan formation in the top photograph on page 40. Richard Grieve of the Canadian Department of Energy, Mines and Resources has made a count of the well-established ancient craters in North America and Europe; on the basis of his count one can estimate that in the past 600 million years 1,500 Apollo objects one kilometer in diameter or larger have struck the earth, about 70 percent of which presumably landed in the oceans. The map is based on a compilation made by Earth Physics Branch of the Department of Energy, Mines and Resources.

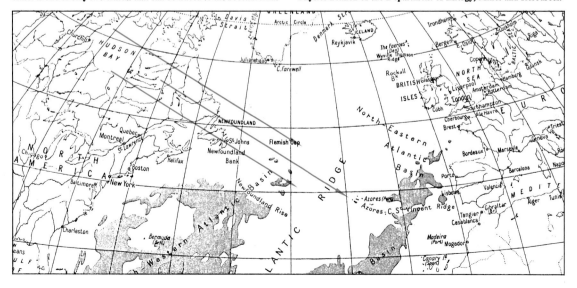

nuclear exchange, we can readily understand the dark period. Did we not find this in the legend – when Isis searched the sun-god for his secret name?

So why should we give time to these considerations in unravelling the mystery of Rennes?

The links are there surely enough in the common ground of the legends and they may be stronger than we at first realized.

Five additional days occurred. In astronomical terms that must indicate the movement of the earth to an orbit of greater circumference – or a greater radius. Was there then another circle at Rennes? If so, was my circle of churches the larger, representing **365** days or the smaller, representing **360** days? I measured the diameter of the circle of churches carefully and converted it to ground measure. I was disappointed – it was neither. The diameter of this circle on the ground was **372,557** inches, or **5.88** miles. I could not resist the temptation to set my compasses to equate with **360,000** inches of ground measure, to see if it would disclose anything significant. It did – I now had an almost equally impressive circle which passed through – the Château d'Hautpoul, the foundations of which dated back to the times of the Visigoths; next came the church of Cassaignes; then the cemetery of Serres and finally the cemetery of Saint Just-et-le-Bézu.

I now had reason to assume that if **360,000** inches was being demonstrated, it was representing the year of **360** days. This was the period of the year before the orbit of the earth was disrupted. Could there be another circle I wondered, one to represent the present year of **365** days? If there was, it was certainly not the circle of churches with its diameter of **372,557** inches. Could it be that my reasoning of a diameter representing the orbit of the earth was wrong? After all it is the circumference of a circle which denotes the orbital period. I investigated the circumferences, but could find nothing significant which would cause me to abandon the idea of the diameter being the vital factor. A diameter of **365,260** inches, which is the precise figure required to represent the current year, produces a circumference of almost exactly **18** miles – which was difficult to ignore. Furthermore, this radius fell short of the circle of churches by only 200 yards. Nevertheless, I was looking for perfection, so I continued my search for another circle. In considering all the evidence, I was drawn to the serpent feature near Peyrolles which was described earlier.

Again I felt the thrill of anticipation and cursed myself for not having seen it before. Isis had taken the saliva of Ra, the sun-god, and mixed it with the dust of the earth to make the venomous serpent which stung him as he followed his daily course through the heaven, his circuit. There must be a circle passing through the head of the serpent. But where was the centre?

I spent a considerable amount of time analysing the possibility that a circle of larger diameter than that of the churches might pass through this ground feature. Geometrically the circle evaded me, and it was in a painting that I found the clue which allowed me to proceed.

While in the valley, I had acquired a book on Rennes-le-Château. It contained a reproduction of a painting showing a bishop and two young men. They may be meant to represent the twins – as the symbol on the bishop's gown between them is the Zodiacal sign for Gemini. The original painting (illus 57) had been kept in the Church of Rennes-les-Bains, but had been lost. I presumed its disappearance was more by design than neglect and that it might therefore hold clues. I was right, there were many, but one in particular was amazing; and it provided me with the key that I sought to the body of Nut and the circuit of Ra.

57. Le Pape – The painting which disappeared from the church at Rennes-les-Bains. It conforms to an actual view from the cemetery of the church. The foreground cross is the Plantard Tomb – the grilled window, a feature still there in the church today. It aligns the famous Menhir Decapite du 'Cap de l'homme' which points directly to the Church at Rennes-le-Château. The significance of decapitation or losing the head is an obvious reference to phallic dismemberment. Significantly this line is that of January 17th in the zodiac of Rennes-les-Bains.

It was possible to identify in the painting specific positions in the valley. The fingers of the bishop indicated that two circles could be drawn passing through Rennes-le-Château. It was a simple matter to reverse the procedure and draw a circle with Rennes-le-Château as centre to see what it passed through and which was of significance on the circumference. And there was no doubt – it was the sister Church of Rennes-les-Bains where the painting had been kept!

I transferred the centre of the circle to Rennes-les-Bains, knowing that it would require only a slight change in radius to fulfil all the requirements; and fulfilled they were, beyond my wildest dreams.

From Rennes-le-Château the circle formed the arc of Nut (illus 58) terminating exactly on the horizontal axis of the circle. *temple* Furthermore it passed through the head of the serpent!

As can be seen from the illustration (59), the boat of Ra follows the curve of Nut's back which marks his circuit. The front of her body was the arc of the heavens corresponding to the circle of churches. Her feet touched the horizon at La Borde de l'Auguste which is the line referred to in the secret doctrine as the feminine division – in our diagram it is also the horizontal axis of the temple.

The imagery was impressive, here I was seeing the inverted crescent of Nut, Queen of the Heavens, and it occurred outside the circle of churches. My mind raced through the preparatory studies I had made of graphical representations of the creation and the states of matter. A circle was used to depict the limit of the understanding of man – the boundary of material existence. The circumference of that circle marks the Abyss; beyond it is the realm of the gods of spirit. If this were so then the position of the arched body of Nut at Rennes conformed exactly with the ancient imagery. I completed the circle which then created another crescent (illus 58). This was inside the material sphere. It was the upturned crescent of the goddess Isis, fingertips and toes touching those of her mother, being born in flesh. It was also correctly placed within the circumference of the Abyss.

The name at the eastern point of contact intrigued me – Bord de l'Auguste. *Bord* means side and is particularly of nautical origin meaning primarily side of a boat. The position was clearly at the side of the 'boat' of Isis. *Augusta* was the feminine style of Augustus the Roman title which was reserved exclusively for the Emperor. Oddly enough this title was first awarded by the Roman Senate on – would you believe it – January 17th, 27 BC. For our purposes it is sufficient to know that Augusta was the highest of all honours attributable to a woman.

Returning to the geometry, I almost feel as though I should apologize for demonstrating yet another 'miracle of the Meridian', but I am duty bound to do so. When the central axis of the temple was extended in a northerly direction it intersected the circuit of Ra, or Nut's back – the extension is exactly one

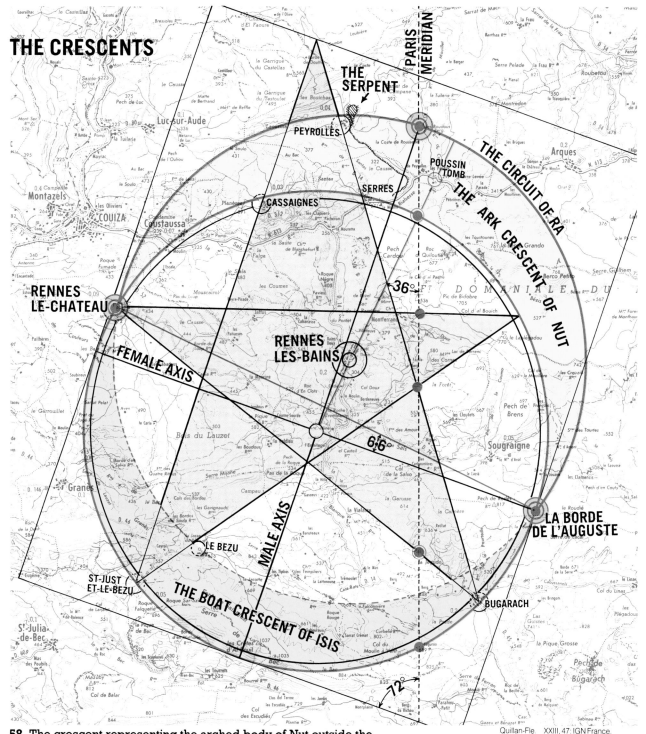

THE CRESCENTS

THE SERPENT

PARIS MERIDIAN

THE CIRCUIT OF RA

THE ARK CRESCENT OF NUT

PEYROLLES

POUSSIN TOMB

SERRES

CASSAIGNES

RENNES LE-CHATEAU

36°

RENNES LES-BAINS

FEMALE AXIS

6.6°

Sougraigne

MALE AXIS

LA BORDE DE L'AUGUSTE

LE BEZU

ST-JUST ET-LE-BEZU

THE BOAT CRESCENT OF ISIS

BUGARACH

72°

Quillan-Fle. XXIII, 47: IGN France.

58. The crescent representing the arched body of Nut outside the circle of churches. The outer curve of this crescent is the back of the goddess and is therefore the circuit of Ra which may be seen to pass through the head of the serpent. Note also that the central or male axis of the temple intersects the Meridian on the circuit of Ra and note the coincidental 36 degree angle of intersection between the axis of Nut and the Paris Meridian.

English mile. But that is not all – it is also the *coup de grâce* for the meridian which crosses the circuit of Ra at exactly the same point! (illus 58).

You will recall that I was searching for a circle which would represent the **365** day year. I had another circle now, but was this the diameter of **365,000** inches? It was not. It was more startling than even that would have been – the radius of the circle was **190,080** inches – **3** miles; a diameter of **6** miles. The number of Ra marking his passage through the heavens! Once more my mind reeled at the astonishing perfection of the construction.

I was beginning to believe this geometry had a mind of its own; that it was not for me to solve it, I merely had to recognize what was being shown to me. Once again I reinforced the images with thicker lines on another map and viewed it from a distance. Again came the realization. The central axis of the temple – the male axis, the phallus – not only passed through the centre of the circle, it went up exactly in between the legs of the pentagram representing the body of a female. I looked to the north where it entered the body of Nut. I knew I would be shown something of significance – and I was, but for the moment it is important that we do not lose sight of the temple layout. In *Le Serpent Rouge* under Scorpio we read:

> . . . What strange mystery is concealed in the new Temple of SOLOMON, . . .

I directed my examination to the Temple of Solomon and to the furniture it contained – in particular the Ark of the Covenant.

59. The creation myth showing the boat of Ra traversing the back of Nut – goddess of the starry heavens.

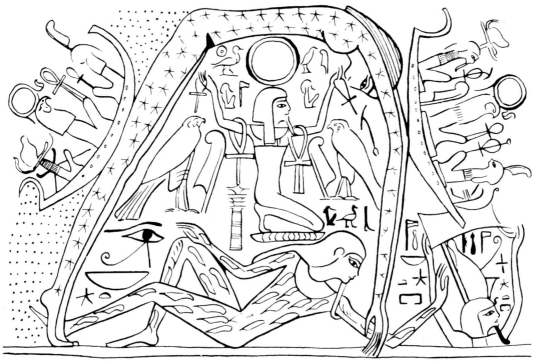

8

The Temple of Solomon

And this I know: whether the one True Light
Kindle to Love, or Wrath – consume me quite.
One Glimpse of It within the Tavern Caught
Better than in the Temple lost outright.

The architect, Hiram Abiff – Solomon and Sheba – the Brazen Sea – π is 3 – the feminine numbers – the menorah – the Ark of the Covenant – the mercy seat – the shew-bread table – the way to the womb.

I had already found the first elements of the straight lines which would form the walls of the temple. In addition to this, I knew from my studies that any temple wall would have to be controlled in one way or another by circular measure for it to be considered to be 'holy'. I turned my attention to the biblical account of the Temple of Solomon to see if I could recognize the message being portrayed at Rennes, either in the Temple or in the description of the Temple furniture.

Looking at the Temple construction logically first, and without wishing to shatter any illusions, the Christians or the Jews may have about it, I would first say that if it took thirty or forty thousand men **7** years to build a Temple of only **60** by **20** cubits – it must have been the most uneconomic project ever. Then to suggest that this pathetic construction should be considered as the dwelling-place of God on earth is the epitome of arrogance – particularly when we examine the next structure of Solomon. This was a palace for his Egyptian wife; it was much larger, grander and took **13** years to construct. The answer to these numbers is revealed, as is everything else, by the secret key of Isis (**18**). Multiply each of these figures (**7** and **13**) by **18** to understand what is implied:

Symbolic numbers – not real time

$$7 \times 18 = 126$$
$$13 \times 18 = 234 \text{ and } 126 + 234 = 360 \text{ the circle}$$
and the symbol of Nut as absolute femininity.

The Temple of Solomon is considered in some religious circles to have been one of the holiest places which ever existed on earth, but I would remind those erudite bodies that the House of God should be indestructible – this Temple was razed to the ground on three separate occasions.

For the moment I would like the reader to join me in considering the legend or account which has always been one of the important parts of Masonic ritual. I refer, of course to the story of the architect of the Temple of Solomon, Hiram Abiff. It is obvious from the honour afforded to him by Solomon that he was not employed, but was rather a person of equal status to Solomon himself. It is quite likely that the layout of the temple, which will be seen to use the female principle predominantly, was decided upon by King David. The close connection which existed between David and a previous Hiram is indisputable, and is confirmed in the Bible, where we are told that when David captured Jerusalem, Hiram, King of Tyre sent carpenters and masons to build him a house. Before its capture, Jerusalem was ruled by the Canaanite Jebusite Kings or Priest-kings who revered the goddess Ishtar and Tammuz in the shape of Adonis. It has even been suggested the name of David was one which the King only acquired after he captured the city. Its meaning is 'the Beloved One' which is beloved of Ishtar.

It has been suggested that David's son, Solomon, transferred his allegiance to Jehovah, but that is obviously wishful thinking and a close study of Solomon's activities shows only too well what his beliefs were. He blatantly erected a temple to Astarte (Ishtar) and as we analyse the Temple of Solomon itself we will be left in no doubt to whom it was dedicated.

Despite the restrictions to which he was subjected by virtue of his desire to achieve unification of the tribes, he erected the Temple of Solomon in a manner which may now be seen to have nothing to do with Jehovah. This achievement demanded a great deal of skill – both in building techniques and in knowledge of the secret doctrine of shapes and numbers. This is why King Hiram sent Hiram Abiff to control the construction of the temple.

In the Lebanon, Hiram would have worshipped at the Temple of Astarte or Ishtar, and this Syrian goddess is closely associated with Cybele or Isis. It was in these temples – the Ishtar-Tammuz doctrine was practised, involving the sacrificial corn-god and his subsequent resurrection. In these rituals the female is the dominant deity, and therefore it was an amazing feat of deception for Hiram to have built a temple for the Jews incorporating all the doctrine from which they were trying to dissociate themselves, thereby invisibly controlling their holiest place. Dedicated as he was to the recognition of the superiority of the female, how could he possibly compromise himself to design and build a temple for people who were reducing women to a subservient status?

The story of Hiram plays an important part in Masonic ritual and briefly it is as follows.

During the construction of the Temple, Solomon was visited by Balkis, the Queen of Sheba, who by all accounts was a woman of exceptional beauty and insatiable sexual appetite. She was said to have posed many questions to Solomon which would normally be considered indelicate for a woman. Generally she exhibited a

60. The two crescents of Nut and Isis showing their relationship to the pentagram and the serpent.

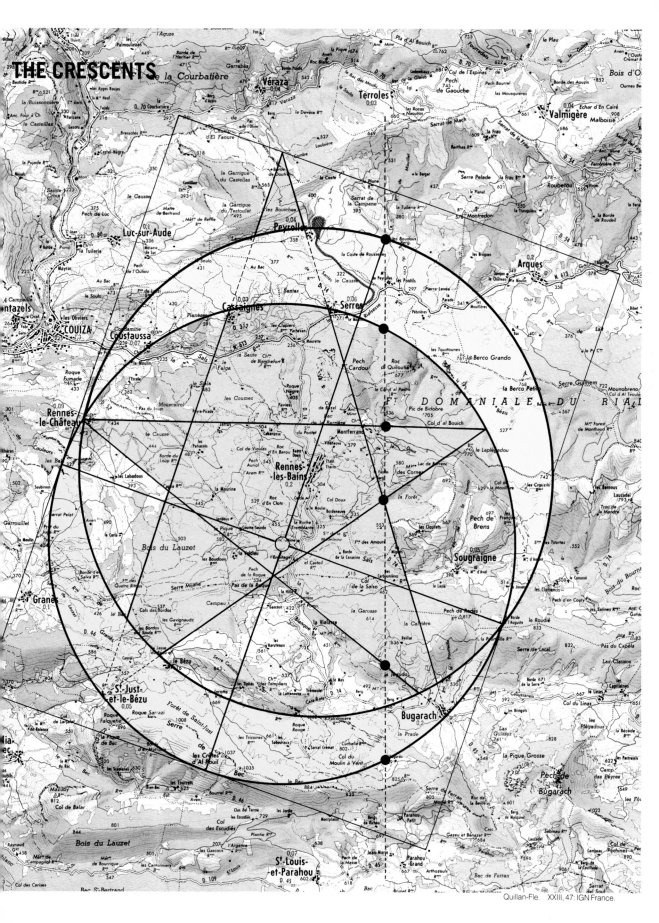

THE CRESCENTS

Quillan-Fle. XXIII, 47: IGN France.

character which in Victorian times would have severely shocked her associates. However, we might be more accurate in our assessment of this lady if we shed any illusions of male supremacy. We should consider her psychology to be more akin to that of the most liberated woman of our own times.

Things went well between Balkis and Solomon, and they were to be married – until she met Hiram with whom she immediately fell in love. Solomon did not like this at all and would have arranged Hiram's demise immediately, but he was dependent upon him for the completion of the temple furniture and, in particular, the Brazen Sea.

Solomon had been informed of a plot in which three dissatisfied apprentices had conspired to murder Hiram but, as it served his purpose, Solomon neglected to warn him. The plot failed and the affair between Sheba and Hiram would have undoubtedly developed but for a second, successful attempt by the apprentices. Before Hiram died, he said he would have many sons who would complete his work – by which he meant the building of other temples – and it requires little imagination to see that the Knights Templar considered themselves to be the appointed architects and custodians of the secret formula.

It would now serve our purpose to consider what great secrets could be concealed in simple geometry and why they should have been in the hands of Hiram Abiff in the first place. C. W. Heckethorne in the *Secret Societies of All Ages and Countries* suggests that Cain was the son of the gods (Elohim) and this was the line from which Hiram Abiff descended. These were the 'fire people' to whom are attributed all the sciences and the secrets contained in their use.

This superior race was supposedly destroyed by the flood with only two exceptions: Tubal-Cain and his son, from whom was descended Nimrod, the Mighty Hunter and in turn Hiram Abiff. It is likely, therefore, that this information is of great antiquity and quite possibly contains secrets of the science of the Elohim.

One of the things which Hiram was responsible for was the casting of the Brazen Sea, and in the process of pouring the metal an error occurred which could have resulted in his death, but he was saved by the spirit of Tubal-Cain. The emphasis which this item receives suggests we should look at it more closely.

In *Kings Ch. VII v23* we are told:

> And he made a molten sea, ten cubits from the one brim to the other, it was round all about, and its height was five cubits and a line of thirty cubits did compass it round about.

We know, and we can be sure the architects of the temple knew, that the value of π was not **3**. But that is what is needed to make the above statement true. It is unlikely for numerical errors to be introduced in translation, therefore we cannot take this discrepancy lightly. I assume it is trying to tell us something. Is this one of those bridges which are needed to relate graphical and numerical values, while still maintaining the identities of the gods?

I considered the circle at Rennes with a diameter of **360,000** inches – the radius is **180,000** and with a symbolic value of **3** for π the circumference would be **1080** thousand inches – a clear repetition of the identities contained in the radius (Isis and Nut). Was this just another coincidence or was I beginning to recognize a symbolic numerical language which would reveal the secrets of the past? It is also worth noting here that if we accept the value of **18** inches for the cubit, the product of the circumference and the height of the Brasen Sea is **2700**; numerals known to be associated with the womb and pregnancy.

At this point we could clear up a confusing factor about Isis. The number of this goddess was previously thought to be **10**, resulting from an interpretation of her Greek name Io. The number of Demeter (diameter) being **20** seems to confirm this, but I believe this to be misinterpretation of the doctrine. The Greeks were a young culture and learned their secrets from the ancient Egyptians who knew the number of Isis was **8** and her active principle was **18**. If we now consider perfection in the circle with a diameter numerically equivalent to the number of degrees in the circle (**360**), the radius is **180**. The number of inches in the cubit of Isis is **18**, hence the radius is **10** cubits and the diameter **20** cubits. The values of **10** and **20** are therefore valid only if one accepts the cubit as **18** inches. However, as we examine the Temple of Solomon and the furniture it contained we will be left with no doubt that the **18** inch cubit of Isis is the 'key' we require.

Kings Ch. VII v15 provides an obvious confirmation. Here we are speaking of the famous pillars Jachin and Boaz cast by Hiram and associated with Freemasonry:

> For he cast two pillars of brass, of eighteen cubits high apiece:
> and a line of twelve cubits did compass either of them about

Many authorities have already considered these pillars to be phallic symbols, in the same way as are the Egyptian obelisks. The height of **18** cubits is an obvious indication of the presence of Isis, and together they reveal the **36** identity of the pentagram or the circle. The circumference of **12** cubits or **216** inches produces a diameter of **72** inches when using the symbolic $\pi = 3$. As **72** degrees is the base angle of the pentagram and the radius would be **36**, again we appear to be confirming femininity. *Kings is full* of dimensions which become 'understandable' when the **18** factor is applied, particularly when examining perimeters. The temple dimensions of **60** × **20** × **30** cubits seem to be meaningless, but converted to inches they become **1080** × **360** × **540** – all strictly in accordance with the female imagery. In *Kings VIII, 2*, we are given the dimensions of Solomon's house as **100** × **50** × **30** cubits, and apart from their obvious sum of **180**, the total length of the edges is **720** (pentagonal again). For the reader who would like to pursue this code I offer another working 'tool'. Having calculated the total perimeter or edge length of a given structure, remember the temple rule that all square constructions must contain circular measure in order to be considered 'holy'. Use the symbolic $\pi = 3$ and then assume that the total perimeter is actually a circumference. Calculate the resulting diameter and radius and you will find the numbers which confirm the cyclic motions of the earth. The processes also confirm that English or Celtic measure was used – 12 inches or feet for those who have the 'understanding'.

For a simple graphical proof of the construction of the temple at Rennes I would refer the reader to another article of furniture from the Temple of Solomon – the menorah, the seven-branched candlestick (illus 61). The three equally spaced concentric circles of Rennes are easily seen if one recognizes the menorah as half of that diagram – or a 180-degree section. There were five such candelabra in the temple, which is to be expected. The three circles of Rennes will be seen to represent the womb, and this is obviously the reason for the design of the menorah. The central or upright branch is the phallus, penetrating to the centre of the womb, precisely as the male axis of the circle does at Rennes. Even the word menorah is worthy of note; *men* is Greek for month and many words associated with the female monthly cycle come to mind. One in particular, menorrha-gia, is used to describe an excessive flow of blood in the menstrual period, but *men*suration is nothing to do with that; it is the process of calculation of geometric shapes and volumes in general. We should also make a *men*tal note that it is the seventh prong of the candelabrum which penetrates the womb and that the number 7 is representing a certain phallus which we must deal with later.

Although it is becoming increasingly clear who the temple was dedicated to, let us now consider the purpose of the temple. Was it a place of worship? Accepted. Was it the dwelling-place of God on earth? Certainly not! It was said that God would never dwell in a place constructed by man. This is the reason for the elaborate story that no sound of hammer or chisel must be heard in the process of building the Temple of Solomon which gave rise to the belief it was built by demons over whom Solomon had control. From this reasoning emanates the great majority of all the 'mumbo-jumbo' of sorcery and witchcraft so condemned by the religion which precipitated it in the first place.

If hideous things existed in the past and there is a mass of evidence to say they did – they were probably the results of genetic experiments to produce hybrid creatures to work in conditions that were unacceptable to their masters. Their intellect, albeit a fraction of their masters', was sufficient to allow them to perform their appointed tasks. And never let it be said that I am confusing this local event of genetic engineering with the work of the Supreme Entity of Creation, the embodiment of all things spiritual and material: THE CREATOR.

61. The Desolation of the Sanctuary (PSALM LXXIV v 6, 7) showing the temple furniture including the Menorah. Inserted is the geometric Menorah showing the seven points – indicative of Set or Satan.

But we digress – was not the major reason for the temple to be the resting place of the Ark of the Covenant?

I can never quite understand when I hear this expression, whether the author is referring to the box or the contents.

I must say that I am greatly indebted to Stephen Spielberg for educating so many people, so quickly, as to the appearance of this intriguing artefact. Unfortunately his creation adheres, possibly too strictly, to the accepted image which in my opinion is incorrect. However, I would congratulate him on conveying the idea that, although seemingly innocuous, it might be a very dangerous object. The Old Testament warns us quite clearly of the possible consequences of tampering with it and I would strongly advise those who investigate the locations of Rennes-le-Château to acquaint themselves with the correct procedures. I can only hope that if it is found it will not, by reason of religious politics, be swept under the carpet as the end of his film implies. But I see only too clearly that this could be the case. The historical records throw no light on the ultimate whereabouts of the Ark of the Covenant and there appears to be little to be gained by examining the fragments of evidence available. the fragments of evidence available.

The 'box' (illus 62) then was constructed according to precise measurements which are given to us in *Exodus, Ch. XXV v10*:

> And they shall make an ark of shittim wood: two cubits and a half shall be the length thereof and a cubit and a half the breadth thereof, a cubit and a half the height thereof.

Before proceeding further I will admit there have been many different opinions as to the number of inches in a cubit, or even as to whether the cubit can be transcribed into exact inch measure. Without wishing to sound cavalier on these points, I nevertheless dismiss them by two simple assumptions. Firstly,

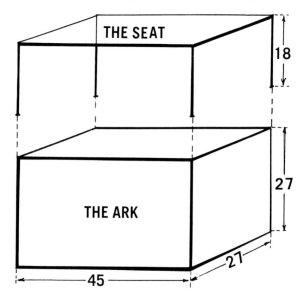

62. The dimensions of the Ark and the Mercy seat.

among those who have studied the subject, one of the most popular values for the cubit is **18** inches (Isis) and this is supported by my own findings which were arrived at by a completely different route. Secondly, that an English inch is related to an Egyptian measure is more easily understood if one can accept both the Celts and Egyptians were that descendants of the same people – possibly even the survivors of the lost continent of Atlantis. This contention is supported by both Celtic myth and the inexplicable fact that the Egyptian culture appears to have been transplanted and shows little or no sign of having developed *in situ* from a primitive race.

If my assumption of the feminine principle concealed in the temple was correct, I felt it would also be evident, albeit hidden in the major reason for the temple being built, the Ark of the Covenant. We will now examine the Ark in inch measure. The length **45** inches, the height and breadth **27** inches. The perimeters are, therefore:

$$4 \times 45 = 180 \text{ (Isis and Nut)}$$
$$4 \times 27 = 108 \text{ (Isis and Nut)}$$
$$4 \times 27 = 108 \text{ (Isis and Nut)}$$

The box was then covered inside and out with gold:

And thou shalt overlay it with pure gold, within and without thou overlay it, and shalt make upon it a crown of gold round about.

Exodus XXV, 11.

And thou shalt put into the Ark the testimony which I shall give thee.

Exodus XXV, 16.

63. The temple furniture showing the normal configuration of the Mercy Seat being the lid of the Ark.

We will discuss later the possible meaning of 'the testimony', for the contents of the box are never made clear and there are many interesting theories as to what it may have contained.

The method by which the box is to be transported is obvious enough. The instructions were that staves of wood should slide through rings to allow two people to carry it.

Now, whenever we see an artist's impression of this construction, the box is surmounted with two cherubim with outstretched wings, but I see no mention of this in the text. By what right or error has the Church allowed all the biblical illustrations to present it in such a fashion (illus 63).

Let us follow the text* a little further:

64. The death of Nadab and Abihu – a warning for those who would tamper with the Ark without the 'understanding'.

> And thou shalt make a mercy-seat of pure gold: two cubits and a half shall be the length thereof, and a cubit and a half the breadth thereof.
>
> And thou shalt make two cherubims of gold, of beaten work shalt thou make them, in the two ends of the mercy-seat.
>
> And make one cherub on the one end, and the other cherub on the other end: even of the mercy-seat shall ye make the cherubims on the two ends thereof.

*Hebrew *Kaporet* means the cover of the Ark. The *Torah* says the Kaporet is one hand breadth in thickness.

And the cherubims shall stretch forth their wings on high, covering the mercy-seat with their wings, and their faces shall look one to another; toward the mercy-seat shall the faces of the cherubim be.

And thou shalt put the mercy-seat above upon the ark; and in the ark thou shalt put the testimony that I shall give thee.

And there I will meet with thee, and I will commune with thee from above the mercy-seat, from between the two cherubims which are upon the ark of the testimony, of all things which I will give thee in commandment unto the children of Israel.

Exodus XXV, 17 to 22.

It would now appear the platform of 45 inches by 27 inches has been assumed to be a lid, but that is certainly not what the text says. Without any shadow of doubt we are being told of another construction, a mercy-seat and a 'seat' is the hieroglyph for Isis as I have previously shown.★ Furthermore, 'mercy' is also indisputably connected with our goddess. Her benevolence is seen in *Le Serpent Rouge* under Leo:

Come to me all ye who labour and are heavy laden and I will give you rest.

In the Babylonian Tablets she appears as Ishtar, who grieves for mankind's destruction and speaks out against the action of the gods in destroying Man by the flood.

When the Ark was grounded, the Queen of Heaven cried out:

O you gods here present, by the lapis-lazuli round my neck I shall remember these days as I remember the jewels of my throat; these days shall I not forget.★

65. The building of the Ark.

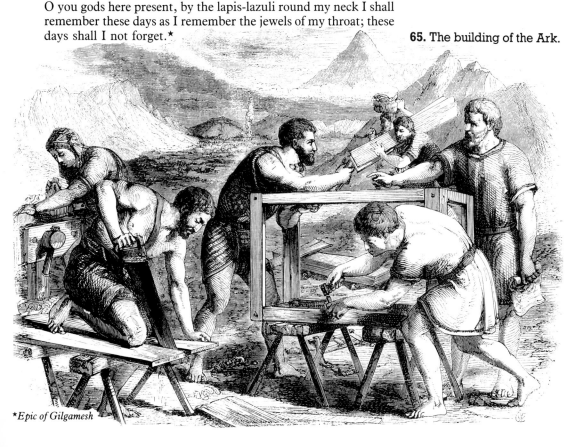

★*Epic of Gilgamesh*

Ishtar obviously knew that mankind was not intended to survive, for she then announced that Enhil must not see those who did, saying:

> He shall not approach this offering, for without reflection he brought the flood, he consigned my people to destruction.

And what is even more significant is the manner in which she associates herself with the remnant of Man:

> . . . but are they not my people, for I brought them forth. Now like the spawn of fish, they float in the ocean.*

She seems to be claiming here to have been responsible for the creation of the human race, and those who designed the temple of Rennes-le-Château leave us in no doubt they also believed this to be the case.

If we return to the text it can be seen that a seat is being constructed, not a lid. The dimensions of the seat are the same as those of the Ark, **45** inches × **27**inches, but there is one dimension missing, for the obvious reason that there would be no need to instruct a carpenter as to what height to make a seat – he would have known it. The measure is **1** cubit or **18** inches (Isis), as are all seats.

Now let us examine this seat of **54** inches × **27** inches × **18** inches.

The perimeter measures are unbelievable:

    4 lengths of **45** = **180** (Isis)
    4 lengths of **27** = **108** (Isis)
    4 lengths of **18** = **72** (Base angle of the female pentagram)

and the total is **360** – the circle. The symbol of the female generative organ is demonstrated once again. The message should be clear: the Ark of the Covenant is the property of Isis and it is clearly marked with her name (illus 66).

It may appear at first sight to be unfair to draw a conclusion from the addition of these perimeters, having made no comment on the sum of the perimeters of the ark.

These were **180** and **216** the total being **396** and are of no apparent significance. However, if we now examine the last item of furniture – the shew-bread table, all will be revealed.

> Thou shalt also make a table of shittim wood: two cubits shall be the length thereof, and a cubit the breadth thereof, and a cubit and half the length thereof.
>
> *Exodus XXV, 23*

Using our **18″** cubit area again the dimensions become **36″** × **18″** × **27″**. The total perimeter measure is therefore:

    4 × **36** = **144** (Pentagonal)
    4 × **18** = **72** (Pentagonal)
    4 × **27** = **108** (Isis and Nut)

*The Epic of Gilgamesh.

66. The author's suggestion as to the implied circular design of the Ark. The wings or labia enclose the vagina, below which is the box or womb.

This total of **324** also happens to be **18** squared.
Let us now add the total perimeter of the three items:

The Ark	**396**
The mercy-seat	**360**
The shew-bread table	**324**
Total	**1080**

Once more we find the female deities Nut and Isis, and furthermore this figure is the circumference of the circle of churches at Rennes-le-Château based upon the $\pi = 3$ value given to us from the Sea of Brass. When this is divided in **15** parts, as the circle at Rennes is, each one becomes **72**. Furthermore **1080**, being the total perimeter of these items produces an average of **360** per article.

Symbolic

The Temple of Solomon and everything it contains is controlled by numerical values associated with sexual doctrine, but always with the female dominant. Furthermore it establishes beyond any shadow of doubt that **18** inches is the value of the cubit required to 'read' the secrets. The more one analyses the values generated by this 'key', the more one realizes that the English or Celtic inch was used to relate cyclic motion to pentagonal geometry. The ultimate secret must lie in the circle – the female generative organ – the womb.

It occurred to me that if the womb were to be a significant factor, pregnancy would also figure in it somewhere. Remembering that the year of **360** days, consisting of **12** months of **30** days would generate a **9**-month pregnancy of **270** days, I was not surprised to find the dimension of **27** demonstrated so clearly on the Ark of the Covenant. Little did I realize at that time just how important those integers would become.

9

The Womb

And that inverted Bowl we call The Sky,
Whereunder crawling coop't we live and die,
Lift not thy hands to it for help – for it
Rolls impotently on as Thou or I.

The point of no return – what is an Ark? – gateway to mystery – the body of Nut – the figures unite – through the labia – the vagina – into the womb of Rennes.

R eturning for a moment to the mercy-seat, the description of the seat or throne also implies that the wings of the angels are considerably larger than the illustrations usually suggest. They encompass the body of whoever sits on the seat and they must therefore form an arch over the seated person's head. The implication is that by sitting in the appointed position, a means of communication is activated. In this way the goddess may receive from, or transmit to, the seated person. If the communication happens not to be with the goddess Isis, the solution will leave us in little doubt as to who, other than her, it could be.

At this point it seems that I have no alternative but to expose the reader to certain information which may cause distress to those who have elected to believe in the stories of orthodox Christianity, and I would sincerely suggest to those people they read no further. Once again I will say that when I decided to attempt to unravel the mystery of Rennes-le-Château, I had no idea where it would lead me, but follow it I must.

As anyone who examines geometrical figures knows, it would serve no purpose whatsoever to construct one line in a proof such as this without supporting it by ground features, or with evidence which is equally corroborative. Having established this, it would be counter-productive to have any preconceived ideas as to what the solution would be. I knew I must follow the proof without excluding any of those areas normally considered taboo, regardless of where it may lead. Even at this stage I realized it would be my duty to publish my findings, despite the contentious nature of the information I was disclosing. The temple of Rennes or, as I now know it to be, the Temple of Isis, demonstrates a degree of skill and knowledge which is astounding, and in publishing this information it is my sincerest hope that experts in many fields will analyse my work and contribute more information than I have been able to obtain. At this stage I cannot be sure whether it will serve mankind for me to go further and expose those secrets which I believe lie behind the solution, but I do so in the hope that it will.

I am reminded of that warning on the Temple of Isis at Sais:

I ISIS AM ALL THAT HAS BEEN, THAT IS OR SHALL BE: NO MORTAL MAN HATH EVER ME UNVEILED.

For those of you who have decided to stay with us, let us proceed, albeit with discretion, to identify the images of the past in a more direct manner.

The cherubim on the Seat of Mercy are Metatron and Sandalphon.* The wings of these cherubim are stretched forth on high, indicating, I would submit that they pass over or encompass the head of the seated person (illus 66). The wings represent the labia or 'lips' of the vagina and the seated person would therefore be simulating a child in the process of being born. The images of the sexual organs in ancient religions are, of course, well known to us, but I would like to focus the mind of the reader on the manner in which a slow transference of ideas and symbols can produce something which, hundreds of years later, may be read as gospel but whose original symbolic truth has been lost.

67. This illustration of Isis incorporates wings to signify the labia and upturned in crescent form to portray the boat or female vulva.

Clavicula Salimonis, Liddell MacGregor Mathers (Routledge & Kegan Paul: London) 1888.

68. The author with one of his team on the head of Les Toustounes – the female head rock.

In Indian temples, where the sexual imagery is displayed more obviously, the Yoni is the female organ and the Linga is the male. The word Yoni is also understood to be the same as Iune and the Iune of the Israelites was the 'dove'. Both of these words can be equated with the Syrian word Io (Isis). The connection between Isis and Magdalene is there again for, as the priestess of Ishtar (Isis), Magdalene was keeper of the doves at Magdala (Place of the Doves) in Galilee.

The Yoni is depicted as a crescent-shaped boat, with or without the mast in position, which is the Linga or phallus. The crescent-shaped boat was also used in religious ceremonies in Delphi, where it was called the Argo – hence the Greek Argonauts. Delphi was in Arcadia and so was Argia – meaning the place of the Argo. Arcadia means Arca or Argha and Dia the sacred Argha. Furthermore, Arca actually means box. The word argha defies simple analysis. That it means female generative power is certain, but it implies much more. It encompasses serpent, boat, cycle, the number **600** and above all the place of the seed or the origin – the womb.

And so back to Rennes-le-Château – the Poussin tomb on the road to Arques depicted in *Les Bergere d'Arcadie* carrying the inscription Et in Arcadia Ego (**14** letters), which was the motto shown on the coat-of-arms of the Plantard family, and Pierre Plantard was, until very recently, the Grand Master of the Priory of Sion. In Poussin's painting one of the shepherds points to the letter R, which is the **18**th letter of the alphabet. We left the geometry of Rennes having established two crescent shapes – one

outside the circle of churches, representing the body of Nut (Queen of the Heavens) and the other inside the circle, with its cusps upward, signifying her daughter Isis. The body of Nut is seen to be beyond the abyss thus denotes that she is a spirit entity. Isis is formed inside the abyss, and this confirms the legends which say she was earth-born, a creature of flesh. Both crescent shapes conform to the Yoni image, representing the female generative organ. Little wonder that René d'Anjou, Grand Master of the Priory of Sion in the 1400s, established the Order of the Crescent, and even more significant was an older order called the Order of the Ship and the Double Crescent.

I could feel now that the mist was clearing and some things had been staring me in the face, even though I had not recognised them. The tomb of Arques carried the secret numbers (**18** and **14**), the tomb is a 'box', Arca means box, Arcadia is 'sacred box' and so is the Ark of the Covenent. This is surmounted by the mercy-seat which carries the secret number of Isis, and her name means seat. The seat of this female can mean her vagina, which is shown by the wings of the cherubs, signfying her labia, shaped like an arc. The ark of Isis is the womb which contains the 'seed of intelligent life' and the Ark of Noah or Ark of Noé was a symbolic reference to life surviving the flood. But it was only symbolic; no animals went in 'two by two', no ark was ever built as described in the scriptures. It would have been impossible for any creature to have preserved unaided, the seed of intelligence through the period of darkness which ensued. Even if a handful of souls had physically survived, with the passage of time they would have reverted to their animal nature and we would be once again in the position of assuming that we were descended from the ape. That is if the line had survived at all.

69. Negotiating the vaginal cavity of Nut, north of Serres.

But it did survive and it was possibly assisted as the legends tell us. Those who assisted us were most probably members of the antediluvian intelligence. Also, something else may have survived which for the moment I would prefer only to hint at. As we progress the reader may recognize some of the bizarre parts of legends involving congress between animals and 'humans' and they may well carry a seed of truth in them. Consider how the seed of intelligence of the superior Nephillin may have, in just a few isolated cases, have escaped the 'cleansing' of the planet and been preserved in animal form.

I returned to the diagram of Rennes-le-Château; no longer could I see this as some massive icon depicting the beliefs of a secret cult. Gone were thoughts of a mathematical treasure map, although I felt certain significant positions may well hold confirmation in material form. This was no Stonehenge or pyramid construction for marking the seasons and the passage of the stars. I was looking at a story transcribed into geometric figures to ensure that it could never be misunderstood again, never be abbreviated, never embellished or 'twisted by knaves to make a trap for fools'. Each figure threaded into another with such precision as to deny the discoverer any chance of superimposing his own beliefs or of using it for his purposes. It was the story of the creation of man and the history of this planet!

For the first time I was not being led through the labyrinth. I looked at the diagram in a different way now. The original pentagram, as the past doctrine suggests, was the body of the female. The male axis of the circle entered her body between the

70. From the vagina looking south towards the womb. The female head rock can be seen on the left.

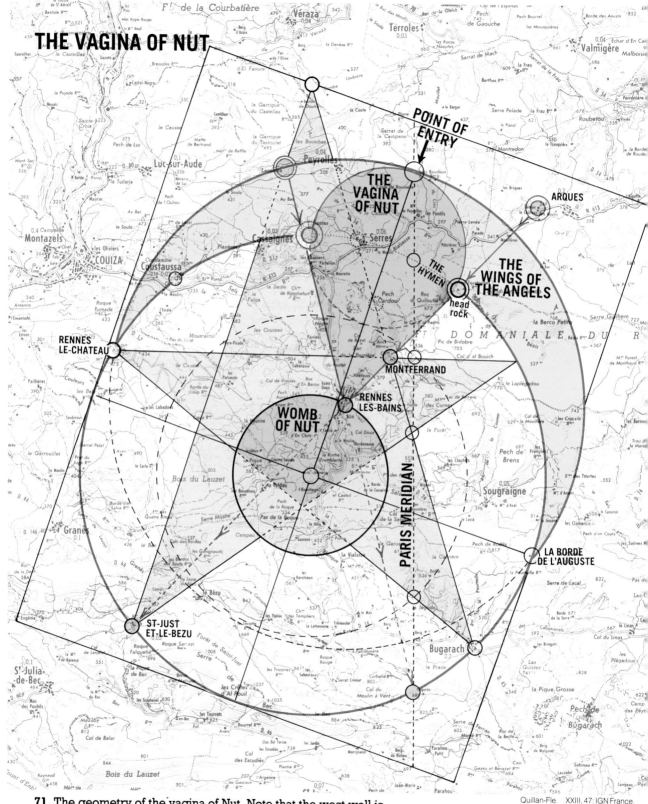

THE VAGINA OF NUT

POINT OF
ENTRY

ARQUES

THE
VAGINA
OF NUT

THE
HYMEN

THE
WINGS OF
THE ANGELS

head
rock

Peyrolles

Cassaignes

Serres

RENNES
LE-CHATEAU

MONTFERRAND

RENNES
LES-BAINS

WOMB
OF NUT

PARIS MERIDIAN

LA BORDE
DE L'AUGUSTE

Sougraigne

Granes

ST-JUST
ET-LE-BEZU

Bugarach

71. The geometry of the vagina of Nut. Note that the west wall is
determined geometrically and the right by prominent features in line.

Quillan-Fle.   XXIII, 47: IGN France.

base legs of that shape. I followed the male axis to the north-half, expecting what I would find there. Many times in studying Egyptian art I had seen the circle of the womb under the crescent body of Nut. I needed another circle which would represent the womb of Nut, and I knew the phallus or male axis would lead me to the centre of it.

At the position where the male, or central, axis of the temple crossed the northern limit of the circle of churches I took a centre. The radius of the new circle was the distance to the intersection of the central axis of the pentagram and the circle of churches.

I traced the circle, Les Toustounes – the rock which looked like the head of a stately female – a touch on the intermediate circle of the temple and then internally tangential to the circuit of Ra. The wings of the cherubs were formed and the female rock feature was

72. The Château d'Arques possibly constructed on the ruins of a 7th century fortress. Its position is eventually found to control the geometry of the secret locations.

at the position of a cherub's head. This was Sandalphon and opposing it was Metatron supposedly the names of the cherubs surmounting the Ark of Covenant. I had found the wings of the guardian angels, but I knew those wings also represented the labia, the lips of the female organ. The circle was a perfect symbol for the womb of Nut and also perfectly placed to conform with Egyptian art. It was however, demonstrating a cavity inside the labia and must therefore be representing a vagina. I look to the north; there could be nothing there, for that was beyond the back of Nut. I looked to the south and in disbelief I saw that in passing through the 'lips' from north to south I was entering a vagina. The walls of the vagina were the inside curves of the wings, formed by my last circle, and could be seen to terminate on the circle of churches. The curvature of this circle between the heads of the angels represented the membrane, or hymen. Behind the membrane lay the mountain top of Pech Cardou, which obviously represents the cervix, or entrance to the womb. (illus 71).

I will return to the construction of the vagina in a moment, but first I would pause to remind the reader to be alert to the fact that several diagrams are interacting here. It will be difficult to grasp the harmony of the final solution, without constantly turning over in the mind how this interaction is moving towards a singular conclusion.

We have seen the pentagram representing the female body viewed as a whole, but we must now partially dismiss this from our minds. Here we are looking at a greatly enlarged plan view of the female genitals. Eventually we will see how the designers of this concept correlated the two images.

One digression which may interest the reader is the meaning behind the name of the mountain I just mentioned, Pech Cardou. I found it in the *Anacalypsis* and Higgins is very good at this sort of research. Cor was the Latin name for heart and wisdom, from this came Cardo (the regulator) which was the north/south line used as the origin to divide land into areas for the collection of tithes. The east/west line was the Decumanus and where it crossed the Cardo was the reference position for all the local divisions.

Now, to find the entrance to the womb!

Almost from the first moment that I had examined a map of the district of Rennes, I had been haunted by a number of features which were exactly aligned. Considering what they were, I knew it could not be coincidental. The first of these was the largest château of the area, the Château d'Arques (illus 72). I was convinced that it would eventually be of significance. It was certainly shown on maps of the 1600s, and in some form or other it most likely existed at the time of the crusades. One feature of its construction was particularly outstanding (illus 73), and I now knew that this position pointed the way to the womb; the feature required no further explanation. The château stood alone **500** metres or more to the west of the village and the position was such that it was exactly aligned with the female rock – next was the fortress of

Montferrand – then the church of Rennes-les-Bains and, finally the church of Saint Just-et-le-Bézu (illus 71). In drawing this line, I realized I was also drawing a tangent to the circle which formed the vagina.

I looked to the other side of the circle to see if any other ground features might denote a tangent on the opposing side but there were none. But what I found was even more remarkable. Would these miracles of geometric construction never cease?

An equivalent symmetrical tangent to the west of the circle of the vagina was marked by the intersection of the western side of the northern extension of the pentagram and the circle of Ra (or back of Nut). The angle formed between the two lines, remarkably enough, was **33°**.

As I followed the line south as the tangent to the circle of the vagina, it passed through the church of Rennes-les-Bains and finally left the circle of churches at an important conjunction. This point is the south-eastern corner of the internal square and therefore, is on the **45°** axis from the centre of the circle. The new line precisely bisects the angle between this axis and the line of the Meridian, which also passes through that point.

The vagina was completed and the location of the entry into the womb was the church of Rennes-les-Bains. The womb was the smallest of the three concentric circles. Was this incredible figure really the work of the Templars? Did they have equipment capable of such observations over mountainous terrain, to this degree of accuracy? From my training as a surveyor (trigonometrical) I had serious doubts. The whole thing still pointed to aerial survey, but that was impossible!

Was I being forced into an acceptance of a past super-race? Preposterous as it seemed at the time, with hindsight I realize how much simpler it would have been to accept that explanation rather than what I now believe to be the ultimate secret of Rennes!

However, there I was, determined to follow every lead to the bitter end, regardless of what it might be. I looked at the crescent of Isis with its upturned cusps. I had seen this imagery before associated with the planet Venus and to me that meant Ishtar and Ishtar meant Isis; so I turned my attention to Venus.

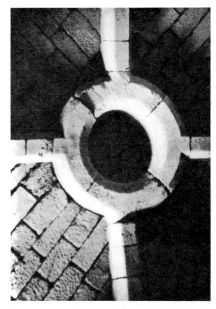

73. An architectural feature of the Château d'Arques which strongly implies something which was finally confirmed – the female organ.

10

Venus – Ishtar – Isis

So while the Vessels one by were speaking,
One spied the little Crescent all were seeking:
And then they jogg'd each other: 'Brother! Brother!
Hark to the Porter's Shoulder-knot a-creaking!'

Celestial identities – the gods are numbers – the planet of Ishtar – its place in legend – the temple prostitutes – more legendary links – first thoughts on the Crucifixion.

There are various theories on the manner in which our solar system was formed, but two are currently favoured.

The first suggests that in the remote past a huge cloud of interstellar gas and dust particles was subjected to an unknown disturbing force. This could have been one of those irresponsible vagabonds of space, the comet or space serpent, playing the dual role of destroyer and creator. Whatever the cause, the cloud began to rotate and condense. The central core, subjected to immense pressures, could account for the sun's formation and a small quantity of the material outside the gravitational field of the mass might have formed the planets. If this were so, one would imagine that a fairly uniform system would be produced. Accepting for the moment that no other interfering forces were present, one would expect to find an orderly disc of planetary bodies with their equators on the same plane and with similar atmospheres, commensurate with their escape velocities. Such is not the case however, our solar system has all the appearances of a battlefield.

Unfortunately, the model of formation suggested above has not stood up too well to the analysis of computer simulation. The nebula tends to prefer to form several nuclei, quite contradictory to our one-star system. I say unfortunately because if this model of formation was correct, we could expect most stars to be surrounded with planets. By virtue of the numbers involved, it would then be reasonable to expect an abundance of life in the universe, much of which could be expected to pre-date us by many thousands of years. Accepting that the environmental factors of Earth are not unique, there would be a fairly good chance that an advanced intelligence evolved which was capable of demonstrating its existence to us. Notwithstanding the 'flying saucer' mystery, this has not happened.

An alternative suggestion was the possibility of an enormous comet in close passage or collision with our sun. In this scenario the planets are the far-flung debris from the disaster – or blessing if

one considers mankind to be a beneficent result of the event. If this
turned out to be true, planetary systems would be rare and the
Christian standpoint of man's uniqueness would be greatly
strengthened. The more we hear of these celestial spectaculars,
the more we gain the impression that nothing exciting ever
happens without being attributed to one of these missiles of the
Almighty – the comet.

I am reminded of the profound knowledge exhibited 'between
the lines' of the *Rubáiyát* of Omar Khayyám:

> The Ball no Question makes of Ayes and Noes,
>   But Right or Left, as strikes the Player goes;
> And He that toss'd Thee down into the Field,
>   *He* knows about it all – *He* knows – HE knows!

However, the solar system *was* formed, and it presents itself as a
fascinating playground for the scientist and the astronomer.
Hopefully, in time, their detailed analysis will reveal the true
history of the planets. For the moment our problem is not
knowing how much the primitive people of Earth knew about
celestial events; at times we see them constructing temples, the
orientation of which proves, beyond doubt, how precisely they
understood the movement of the stars. These repetitive cyclic
movements were predicted surprisingly well, and they obviously
realized that these gyrations would continue. But on the walls of
those same temples we see stories of gods behaving at times in a
very erratic manner. One may concede that ancient knowledge of
these heavenly bodies was limited, but I am sure they could never
have thought of them as locations of rational knowledge, as living
creatures, exhibiting all the emotions to be found in man. Despite
the contradiction, this is the way we seem to view it today. Could
we have missed the simple fact that they used the stars for two
purposes? Firstly, as a calendar and watch, which is generally
accepted; but secondly, as a symbolic reminder of vaguely
remembered events passed down from generation to generation.

Could they be warning us that at times these majestic heavenly
bodies behave in a totally irrational manner, as if they had minds
of their own? So irrational in fact, they 'appear' to be human.
Could they have devised a method which, by attributing numbers
to the participants, would record for eternity the actual sequence
of events. To some degree this process would serve the purpose
but, to leave no doubt in the minds of the recipients, it would be
necessary to portray these events graphically. Here the designers
were faced with a seemingly impossible task for nothing could
survive the erosive process of time in an atmosphere such as that of
Earth. Added to this would have been the near-certainty of the
destruction of the surface of the planet, or some part of it, by
celestial mishap.

The most logical, if not the only, way to convey knowledge
across a void of time to a creature who at that moment was a
primitive savage, would be to establish numerical identities which

also related to geometric figures. If it then turned out that the creature survived the ravages of this tempestuous solar system, and at some point emerged as a primitive intelligence, it would of necessity, discover simple numerical and geometrical processes.

Here then is the means of communication – to implant or programme the mind of the creature with intuitive equivalents. The geometry is axiomatic, but the numerical values could to some degree be devised to suit it, and those values had to be given identities, human or god-like.

With the invariability of geometric relationships, what other invariables would have to be accommodated? The answer is inexorably self-evident – the cyclic process of the heavenly bodies themselves. The **360** day voyage of Earth round the sun must determine the degrees of the circle. Whether Earth ever performed such an orbit is irrelevant. The actual orbit was numerically close enough to equate with that which the symbolic geometry demanded. The actual relationship between the diameter of the circle and its circumference posed the same problem, and it is for this reason that the symbolic value of π being **3** was chosen, and demonstrated in the Bible. But what of the rotation of the planet itself? It was essential that this cyclic motion be divided into units, the number of which would form a bridge between the progression of numbers which were the invariables of geometry and celestial cycles. It was the only area of free choice available and, for those who have the 'understanding', it could only be **24**, with sub-divisions of **60**.★ Following the most elementary use of **24** certain revelations occur; the divisions of the circle of **360** by this number produces the manner in which the circle of churches at Rennes is divided (**360** divided by **24** = **15**). This division produces the **15** of Osiris who lost his phallus, which in turn brings us to the Ishtar-Tammuz legend so closely related to that of Isis and Osiris. Ishtar's planetary connection is Venus, and to ensure no stone is left unturned we will now look in more detail at Venus, a close neighbour of Earth and clouded in more than its fair share of mystery. Until quite recently it defied examination – being covered in dense clouds which prevented our telescopes from seeing the surface. It is slightly smaller than Earth and it is approximately 72 per cent of the distance of Earth from the sun. We must immediately dismiss any idea of similarity of surface conditions between Venus and Earth. The pressure and the surface of Venus would be unbearable to most life-forms, and the atmosphere is largely carbon dioxide – so we can rule out any ideas of Venusian flying saucers.

Uninviting as Venus appears, it has played an important role in mythology and that role is even stranger than the planet's physical characteristics. The name Venus conjures up ideas of love and beauty, strengthened by its early association with Aphrodite, a mother goddess; but it was also linked in Roman times with another facet of love – prostitution. We will concern ourselves with a much earlier dedication of the planet, which was to the

★This forms part of the mathematical blueprint of creation, which I will explain in a later book.

Babylonian goddess Ishtar who is unmistakably linked with Isis. It pleases me to see that the ground features recently identified by radar survey are named Ishtar and Aphrodite in keeping with the legends. These legends show Astarte or Ishtar as a goddess of incredible power. She was inclined to have symbolic love affairs with earthly men, who were apt to suffer considerably if they took this lady too casually. She permeates the legends of Adonis. She is there in association with Hiram Abiff, the builder of Solomon's Temple, who had constructed other temples dedicated to her. It is understandable that Hiram would be very careful to do nothing to offend her and would, therefore, ensure that the Temple of Solomon was constructed to her measure, regardless of what name the Jews cared to put over the doorway. As we know, Venus is seen as a brilliant 'star' in the morning and in the evening, at which times it dominates the sky. In the past it was referred to quite rightly as having 'horns' and this is an accurate description of the planet as seen through the telescope. The crescent in the southern aspect manifests cusps which have the appearance of horns. This, however, is something which is obvious only with optical magnification, and if this had been noticed before Galileo's telescope we would have cause to wonder whether it could have been seen by the naked eye. Even at its closest approach to Earth, it cannot be easily discerned. I wondered if perhaps in past times it had come much closer to Earth?

Velikovsky made an impressive list of references to this in his *Worlds in Collision*:[*]

> The star that smoked – a Mexican reference.
> The star with a beard – a Chaldean reference.
> A star which scatters its flame in fire – an Egyptian reference.
> The star with hair – a Babylonian reference.

To those who have studied the ancient symbols, this crescent shape with upward pointing cusps is immediately recognizable as the 'boat' or female organ – the 'holiest of holes' or the entrance to the 'holy of holies', the sanctuary of creation.

Any number of symbols can be identified as having been associated with Venus, but above all was the blazing star of the pentagram.

Overriding all these images was the fear which this planet evoked in primitive people. Some authors have attributed this lengendary fear to the possibility of an actual memory of the time when Venus ravaged Earth by coming too close to it. I do not wish to become involved in attempting to identify Venus as the root cause of our disrupted solar system, or even to attempt to attribute magical powers to its celestial movements. However, it does seem clear to me that its significance in legend is disproportionate to its appearance and to its usefulness as a navigational beacon or chronological marker. I am also totally mystified by the fact that long before its precise alignments could have been expected to be known, it was identified with the pentagram.

* Velikovsky, *Worlds in Collision* (Gollancz: London) 1950.

The occultations of Venus with the sun were admirably demonstrated in Henry Lincoln's film, *The Shadow of the Templars*, and the diagram illustrates how in every **8** years (the number of Isis) the **5**-pointed star (a female body) is traced in the sky (illus 74).

With the Earth as the centre of the circle, the moment when Venus is directly behind the sun is seen at position A. As the sun apparently follows the clockwise course, Venus is next in occultation at position B having completed two fifths of the circle. This process continues through C, D and E, finally returning to A having made five movements of two fifths of the circuit to mark the pentagram in the heavens. This movement is therefore two complete revolutions of a circle in **8** years.

In the circle of perfection using symbolic $\pi = 3$ with a diameter of **360** the circumference is **1080**. Therefore in one year the distance travelled is **2160** divided by **8**; once again we see the **270** signifying the period of pregnancy (**9** months of **30** days).

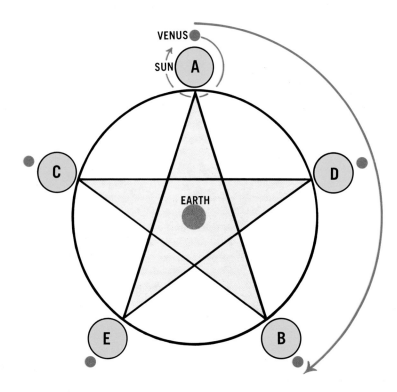

74. The occultations of Venus occuring in the shape of a regular pentagram in the sequence shown by the letters. The complete figure is formed every 8 years having completed two apparent rotations.

When was this movement first identified? Why is this the most persistent of all the symbols of the occult? And above all, for our purposes, why is the pentagram the controlling structure of the geometry in the temple at Rennes-le-Château?

Here we may find another thread in the tapestry. Venus is closely associated with Magdalene, supposedly a redeemed prostitute, but nevertheless the love connection is there. Could it be that Christian doctrine would wish to label her in this fashion to prevent further investigation into her activities? We have already spoken of Magdalene's connections with the Temple of Ishtar, and at the temple of Aphrodite (Ishtar) in Cyprus it was the custom for women to prostitute themselves to strangers prior to their becoming married. Frazer tells us in *The Golden Bough*★ that in Babylon, regardless of their social status, women were obliged to submit themselves to strangers at the temple of Mylitta (Ishtar), and money received for these services was donated to the goddess. But it has also been suggested the practice was a symbolic remnant of a time when it was imperative to increase the population of the world, and this would have served the purpose admirably. It would also have ensured at the same time that cross-fertilization occurred between persons who would not normally have associated with each other. It was the continuation of this ritual in the Temple of Ishtar which has been misinterpreted by Christianity and has resulted in the women who were associated with it being labelled prostitutes, Magdalene being a prime example. This also partially explains the function of the so-called 'virgins' in holy places. Their role was understood to be purely sexual, and I have no doubt this may have been so, but there was possibly another function for these ladies; one which is far less obvious, and which has remained a closely guarded secret!

Once again in following the trail of the mystery of Rennes I was led back to the undeniable predominance of the female principle. I could have made the mistake of attributing all these sexual connections to primitive pagan beliefs, but this would have been a misleading simplification, for beyond the protective veil lies something far more profound which would shock the puritans. In its geometric function in the temple, the pentagram represents the shape of a female body with five extensions. The male body, with the phallus has six extensions and is represented by the six-pointed star (illus 75). This is the symbol adopted by Judaism in its policy of suppressing the female predominance in holy doctrine. They often claim that it represents the Seal of Solomon, whereas in truth it was only the motif displayed on his shield. The actual seal was a pentagram demonstrating that his devotion, like that of his father King David, was to the female principle. Knowing, as I am sure they did, the full significance of the Ark of the Covenant, their allegiance could not have been otherwise. We must look in more detail at the powerful deity Ishtar, so closely related to the planet Venus, and at the legends associated with her.

Ishtar, like Isis, had a male partner Dumu-zi; in Syria he was

★Macmillan & Co Ltd, London 1925.

Tammuz and to the Greeks, Adonis. In these legends we find
Ishtar as the corn-goddess and her lover, represented by the
priest-king. The relationship of these lovers was an annual ritual,
and their period of 'love-making' continued throughout the spring
and summer, at the end of which Dumu-zi died. Ishtar
brokenhearted descended, as did the planet Venus, into the
underworld to search for her lover. To reach her goal she had to
pass through seven gates. At each gate, since she was forced to pay
a price to the keeper of the gate, she removed an item of clothing,
possibly a veil. Whether one understands this as a journey or as a
dance, the outcome is the same. Ishtar stands naked and pleads
her case. She fails and is scorned in the underworld. Then the gods
intervene and demand that Ishtar and Dumu-zi be permitted to
return to the surface. Venus rises and the celebrations of spring
begin – the corn seed has survived and resurrection is achieved.
Once again it would appear that Omar Khayyám was well
informed:

> Up from Earth's Centre through the Seventh Gate
> I rose, and on the Throne of Saturn sate,
> And many Knots unravel'd by the Road;
> But not the Knot of Human Death and Fate.
> (*Rubáiyát* of Omar Khayyám)

There is no doubt that this ritual was re-enacted annually with
the priest-king being sacrificed to ensure a successful harvest the
following year. Obviously, where a ruling king existed he needed

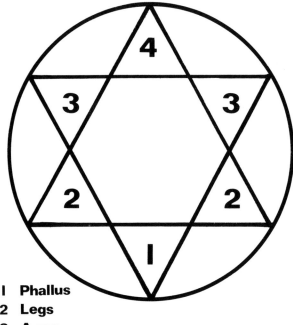

1 **Phallus**
2 **Legs**
3 **Arms**
4 **Head**

75. The parts of the male body as
identified with the regular
hexagram.

to ensure he was not the focal point of this ritual, and because of this we find a process of substitution being employed.

This resulted in Harvest Lords or Priest Kings being elected and it would appear that for one year they lived like kings. No woman refused them, for in the sexual act she was performing the function of the goddess Ishtar. The priest-king enjoyed the best of everything that the community could provide, and then came winter, the time of sacrifice. A great festival marked this occasion, and the methods by which the unfortunate individual was dispatched varied from place to place. Suffice to say, at times his demise was achieved by the removal of his penis.

It is gratifying to learn this ritual was eventually replaced by further substitution in the form of 'corn cakes' fashioned in the image of a phallus. Apparently it was better to worship this goddess at a distance. Too close an association implied payment of a penalty, and this has been been recorded in numerous legends. Wherever, 'wounding in the thigh' or 'in the side' is mentioned it is likely to imply removal of the phallus and its donation to the goddess. Circumcision is probably a remnant of this ritual. One may begin to recognize many features of these beliefs associated with Jesus. The true story of Jesus will probably never be told, but today there are those who examine the story of Our Lord, uninhibited by previous indoctrination. Gone are the days when self-appointed preachers could insist on blind belief against truth or reason.

Enough doubt has already been cast on the identity of Jesus to lead one to question the validity of the New Testament in its entirety and, even when the desire to believe is present, many questions arise. Jesus appears to have been closely associated with, and respected by, people of high standing and he might have been instructed in Egypt. He was closely associated with Magdalene of the Ishtar temple. She may have been considered a prostitute later in Christian history but, as we have seen, any woman who was so connected would have adhered to the rule of the temple. Accepting that Jesus was of the royal blood line of David and Solomon, one might expect him to have the same beliefs and they are clearly defined in the geometry of Solomon's Temple and the Ark of the Covenant. His close friend Joseph of Aramathea supposedly visited England which gave rise to the mass of 'legends' which have associated King Arthur and his Knights with the mystery of the Holy Grail.

Knights of the 'round' table, devoted to the female principle as they were, could not have chosen a table of any other shape. And behind the pure hearts, bravery, combat, chivalry and pageantry, we can see all too clearly they were totally subservient to their ladies. The quest for the Holy Grail is a dominant feature of their history, and I will not shirk the issue. Later the reader will understand how that mysterious 'vessel' does no more than confirm all the other images of the temple at Rennes-le-Château. Surely all these interrelated fragments are not explicable except in terms of their having a common origin.

The Crucifixion of Jesus is probably another enactment of the ritualistic killing of the 'king'. The wound 'in the side' and many other coincidental factors will be dealt with later, but for the moment we should consider that there may have been a substitution arranged even on this occasion.

I would refer the reader here to *The Holy Blood and The Holy Grail*, in which the authors have presented a very convincing argument for such a scenario. This culminates in an extract from the Nag Hammadi scrolls, which purports to be a quotation of the actual words of Jesus:

> I did not succumb to them as they had planned . . . And I did not die in reality but in appearance, lest I be put to shame by them . . . For my death which they think happened (happened) to them in their error and blindness, since they nailed their man unto their death . . . It was another, their father, who drank the gall and the vinegar; it was not I. They struck me with the reed it was another, Simon, who bore the cross on his shoulder. It was another upon whom they placed the crown of thorns . . . And I was laughing at their ignorance.

So Jesus may have survived this 'crucifixion', and if he did there was every possibility of the Languedoc being the place to which he fled. A painting in the church of Rennes-les-Bains (*Le Christ au lièvre*) shows Jesus in a cave, and outside can be seen a distinctive rock which exists near to the church (illus 76).

Another interesting link between Ishtar and our mystery was found in the tomb of a Merovingian king, Childeric I.

The tomb of Childeric I was discovered in 1653 and was found to contain 300 solid gold bees. The bee was the sacred symbol of the Merovingians. But it was also a symbol of the goddess Ishtar, the queen bee, and I am sure the reader knows that the queen rules the hive; the female is predominant. Furthermore, when she mates in flight the sex organ of the drone is torn from his body and remains in the queen and the drone then dies. Once again we realize how closely the mystery of Rennes is connected to the Ishtar rites.

Another item of interest which the tomb produced was the golden head of a bull; the horns again connect with Venus, Ishtar and Isis. The last item which could possibly be quite significant was a crystal ball, but that connection is too involved to deal with here.

One of the enigmatic ciphers mentioned earlier refers to Dagobert II, who was also a Merovingian and was married to a Celtic princess.

TO DAGOBERT II, KING, AND TO SION BELONGS
THIS TREASURE AND HE IS THERE DEAD

The authors of *The Holy Blood and The Holy Grail* provide us with a detailed history of the Merovingians and the relationship between them and the Priory of Sion and consequently to the mystery of Rennes-le-Château.

Finally there is the Virgin Mother, an image even the most conservative of the experts is willing to concede was taken directly from Isis. We are told that the worship of Isis persisted into Christian times, when it was represented by Mary, Mother of Jesus.

The trails divide again and again, but they are never dead-ends, leading nowhere. They always come back to some familiar landmark in history or myth, or to some significant location.

The picture is vague and distorted, but the links *are* there. If Jesus survived, if Magdalene was his wife, if he had children and if they fled from Jerusalem to the Languedoc, then many apparently unrelated pieces of the puzzle come together. I feel certain we will find the evidence we need in the secret locations of the geometric temple at Rennes-le-Château. I am also convinced that this was known to the Vatican. That they censored the gospels, almost out of recognition, is generally agreed, but there is every possibility that they shut the gate only to find that the horse had already gone. There is much to suggest that this was not fully realized until evidence came to light that the Knights Templar held a great secret. The Knights Templar considered Jesus to be a brother knight, and as we progress their reasoning for this will become very clear.

76. *Le Christ au lievre* is a copy of a painting by Van Dyck. The distinctive rock outside is a well known feature near Rennes-les-Bains, but it did not occur in the original painting. Does this imply the body of Christ is buried somewhere in the temple?

11

The Knights Templar

That ev'n my buried Ashes such a Snare
Of Perfume shall fling up into the Air,
As not a True Believer passing by
But shall be overtaken unaware.

Their crusades – the charges against them – confession? – their beliefs – their secrets –
the skull of Baphomet – the cat – a link with Egypt – the female Satan?

The Knights Templar were a religious military order. According to historical records, the order was founded in 1118, but recent research seems to point to connections with the Holy Land at a far earlier date. It was said that nine (**9**) knights established the order to protect Christian pilgrims. Then for nine (**9**) years no new members were permitted to join. During the 12th and 13th centuries their popularity and power grew rapidly following the success of the early crusades. They acquired an extensive amount of property and land wherever they operated, and were particularly wealthy in France. They were responsible not to the kings of the country where they lived, but directly to the Pope. Less obviously, they were dedicated to the Patriarchy of Constantinople, and that body was not on the best of terms with the Church of Rome.

Equally controversial was the total rejection of women by the order, which was supposedly the reason for their white mantles of chastity. This principle seems to me to be totally contradictory to the secret beliefs of the Templars and the legendary dedication they showed to their ladies, or indeed to any lady in distress. I confess it surprises me how historical accounts of their achievements, their eventual arrests, the accusations, and the trial and condemnation of the Templars, all avoid mentioning that this celibate attitude was merely a façade. I am sure the historians had access to the same information which I had, and it quite conclusively points to the fact that the Templars were dedicated to the female principle.

With the loss of Palestine in 1291 to the Mameluks of Egypt, the image of the Templars was a little tarnished and as the years passed, some people considered that they were resting on their laurels and serving little or no purpose. They had acquired, by this time, immense wealth, acting as conveyors of property and, as bankers. They were also undoubtedly the safest couriers for moving money from one place to another. The King of France,

Philippe IV, on the other hand, was in dire financial trouble, and could not resist the temptation to seize the Templar wealth. Knowing this would be a direct affront to the Pope Clement V, he infiltrated the ranks of the Templars with spies. What they supposedly discovered was that the Templars were homosexuals, that they denied Christ, spat and urinated on the cross, worshipped a skull, kissed the anus of a cat, or goat, and committed numerous other offences which would leave the Pope no alternative but to turn against his knights.

The Pope conceded and added his authority to Philippe's; the Templars were arrested, tried, tortured and, supposedly having confessed, were disbanded. Their extensive property and wealth, or most of it, fell into the hands of the king and the Pope. The knights, in the south of France and just over the border in Spain, appear to have escaped the net for a while and by all accounts a lot of their gold disappeared; possibly this is one of the treasures of Rennes.

As the only records are those of the persecutors, we are obviously not hearing the full story. I feel it my duty to offer some information which may help the reader to make a better judgement.

First let us examine the hidden intention of the Templars, which was to rebuild the Temple of Solomon according to the plans of Ezekiel. They were, therefore, builders and masons as well as soldiers, and the trowel plays an important part in the symbolism associated with them. Some have said that the Templars derived their name from this avowed aim. Others say that Baldwin II, King of Jerusalem, gave them a house near the Temple of Solomon in recognition of their services. But Eliphas Lévi points out this could not have been so, as the Temple had ceased to exist and even the site was uncertain. In fact, current research may eventually prove that Jerusalem was not the site of the Temple of Solomon at all. I think for the explanation of the name, we would be better advised by Higgins, who points out that all temples were supposed to represent the cosmos. They were surrounded with pillars indicating the positions of heavenly bodies or, in other cases, numerically recording the cyclic motion of them. He claims all those periods are demonstrated in one temple or the other with the exception of **666** – a number which is always concealed.

Leaving aside for the moment the French word for knight, we find a coincidental equation which links English and French phonetics. Knight = night = *la nuit* (French for night). Most of the ancient temples were open to the night sky, and the Queen of the Starry Heavens was Nut. Coincidentally, an alternative spelling of the name of this goddess is Nuit. The feminine gender of *la nuit* is not surprising, and it follows that the day (*le jour*) is under the jurisdiction of Ra, and should be masculine.

Therefore, the model of a temple was to represent the Templum, the starry dome of the heavens. As such it was merely a microcosm of the true Temple built by the Architect of the Universe. Some temples exhibit **360** pillars, which does not surprise me, and one such temple in Scotland is called Iona, which also is predictable.

Higgins considers the Templars' history goes a good deal further back than historians have recognized, and in this history one could find a reason for the paradox of their dealings with the Assassins and their bitter enemies the Mohammedans. These transactions were largely concerned with acquiring land in which the Templars could function free from any interference by the Pope, or the kings under his influence. There is no doubt that the Templars had the intention of ruling the world, and one can only contemplate how advantageous this might have been to mankind compared to the chaos of the last thousand years.

To unravel the history of the beliefs of the Knights Templar is, indeed, a daunting task. They are remembered from one standpoint, as one of the most evil bodies of men who ever drew breath. On the other hand, they were courageous and chivalrous knights who, as far as their strength permitted, kept the roads and highways safe for the passage of Christian pilgrims.

Soldiers of Christ? Quite possibly they were, but they certainly did not consider Him to be the Son of God. Jacques de Molay, Grand Master of the Order told them to believe in the great omnipotent God, who created heaven and earth, and not in the Crucifixion. Believing in God was obviously not approved of, for the order was broken by Philippe le Bel, certainly with the blessing of the Pope, on that fateful day, Friday 13th October 1307. The members of this religious order, who apparently served the Pope's purpose, were arrested in a well-timed operation which would be commensurate with a present-day drug squad 'round-up'. How did Philippe le Bel convince the Pope that the most efficient body of fighting men he had ever been served by should be so broken? The motives of the king can well be understood, for the wealth of the Templars was common knowledge. It was said it was their intention to purchase the world, and if one studies their history, they were certainly achieving their aims. As a principle, however, this would not have offended the Vatican whose aims are, or were, much the same.

Simply, the moves of Philippe le Bel were to disband the Templars and, by so doing, to seize the vast number of estates which they had acquired. Furthermore, the 'cash in hand' of the Templars was considered to be an incredible hoard of gold, which, if true, would be reason enough for him to act as he did. However, to obtain the co-operation of the Pope it was necessary to discredit this organization on ethical grounds. The complicity of the Pope is demonstrated by the fact that his action was not confined to France alone. If the Roman Church was to claim it was misled by Philippe le Bel, in that country, it would not explain why Clement V insisted that the Templars in England and Spain should also be seized.

Although Edward II grudgingly agreed to allow the papal inquisitors to come to England, they failed miserably. To their utter dismay they were not allowed to torture the accused and, in consequence, failed to obtain the 'confessions' they had achieved in France. There, the Templars apparently confessed to all the ridiculous charges made against them. This is most probably true, considering that they were being roasted alive at the time.

I feel I must credit Pope Clement with enough intelligence to know these charges were fictitious, but like all good lies they carried an element of truth in them. Philippe le Bel's spies found it simple enough to represent their rituals in a manner which would be offensive to the unknowing world. For example, anyone who has been involved in military action will know that strict compliance with orders, regardless of individual opinion, is essential to the success of any operation. I am sure I will not be guilty of disclosing too much if I inform the reader of a possible method devised by the Templars to ensure that new members were totally obedient. If the initiate was led into the Temple where he was shown a goat and then asked to kneel and kiss the anal region of the animal, you must admit that if the initiate did as instructed, it would be proof of his willingness to obey. To alleviate repulsion the initiate was suffering, he could be blindfolded and, after due ceremony, would be asked to proceed. If during the interval the goat had been removed, and something far more attractive had been substituted, it could then be made apparent to the initiate upon his completion of the task by removing the blindfold. I trust the reader will now appreciate why this ritual was such a closely guarded secret. For if the initiate was aware of the final outcome, it would serve no purpose whatsoever. I am sure the reader now insists I disclose the identity of the substitute, but I will not – let the geometry of Rennes-le-Château reveal it for you. What it will also reveal is, although the charges were fictitious, the Pope may have acquired information that the Templars were the custodians of secrets so powerful that they could not even be mentioned in the trials. These secrets had to be totally erased from history, and they were – until now.

I wondered if any of the accusers had been careless enough to include a reference to those items which the Pope found so dangerous. Given that the doctrine was highly secret, such a mistake could have occurred quite innocently – and it did. In some trials the Templars were charged with having kissed the 'ass' or anus of a cat in the initiation ceremony. I remembered reading an explanation for the word Cathars in *The Trials of the Templars*★ by Malcolm Barber, where he quoted a description of the Cathars by Walter Map (1182):

> . . . a sect which he called Publicans or Paterines, who worshipped a huge cat which descended to them on a rope. This cat they kissed on the feet or under the tail or on the private parts, an act which inflamed them with lust. The usual sexual orgy followed. In his defence of the faith against the Cathars, written in the late twelfth

★(Cambridge University Press: London) 1978.

century, Alain de Lille drew on the same tradition, asserting, among his explanations of the name 'Cathars', that they were so called from 'cat' because they kissed the hind quarters of a cat, in whose form, it was said, Lucifer appeared to them.

Here is a link indeed, for the Cathars were the victims of the Albigensian Crusade, persecuted for, amongst other things, believing that the material world was the creation of Rex Mundi (Satan-King of the Earth) who was equally responsible, therefore, for the creation of the body of Jesus. The Cathars were closely associated with the Templars in the Languedoc.

Next, we should consider the innumerable pointers which indicate that the Templars worshipped the goddess Isis and her husband Osiris, and we will soon realize the significance of the cat.

Apart from its obvious connection with the female, the cat was one of the most sacred creatures of Egypt, being considered the personification of the Goddess Bast (the soul of Isis), and represented as a female with the head of a cat. She ruled in the city of Bubastis where all cats were supposed to be buried. The creature was considered so sacred, it was embalmed as if it were human and anyone who killed a cat was condemned to die.

In the *Book of the Dead* (Chapter XVII), we are told the Cat was in the Persea tree of Heliopolis on the night when the enemies of Osiris were killed. In male form the Cat equates with Ra himself in the name of Mau. Elsewhere in the *Book of the Dead* the Ass speaks 'the mighty word' to the Cat and this 'Cat-ass' is a form of the sun-god, who provides the words for the dead to protect themselves from the powers of darkness. The Persea tree seems to equate with the mythological sycamore of Nut at Heliopolis, at the foot of which the Great Cat, Ra, slayed the evil serpent Apep. Wallis Budge* considers this may well have been the archetype of the tree where the Virgin Mary rested during her flight to Egypt. Once more the links join, and we are able to see the close connection of the Templars to Egyptian mythology.

For the moment, let us glance in a lighter mood at more Templar imagery – the seal showing two knights on one horse. One suggestion was that they represent Geoffrey de Saint-Omer and Hugh de Payens as the founders; another, that it shows them to be the 'poor knights' who had insufficient horses to allow them one each. Another Castor and Pollux – Hussein and some other fellow whose name I cannot remember. I suppose in a few hundred years' time someone might say it was Laurel and Hardy; even that would not be as ridiculous as some of the substitutions which have occurred. For the purpose of casting the maximum discredit, Philippe le Bel came up with the craziest idea of all. Two knights on one horse, he claimed, was indicative of homosexuality. Give us credit, Phillippe, we know better. A knight is **9** and we need two of them to make **18**. I need say no more at present, but the full meaning of this will be demonstrated when we deal with the numerical language of the gods.

*The Gods of the Egyptians. Vol. 2. p.107 (Dover Publications: New York)

Admittedly, the Templars were disgusted by the Christian devotion to the symbol of the cross. But is this so hard to understand? Would any clear-thinking organization worship the instrument with which their hero was murdered? We must remember that Jesus was, to the Templars, a brother knight.

The next accusation was that the Templars worshipped a huge skull named Baphomet which respresented the devil. We should not dismiss this lightly, as a skull in some form or other did exist, and it occurs time and time again in the Rennes mystery. Many authors have discussed the skull of Baphomet. Some have concluded it is entirely fictitious, while others describe it as a terrifying force of evil. Remembering that there are 'none so blind' as those who will not see, if we disregard the extremes of religious fanaticism, we may be able to arrive at something nearer to the truth. Let us look at one author who appeared to be well informed on the subject.

Alphonse Louis Constant began his career as a priest in the Roman Catholic Church and then took an interest in things which should not have concerned him – he began to study the occult. He wrote on the subject under the pseudonym of Eliphas Lévi and gave up the Church. Eventually, he returned to the Catholic fold late in life. I suppose he must have considered there were really only two horses in the race, and that by backing them both he stood a reasonable chance in the hereafter. It is arguable whether anything is gained by studying the words of a 'double agent', but I believe he was a genuine searcher and much that he said had an element of truth in it. I am sure that a good deal he wrote he subsequently wished he had not, but 'the moving finger writes and having writ moves on', and we have the benefit of his inquiries. At one point he states, 'without evasion', the Great Magical Current – the double current of life – the living and astral fire of the earth, equates with the brazen serpent of Moses, which was twined round the symbol of the Tau – the Caduceus – the Linga – and the Baphomet of the Templars. Regrettably, he does not explain how he came by this equation, but my investigations certainly agree with his, and they could never have shared the same origin.

I am sure the reader will see the connections:

Moses – Egyptian priest – Isis
Caduceus – **8** and **1** – Isis
Linga – crescent – boat – female – Isis
Baphomet – ?

Elsewhere, his emotions control his pen and I feel I must give the reader the benefit of the result, trusting that it will amuse him as it did me.

> We recur once more to that terrible number fifteen, symbolized in the Tarot by a monster throned upon an altar, mitred and horned, having a woman's breast and the generative organs of a man – a chimera, a malformed sphinx, a synthesis of deformities. Below

this figure we read a frank and simple description – THE DEVIL. Yes, we confront here that phantom of all terrors, the dragon of all theogonies, the Ahriman of the Persians, the Typhon of the Egyptians, the Python of the Greeks, the old serpent of the Hebrews, the fantastic monster, the nightmare, the Croquemitaine, the gargoyle, the great beast of the Middle Ages, – and worse than all these – the Baphomet of the Templars, the bearded idol of the alchemist, the obscene deity of Mendes, the goat of the Sabbath (illus 77).

Very eloquent Eliphas and I admit not the sort of thing I would like to meet at night down a dark alley. But if it is so repugnant to you, why did you create it? Or alternatively, publicize it to such a degree it was adopted by a lunatic fringe of humanity who practise the so-called black arts? Or did you create an image which was expected of you? Repulsive as it is, it carries all the symbols of perfection. This is an androgyny divided into male and female. But it tells us more, the cloven hoof and horns suggest that an animal was utilized to achieve this division. The crescents of Nut and Isis are easily recognized, as is the pentagram in the crown of Lucifer. Certainly this creature brings light in the darkness. If that light signifies intelligence, it is confirmed by the caduceus. The serpents entwined round the phallic rod to illustrate the presence of Isis and, by way of confirmation, they surmount the circle, positioned as a womb, and symbol of the female generative organ. The wings seem inappropriate for a goat, but they also confirm the goddess Isis. Little wonder that the hands depict the sign of excommunication.

Rest easy Eliphas – your message is clear – the time has come at last – there are those who understand!

On the question of **15**, words fail me, should we cross ourselves whenever it appears? What of those poor unfortunate souls that live at number **15** in some street or the other, are they cursed?

I wonder if the evil of the number **15** could be anything to do with the **14** parts of the body of Osiris, and the phallus, the fifteenth part that was never found?

So the picture, according to Eliphas Lévi, looks pretty black for the Templars. But now he becomes confused, for in the same book he offers an explanation of the word Baphomet which appears to be quite complimentary. He states that it should be spelt cabalistically backwards, as three abbreviations TEM.OHP.AB:

TEMPLI OMNIUM HOMINUM PACIS ABBAS
Father of the Temple of Peace of all men.

This seems to me to be at variance with the image he painted previously, and it causes A. E. Waite, who translated the book into English, to become equally emotional, for in a footnote he says:

There are three things to be said on this fantastic explanation (1) that there is no reason assigned or assignable for reading Baphomet

77. The Sabbatic Goat of Eliphos Levi. An androgynous image incorporating all the imagery of Set, Isis and the gods of creation.

backwards; (2) that the Latin produced from the alleged abbreviation is incredibly bad; and (3) that its import has no application to the Templars, either as a chivalry or an occult sect. From neither point of view can they be regarded as apostles of peace.

Now if Mr Waite can ridicule in this fashion, let us comment on his words. In his first statement, I would suggest that he looks again at the methods used by most great men of science, and at the rituals of societies who were driven underground by the persecution of the church. They all used reflected or reversed images to conceal identities from the eyes of the profane.

Secondly, the Latin is bad, but surely it was said the Templars were largely uneducated, so it is not such a poor attempt. Also I would remind him that if we were to judge the reliability of a document by the quality of the grammar, many more pieces of 'documentary truth' would have to be disregarded.

Waite's last remark is so banal it is not worthy of comment, but I would say just this: the Templars aim was to build a Temple – so *there* is one application. It is also obvious that they were tolerant and that they respected all beliefs, considering them all to have a common origin.

On the question of chivalry, how can he deny that, despite the accusations of the Pope and Philippe le Bel, the Knights Templar are considered to this day to be the very personification of courage and chivalry. Furthermore, if their society was not occult (and by this I mean hidden not evil), how is it they form such a large part of the literature of the subject?

On the question of the skull, Henry Lincoln shows us another possibility which has a ring of truth to it. He likens Baphomet to the phonetic pronunciation of an Arabic word *bufihimat* and, with good scholarship suggests that Father of Wisdom is the meaning and father in this sense could mean source.

His next sentence intrigued me. It begins:

If this is indeed the origin of Baphomet . . .

may I suggest that he could have said: If this is so Baphomet is indeed the origin!.

The implication points, he admits, to a being of divine origin, but he questions who or what he was?

We have seen that other scholars seem to have no doubt who he was – he was the Devil. But who, may I ask, was the Devil? Surely he was a mythical figure created by religious fanatics to personify the evil in the world – the 'bogey man' who will get you if you do not go to church? Here is the 'scapegoat' to excuse us of the responsibility for our own evil. (We seem unable to avoid this goat.) I am sure some well-meaning Christians would now wish to remind me the devil is Satan, whose presence is indisputably recorded in ancient doctrine. So it is; but the equation Devil = Satan is not!

I know it would be unfair to leave the reader with this conundrum, so I will return to it later. For the moment let us look at something else mentioned by Henry Lincoln. When the Templars were disbanded, a silver head of a woman was found in a preceptory in Paris, and it bore an inscription CAPUT LVIIIM (58m). Henry Lincoln suggests that the M may be implying the symbol for Virgo, the virgin, and he may well be right, for the original virgin was Isis, Goddess of the Templars. The number **58** is less puzzling if one remembers that five (**5**) is the number of the pentagram and eight (**8**) is indicative of Isis. We may now complete the simple equation which exposes her secret number:

$$5 \times 8 = 40 = 58 - 18 \text{ ISIS}$$

The numbers **5** and **8** are also exhibited in the beliefs of the 'Brothers of the Rose Cross', where the rose is constructed with a centre of five petals, surrounded by eight petals. When the language of the gods is revealed later, the reason for the number 58 will be even more apparent.

But now let us return to the huge skull Baphomet. Could it be a gigantic skull which would prove beyond doubt that a being of such proportions had actually lived on this planet. Was this truly the source, or origin, or father of the human race? Could this be one of the secret artefacts hidden in the valley of Rennes-le-Château?

Is it being implied that Baphomet is Satan? In order to conceal his identity, has Satan been intentionally associated with the Devil?

Is it coincidence, once more, that simply by allocating the numerical value of the letters in the English alphabet to the letters of Baphomet (**2 + 1 + 16 + 8 + 15 + 13 + 5 + 20**) the total is **80** (Isis and Nut)? An 8-letter word totalling **80**. I have little doubt that the final investigation of the Baphomet skull will reveal it to be female; possibly the actual, or the symbolic equivalent, of the skull of Isis – the Supreme feminine intellect responsible for our elevation from animal form †.

Finally, I am delighted to find that in *Nightside of Eden*,* Kenneth Grant describes Baphomet thus:

> . . . adored by the Templars in the form of a Head. That it had a feminine origin is shown by Gerald Massey who writes 'METE was the BAPHOMET or mother of breath'. According to Von Hammer, the formula of faith inscribed on a chalice belonging to the Templars is as follows: Let METE be exalted who causes all things to bud and blossom, it is our root; it is one and seven; it is octinimous, the eight-fold name.

What have we here? the **8** of Isis and the persistent **17** of the mystery of Rennes-le-Château and more confirmation of

† *Publisher's Note* – Immediately prior to our going to press, the author's findings have been substantiated by Hugh Schonfield in *The Essene Odyssy*, published by Element Books (p. 164). He showed that by applying the Hebrew Atbash code to the name Baphomet, the name Sophia, female wisdom, is revealed. Sophia is equated with Isis by Plutarch.

*(Frederick Muller Ltd: London), 1977.

Baphomet being female. If **17** is to be associated with Isis I can suggest another fragment for our puzzle. It was in the month of Hathor (Isis) that Osiris was murdered and, coincidentally, this occurred on the 17th! Even stranger, when Isis first received report of his death she was in the city of Coptos, later Sidon. It was a Lord of Sidon who in Templar legend had intercourse with the dead body of his wife or mistress.* After this act, a voice bade him return in **9** months, which he did, and found a skull lying between the legs of the woman. This has a strong association with the skull adored by the Templars. We are seeing here a more conventional act of necrophilia than that described in the Egyptian legend of Isis and Osiris but, although there is confusion of identities, I wondered if it could be intentional. The Christian Satan has been equated with the Chaldaic Sheitan and in turn with the Egyptian Set, who was the 'brother' of Isis. Could these problems of gender mean we are overlooking Eliphas Lévi's simple message – they were androgenous! I feel we should look more closely at this Satan of ours.

*See p.181 (The Ass).

12

Satan

Up from Earth's Centre through the Seventh Gate
I rose, and on the Throne of Saturn sate,
And many Knots unravel'd by the Road;
But not the Knot of Human Death and Fate.

In all that is Holy, who was Satan?
In all that was Holy, was Satan.

In *Isis Unveiled*, Madam Blavastky outspokenly stated, 'How little the philosophy of the old secret doctrine was understood is illustrated in the atrocious persecution of the Templars by the Church and in the accusation that they worshipped the devil in the shape of the goat, Baphomet'. The explanation of this confusion of images has already been explained, but any student of the occult will tell you that this devil, by whatever he may be called, is the symbol of God's representative and the purest creation on earth.

If we turn to the *Encyclopaedia Britannica* for guidance on the identity of the devil, we are told he is 'the supreme spirit of evil' and the reference runs to a thousand words or more, and yet, the word devil rapidly disappears and is replaced by 'Satan'. Now surely we could not be so confused? The devil is the imaginary entity which represents evil, certainly not Satan. The word Satan, stangely enough, is not listed in the *Encyclopaedia Britannica*, nor is there any cross-reference to Lucifer or the Devil and yet as we read on under 'the Devil' we find that in the Jewish Targums Sammael is 'the highest angel that stands before God's throne and caused the serpent to seduce the woman'.

The birth of Cain, it continues, is ascribed to a union of Satan and Eve. And with Cain we return to the mystery of Rennes-le-Château, for the architect of the Temple of Solomon so revered by the Templars was Hiram Abiff. He descended from the line of Cain through Tubal-Cain who, with his son, was said to be the only survivor of the superior race after the flood. That race, we are told was, or was created by, the Elohim, 'the serpent people', those of the fire snake.

In *The Holy Blood and The Holy Grail* we find another unusual association with the entity Satan. We are shown a poem by Charles Péguy who, it is suggested, could be associated with the Priory of Sion and thereby with the Rennes mystery.

The arms of Jesus are the Cross of Lorraine,
Both the blood in the artery and blood in the vein,
Both the source of grace and the clear fountain;

The arms of Satan are the Cross of Lorraine,
And the same artery and the same vein,
And the same blood and the troubled fountain;

There is certainly nothing veiled in this equation:

Jesus = the Cross of Lorraine = Satan

Is this heresy? There was a time when statements such as these would have condemned the author to the fire.

The statement is certainly in keeping with the beliefs of the Cathars, who consider all created matter is the work of REX MUNDI – SATAN and, as flesh, Jesus could only be so related. This is a simplification of the teaching but it is not difficult to read into it the message conveyed. It implies we may all be the 'creation of' or 'descendants of' Satan. This may seem to be blasphemous from a Christian point of view, but only if we accept the Christian association of the Devil with Satan. Much would indicate their equation is wrong. Even in the opinion of a Christian scholar, G. H. Pember, M.A.

In *Earth's Earliest Ages** he explains there is 'no personal Devil' and whereas God is positive, the Devil is negative. Then he states:

> the Devil is not to be confused with Satan, though they are sometimes spoken of in Scripture as if they were identical. In such cases, however, Scripture represents but the popular belief.
> The truth concerning Satan belongs to those greater mysteries which have always been reserved from general cognition. The ancient rule in this respect is still in force.

He then goes on to say that it is not likely always to remain so and as the education level of the world progresses, it will be ready to receive the great secret. He continues:

> There is little doubt that the culmination of the mysteries was the worship of Satan himself.

He does not specify on what this 'great secret' is, but suggests to the reader that it is probably connected to a footnote earlier in his book, and I reproduce that footnote here:

> May there not be great significance in the fact that the very name of Satan passes, through its Chaldaic form Sheitan, into the Greek Titan, which last word is used by Greek and Latin poets as a designation of the Sun-god?
> Indeed it would almost seem as if this connection were understood in the dark ages: for Didron, in his Christian Iconography, describes three Byzantine miniatures of the tenth century, in which Satan is depicted with a nimbus, or circular glory, the recognized sign of the Sun-god in Pagan times.
> As the Church became Paganized, the nimbus began to appear in images and pictures of Christ and the saints. At the same time the Church was corrupted by the introduction of other customs, such as the circular tonsure, and the practice of turning to the East, which had been connected with sun-worship from hoar antiquity.

*Hodder & Stoughton: London 1907

It would seem from this, that even the most cherished of Christian symbols, Christ's aura, was borrowed from the King of the Earth. If on the other hand, Jesus was the epitome of purity, as Satan was, he would certainly be entitled to wear this crown.

I will give a few more quotations from this revealing book:

> And it is an ominous fact, that, after the fall, the first inventors of the arts and sciences were the descendants, not of the believing Seth, but of the deist and murderer Cain.

I am sure the reader will realize that this statement is in complete agreement with Masonic teaching and the secret doctrine in the same way as the following:

> . . . so we should naturally conclude that superior beings inhabited and ruled that former world and, like Adam, transgressed the laws of their Creator.

(Note the distinction 'their Creator' and not the Creator.)

The nature of this 'transgression' must be defined if we are to achieve an understanding of the position that humanity occupies in the scale of creation. The beliefs of the Cathars are strongly supported by Pember's next statement:

> If, then, we glance at the few particulars of Satan's history which have been revealed to us we cannot fail to observe that, besides the actual power attributed to him, he manifestly holds the legitimate title of 'Prince of this World'; or, in other words, that this dignity, together with the royal prerogatives which of right pertain to it, was conferred upon him by God Himself.

Finally we are given an insight into the possibility that the human is a 'hybrid' – an animal which, having been impregnated by a creature of intellect, is only half-human:

> Then a new and startling event burst upon the world, and fearfully accelerated the already rapid progress of evil. 'The sons of God saw the daughters of men that they were fair; and they took them wives of all which they chose.' (Elohim) These words are often explained to signify nothing more than the intermarriage of the descendants of Cain and Seth; but a careful examination of the passage will elicit a far deeper meaning.
>
> When men, we are told, began to multiply on the face of the earth, and daughters were born unto them, the sons of God (Elohim) saw the daughters of men. Now by 'men' in each case the whole human race is evidently signified, the descendants of Cain and Seth alike. Hence the 'sons of God' are plainly distinguished from the generation of Adam.

The more thoroughly we examine this book, the more it appears that the truth has been known for a long time and it is confirming all that the solution at Rennes is leading us to:

God created Satan the fairest and wisest of all His creatures in this part of His universe and made him Prince of the World and of the Power of the Air. Since his wisdom would be chiefly used in expounding the will and ways of God, we can probably discern in its mention his office of prophet. He was placed in an Eden, or region of delight, which was both far anterior to the Eden of *Genesis* – for he was perfect in all his ways when he entered it – and also, apparently, of an altogether different and more substantial character, resembling the New Jerusalem as described in the Apocalypse.

In the scanty account given to us of this Eden we may, perhaps, trace the lineaments of the heavenly Tabernacle. For, from the second chapter of *Genesis*, we find that Eden was a district, and the garden an enclosure within it. Following this analogy we discover in Satan's habitation three enclosures, Eden, the Garden of God, and the Holy Mountain of God, corresponding, possibly, to the Outer Court of the Tabernacle, the Holy Place, and the Holy of Holies, respectively. And this idea is strengthened by the fact that Satan is said to have been upon the Holy Mountain of God as the Anointed Cherub that covereth; just as the images of the covering Cherubim were placed in the Holy of Holies.

It would appear that we have seriously misjudged Satan. The implication is that he is something less than the Creator but, let us have no doubt, he is infinitely superior to us and it would seem that his transgression was to create human beings. How then can we degrade his image, when but for him we would not exist? Legend has often intimated that sexual union between certain animals and man may, under special circumstances, produce a superior being. This obviously supposes that the seed of the Nephilim lies dormant in some animals. Let us consider a legend where an exceptional person was said to have been so conceived: the birth to which I am referring is that of Jesus, and I will quote from Eliphas Lévi:

A young girl of Nazareth, named Miriam, betrothed to a young man of her own tribe, named Jochanan, was surprised by a certain Pandira, or Panther, who entered her chamber in the garb and under the name of her lover and by force fulfilled his desires. Jochanan, becoming acquainted with her misfortune, left her without compromising her because as a fact she was innocent; and the girl was delivered of a son, who received the name of Joshua or Jesus. The infant was adopted by a Rabbi named Joseph, who carried him into Egypt, where he was initiated into the secret sciences, and the priests of Osiris, recognizing that he was the true incarnation of Horus so long promised to the adepts, consecrated him sovereign pontiff of the universal religion. Joshua and Joseph returned to Judea, where the knowledge and virtue of the young man excited very soon the envy and hatred of the priests, who one day reproached him publicly with the illegitimacy of his birth. Joshua, who loved and venerated his mother, questioned his master and learned the whole history respecting the crime of Pandira and the misfortune of Miriam. His first impulse was to deny her in public, when he said in the middle of a marriage-feast:

'Woman, what is there in common between you and me?' But afterwards, realising that an unfortunate woman must not be punished for having suffered what she could not prevent, he cried: 'My mother has in no wise sinned, nor has she lost her innocence; she is virgin and yet is mother: let the twofold honour be paid to her. As for me, I have no father on earth; I am the son of God and humanity.'*

Could it be the truth has been there all the time – waiting for someone to have the courage to state it clearly? Is this the first time it could be published without the authors being mysteriously found hanged or burned at the stake? I sincerely hope so.

The circle turns again, but always it would seem that we are only trying to identify these entities of myth and history by removing the cloaks which have been covering them; cloaks that enhance or degrade according to the requirements of the sect which designs them. At one time I would have said that to study this subject one needed to be an agnostic, but the true meaning of that word still implies a belief – albeit a negative one. It is difficult to say one is gnostic without being accused of believing in all manner of things which the word is now considered to encompass.

Were it possible to create a word like 'truthic', which would mean one who, free of dogma, could analyse impassively all the doctrines and sciences which could solve the story of the origin of man, we might be looking at the loneliest person in the world. Does it not seem that mankind is avoiding the truth? Are we not creating fanciful stories of our origin which we find more palatable than the truth? Furthermore, even if the strict discipline of truth were adhered to, it would still be necessary to recognize that our mind – the tool with which we analyse – is intentionally blunted.

Whether in time the higher echelons of the Templars would have been capable of such analysis we will never know. But as they dissolved, small streams of their knowledge trickled away 'underground' and can be seen to surface at times in the Priory of Sion, The Brotherhood of the Rosy Cross, the Illuminati and other bodies who considered they have the secrets of the past. One of their 'modern' counterparts A.M.O.R.C. (Ancient and Mystical Order Rosae Crucis) appear to preserve significant images. By the use of the word 'modern' I mean surviving at this time. I do not, of course, intend to cast doubt on their claim to have been founded in the year 1693. In fact, I would have been inclined to suggest the actual origin is of greater antiquity than they claim. My research has led me into areas which I am sure would be found in the part of their doctrine which is secret, and for this reason I would not directly identify it. Suffice to say, I have the greatest respect for their principles and would refer to one detail, to which I am sure they would have no objection as it is freely available in their Manual:

The ancient law that each 108 years was a cycle of rebirth, activity, rest and waiting, made the great work in America come to a close,

*The History of Magic (Rider: London) 1913.

as far as public activities were concerned, in 1801 (108 years after the founders left Europe). Then for another 108 years the Order in this country was in its rest period with only certain descendants of the last initiates passing to one another the rare records and official documents.

For our purposes the numbers **1 – 8 – 0** are obvious and they demonstrate the presence of Isis and Nut, and here they must be linked to the Rose Cross!

13

The Rose Cross

Indeed, indeed, Repentance oft before
I swore – but was I sober when I swore?
And then and then came Spring, and Rose-in-hand
My threadbare Penitence apieces tore.

The blood-red rose – the secretive lily – its secret valley – Solomon and Sheba knew – the Grand Masters knew – great names in association – the love of Magdalene – the sacrifice of Jesus.

To attempt a specific analysis of the two emblems in question, the rose and the cross, would fill volumes. The antiquity of the cross as a pre-Christian symbol has been proven beyond question and a close examination of the rose equally convinces one that it was chosen to represent all manner of things in the past.

In Egypt the rose signified regeneration and in Persia we have the macabre suggestion of the rose incarnadine being so coloured by virtue of the blood upon which it thrives.

I sometimes think that never blows so red
The Rose as where some buried Caesar bled;
That every Hyacinth the Garden wears
Dropt in its Lap from some once lovely Head.
(*Rubáiyát of Omar Khayyám*)

As a symbol of love, both sexual and romantic, it still survives today; but it is equally at home in a graveyard. The use of the rosary both in Christianity and in eastern religions, needs no further comment other than that in its function, it was a device for counting! Eroticism is implied in expressions which relate womanhood to the blossoming rose, and the equation of the rose with the vagina is obvious. There may be some esoteric value in relating the rose to the sun, and many poets have chosen this comparison. It would explain, to some degree, the glory surrounding the rose, and where it is surrounded by a ring of thorns, these may be a simplified material representation of the rays of light. The sun equation is noted by G. Higgins where he demonstrated the sun god (RA) as RAS = ROSE = ROZ. The cabbalistic value of ROZ is **360** which is in keeping with the cyclic female doctrine.

The symbol of the rose united with the cross has been discussed by 'experts' for centuries and the rose fluctuates from red to white as the cross does from gold to red. As the 'rose of Sharon' it sometimes unites with the 'lily of the valley'.

Some say this imagery implies a crucified rose, drained of blood, leaving us with the white lily, a Christian doctrine with obvious connections; the rose represents the body of Christ and the shedding of his divine blood. It has been suggested that the blood from the 'side' of Jesus could be the fluid content of that enigmatic vessel, 'The Holy Grail', but later we will discover that it is not. *semen → womb* Nothing would please me more than to see no contradiction in these 'convenient' allegories, but this is not the case.

Once again, as in all Christian teaching, we find the truth is of far greater antiquity and we are examining imagery which has been adopted in comparatively recent times, then 'overlaid' on the original meaning. Even if one accepts the Christian teaching, is it not paradoxical to find the very organizations who had the highest regard for these symbols being sought out and persecuted by the Catholic Church? Furthermore the study of the Rose Cross leads us into beliefs which deny Jesus as the Son of God and even the possibility of there having been a crucifixion of the type suggested. Many great names come to mind as having been connected in some way or the other with the legends of the Rose Cross, and some of these names appear in the list of Grand Masters of the Priory of Sion. Here we are back on the 'slippery slope' again, moving towards alchemy, the Templars, Rennes-le-Château and the Temple of Solomon. And as if to ensure we do not leave the circle we find in *The Song of Solomon*

> I am the rose of Sharon, and the lily of the valleys

There can be little doubt who is speaking, it is Sheba, Ishtar, Isis, and elsewhere the reference to her being 'black but comely' reinforces the Black Madonna=Isis equation.

Solomon and Sheba appeared to be able to overcome their religious differences by the simple process of bodily contact, and we will investigate this in more detail later, but for the moment let us refer to something Nicolas Flamel wrote:

> The mystic rose
> of Hermic lore, which issues bright and fair,
> Strange virtues circling with the sap therein,
> Beneath the Universal Spirit's breath,
> From the Mercurial Stone.

Flamel was an alchemist, and this body of men have always been misunderstood as being an eccentric bunch who sought a formula whereby they could convert a base metal – usually lead, into gold. Others claiming to be better informed say their aim was to discover the Elixir, something which would transmute base man to a creature of higher intellect or even to an entity of pure spirit. This may seem a fanciful idea, but we must give credit to the work of the alchemists. A good deal of our chemical knowledge stems from them and it is probable we have not fully appreciated the methods they employed to achieve their goal. Furthermore, there is strong evidence to suggest that in some cases they achieved all they set out to at both levels of transmutation.

The alchemists perpetually employed the cross and the rose in the illustrations which conceal their secret processes, but the designs vary considerably. Where possible, the design of the rose on the centre of the cross is often surrounded by a glory, a brilliant light of understanding. The rose is composed of five petals surrounded by eight petals. I think we can safely assume the **5** is indicating a female presence and the **8** signifies Isis. Many students consider this design to have been a development of the much earlier emblem the Crux Ansata (illus 78). This is the Tau surmounted by the symbol of the female organ and together they represent birth or, alternatively, rebirth with knowledge of the hereafter. The Crux Ansata may be seen in another easily recognized emblem, the planet Venus, where it is crowned by the crescent or Linga (illus 79). Alchemically this is the sign of copper-red metal; not only does this perform an important function in their chemistry, but the colour also agrees with Venus as a rose.

Another Christian equation of a white rose representing the Virgin Mary is really of no better foundation than the legend which attributes the red rose to the blood of Aphrodite (Ishtar) staining a white rose, and any number of legends may be found in this category. I think it is very unlikely we will learn any secrets by studying these associations which, by their very nature, are 'occult', or not to be spoken of. The vow of silence, *sub rosa*, in

78. The Crux Ansata.

134

Genisis

Roman times was not a vow to be taken lightly, and silence was
again implied by the attitude of the Egyptian god Harpocrates,
supposedly the 'god of silence'. This could, however, be mistaken
imagery as the Egyptians may be depicting him with his finger to
his mouth to emphasize that he was a child and thereby avoid
confusion with Horus; but this gesture was mistakenly assumed to
symbolize the sealing of the lips.

We can now summarize the image: the rose comprises a five-
pointed display surrounded by one of eight points. Geometrically
the primary image is therefore a pentagram and the secondary
image an eight-pointed star. The latter (illus 80) was worn as a
silver star on a red sash by the crusading Templars and I believe it
is the Star of Isis. Once again we should not overlook coincidence –
if we rotate it twenty-two and a half degrees we have the star of the
beast – **666**! The D.O.M.A. manuscript (*c*.1700) ensures that this
figure is not inadvertently constructed incorrectly and thereby
loses the significance of its association to the feminine circle. The
basic structure of this star is achieved by two sets of 'tramlines'
crossed at right angles – this design is then rotated by twenty-two
and a half degrees and superimposed on the orginal one. It is used,
sometimes slightly modified, in architectural features, to obscure
its true identity. The example given (illus 81) is the rose window at
Nürnberg in Germany. In the centre the eight-petalled rose is
obvious, and could be considered to be automatically generated by
the symmetry of the design. However, the division of the circle
into twenty-eight (**28**) radiating features is not easily explained
other than by accepting the inevitable, it represents the female

79. The symbol of Venus.

81. The Rose Window (1350) 30 ft in
diameter above the west portal of
St. Lorenzkirche, Nurenberg,
Germany.

80. The Star of Isis.

cycle. The window is **30** feet in diameter or **15** feet radius and we recall the numerical reciprocal of **15** is **666**. Convert the **30** feet diameter into inches and you have the **360**-inch diameter signifying the circle of perfection shown to us at Rennes.

Once again we start to collect the apparently unrelated pieces and find they are all part of the same puzzle. It has been suggested that alchemy most probably originated in Egypt – or alternatively from the place the Egyptians came from. We are told the Rose Cross possibly developed from the Crux Ansata and could therefore have shared the same origin. If secrets are contained within this symbolism, it could have passed into various countries by way of famous names in antiquity who all appear to have been associated with Egypt and this may even be the basis of the mystery which surrounds them. Hiram Abiff – Solomon – Ezekiel – Plato – Pythagorus and Jesus are but a few who were instructed in the 'Egyptian Mysteries'. At the centre of these is Isis, or her Syrian counterpart Ishtar.

We could assume these mysteries would now be considered as elementary science and that having the knowledge to manipulate metals to form jewellery and weapons would be in the category of a 'trade secret'. The apprentice or initiate would serve his master for years, slowly acquiring these secrets and other scientific 'know-how' which could have included mathematics, astronomy and medicine. Even if this were so, it would not explain the secrecy which still pervaded these subjects long after they became common knowledge. It would appear that, to the initiated, all the sciences were a manifestation of the same power and, unacceptable as it was in the nineteenth century, the alchemical belief in the universal structure of matter has certainly been confirmed by the physicists of today.

If the innumerable beliefs of the world had been left to their own devices, it would now be possible to trace the remnants of the original knowledge and to recompose it. History, however, decided otherwise. Constantine created a conglomerate religion for the sake of unity and into the boiling-pot of compromise went most of the old knowledge, and by the time it came out it was unrecognizable. Those parts which escaped the 'pot' were hunted down, reconstructed or destroyed to ensure that power remained in the hands of the few. Our problem is to determine whether this knowledge, or any part of it, survived the centuries. If so, where was it and who were the custodians?

Rosicrucian societies exist all over the world today and, in most cases, the members also attend a church. They do not see their society membership as contradictory to their religious beliefs. Paradoxically, their common ground is belief in the existence of a secret doctrine which has been handed down from great antiquity and, as a consequence, is pre-Christian and therefore pagan. Some seem to claim that they hold the secrets, others that they are searching for them. Some societies compromise the whole situation, believing they are teaching a philosophy which, if

Ask what the following numbers mean? With which the whole Holy Scripture and the New Testament is filled, i.e. The Great Wonder-Beast 666.

strictly adhered to, will enlighten the initiate and open a path to the greater mysteries. I have yet to meet anyone who has demonstrably achieved this goal in recent times.

Whatever position these societies adopt, they could never establish continuity in their rituals by normal means beyond the time which I will refer to as the 'recent revival' of Rosicrucianism. This period begins at best in the early part of the 17th century. The event which marks this time is the publication of the *Fama Fraternitatis* in 1614 or thereabouts. Neither the exact date nor the authorship of this work has ever been finally determined. Officially this, together with other Rosicrucian works, is attributed to Johann Valentine Andreae. Initially he denied writing it. Next he admitted to being the author but claimed it was written as a joke. Finally, after his death, a document was found in which he admits being the author, but makes the unlikely claim that it was written when he was only sixteen years of age. Considering his respected position in the Lutheran Church, his denial is understandable. If it was a joke, it was a very clever one, for it started a revival of interest in searching for lost knowledge. A search which still continues today.

The *Fama Fraternitatis* is the story of a boy who accompanied a monk on a journey to the Holy Land. The monk died and the boy was left to fend for himself. He journeyed through the east acquiring great secrets from the adepts. On his return he passed the knowledge to three trusted friends who, in turn, passed it to another eight. The person in question was referred to in the document as C.R.C. and, subsequently in another Rosicrucian publication, his identity was revealed as Christian Rosenkreutz. There is no good authority that this journey ever took place and we would be better advised to classify the work as an allegory purporting to prove the presence in the east of a secret doctrine. Alternatively, we cannot rule out the possibility of this being an intentional disclosure, fictitious or otherwise, designed to cause people of similar thinking to band together. Discussion at least would be bound to result from it.

The mysterious author, under the pseudonym of Christian Rosenkreutz, published *The Chemical Wedding*, which is a masterpiece of allegorical writing. The author is invited to a royal wedding and on every page we can find hints of the secret doctrine, but I would direct the reader to one in particular which is pertinent to our solution. Christian Rosenkreutz, being a wedding guest at the castle, awoke very early on the fifth day. Finding nobody else awake, he asked a page to show him round the castle. We join them in the act of entering the King's treasury:

> After this door was opened, the Page led me by the hand through a very dark passasge till we came to a little door now only put too, for as the Page informed me, it was first opened yesterday when the coffins were taken out, and had not since been shut.
> As soon as we stepped in I espied the most precious thing that

Nature ever created, for this vault had no other light but from certain huge carbuncles. This was the King's Treasury, but the most glorious and principal thing was a sepulchre in the middle, so rich that I wondered it was no better guarded, whereunto the Page answered me, that I had good reason to be thankful to my planet, by whose influence I had now seen certain pieces which no human eye (except those of the King's family) had ever viewed. This sepulchre was triangular, and had in the middle of it a kettle of polished copper, the rest was of pure gold and precious stones. In the kettle stood an angel who held in his arms an unknown tree, whose fruit continually falling into the kettle, turned into water therein, and ran out into three small golden kettles standing by. This little altar was supported by an eagle, an ox, and a lion, which stood on an exceeding costly base. I asked my Page what this might signify. 'Here,' said he, 'lies buried Lady Venus, that beauty which hath undone many a great man, both in fortune, honour, blessing and prosperity'; after which he showed me a copper door in the pavement, saying, 'Here, if you please, we may go further down.' We descended the steps, where it was exceeding dark, but the Page immediately opened a little chest in which stood a small ever-burning taper, wherefrom he kindled one of the many torches that lay by. I was mightily terrified and asked how he durst do this. He gave me for answer, 'as long as the Royal Persons are still at rest I have nothing to fear.' Herewith I espied a rich bed ready made, hung about with curious curtains, one of which he drew, and I saw the Lady Venus stark naked (for he heaved up the coverlets too), lying there in such beauty, and a fashion so surprising, that I was almost beside myself, neither do I yet know whether it was a piece thus carved, or an human corpse that lay dead there, for she was altogether immoveable, and yet I durst not touch her. So she was again covered, yet she was still as it were, in my eye.

Here then is 'the place where beauty sleeps' (*Le Serpent Rouge*).

There can be no mistaking the allegory – Lady Venus – Isis, who no mortal man hath ever unveiled – being here symbolically unveiled. Her identity is further proven in the Ishtar association, the great danger of being taken as her lover: 'which hath undone many a great man'. The reader will need no persuasion to concede the connection of the support to the altar: 'an eagle, and ox and a lion' and we find it in the pentacle of Solomon illustrated by Eliphas Levi.

And it is there in *The Revelation of St John the Divine* (IV, 7):

And the first beast was like a lion, and the second beast like a calf, and the third beast had a face as a man, and the fourth beast was like a flying eagle.

And can one doubt whence these creatures are issuing forth? Look closely at the illustration (illus 82) it is a representation of the female vulva.

Earth, fire, air, and water – alchemy – in a Rosicrucian allegory – demonstrating the source of life and Man – no less, but no more, than part of a secondary act of creation. The more one examines the text, the more one recognizes symbolic connections which will become clear to the reader as we progress. Copper – kettle – ever-burning tapers – death and all the trappings of the Isis-Osiris legend, are to be found here.

82. The Star of David incorporating the female vulva and showing the emergence of man and beast.

So let us vacillate no longer, the blood-red rose of the mysteries, and the lily of which valley? Fourteen and fourteen is now known to us, the menstrual cycle of the female, half-red, half-white. And in part this is *The Song of Solomon*:

Let him kiss me with the kisses of his mouth
The upright love thee
I am black but comely
But mine own vineyard have I not kept
I am the Rose of Sharon and the Lily of the valleys.
O my dove, that art in the clefts of the rock, in the secret places of the stairs,
He feedeth among the lilies
I held him and would not let him go, until I had brought him into my mother's house,
And into the chamber of her that conceived me.
Every man hath his sword upon his thigh
Thy lips are like a thread of scarlet
Let my beloved come into his garden,
And eat his pleasant fruits.

Surely no one could misunderstand the implication, but let us be clear on one thing: if any should believe that in this I reduce the mysteries to nothing more than sexual imagery, they would be guilty of being blind to that which lies beyond the veil. In

Victorian times this veil of sex would have sufficed to dissuade the reader from pursuing the truth, but our journey has only just begun.

No logical mind could believe in Cathars, Templars and Rosicrucians giving their lives to conceal the simple biological fact that women make love and have a menstrual cycle. Even the Roman Catholic Church would permit the female this part of her natural bodily processes. So what else did they know? For what were they tortured and burned, and for what did they die in thousands?

To be sure, the suppression of anything which connected the female with matters esoteric was the prime concern of the Church. This indicates to me that they knew a woman was capable of producing something more potent than a baby!

With this enlightenment, I hope the enigmatic engravings (illus 83) of the Rosicrucians will be more understandable to the so called 'uninformed'. The Gate of Eternal Wisdom is no longer a mystery, and the eight radiating features (including the steps) leave us in no doubt of the accuracy of our judgement. Even the *Rubáiyát of Omar Khayyám* may hold new meaning when read by

83. The Gate of Eternal Wisdom – another representation of the female organ. Note the seven radiating features identifying Set. By including the steps it becomes 8 – Isis. Also note there are 14 ligature-like shapes surrounding the hole.

the light of the moon:

> Look to the Rose that blows about us – Lo,
> Laughing, she says, into the World I blow:
> At once the silken Tassel of my Purse
> Tear, and its Treasure on the Garden throw.

It may seem unlikely to the casual reader for the *Rubáiyat* to even be associated with our subject, but such is not the case. Later we will see that Omar Khayyám too was associated with our mystery.

However, we are looking for the thread which connects the ancient knowledge with the Rosicrucian revival of the 1600s.

Rennes-le-Château will show us the Templars had the secrets and the exhaustive research of the authors of *The Holy Blood and The Holy Grail* may provide the connection we require. It is there in the Priory of Sion. And in the *Dossiers Secrets* they discovered the list of Grand Masters, and in these names we can find all we require and a good deal more. Whether these great names ever sat in council is irrelevant. If a man is known to have achieved a level of understanding of the forces of nature, his appointment is taken for granted, as would have been all the great names in history who could have been considered its founders:

Jean de Gisors	1188–1220
Marie de Saint-Clair	1220–66
Guillaume de Gisors	1266–1307
Edouard de Bar	1307–36
Jeanne de Bar	1336–51
Jean de Saint-Clair	1351–66
Blanche d'Evreux	1366–98
Nicolas Flamel	1398–1418
René d'Anjou	1418–80
Iolande de Bar	1480–83
Sandro Filipepi	1483–1510
Leonardo da Vinci	1510–19
Connectable de Bourbon	1519–27
Ferdinand de Bonzague	1527–75
Louis de Nevers	1575–95
Robert Fludd	1595–1637
J. Valentin Andrea	1637–54
Robert Boyle	1654–91
Issac Newton	1691–1727
Charles Redclyffe	1727–46
Charles de Lorraine	1746–80
Maximilien de Lorraine	1780–1801
Charles Nodier	1801–44
Victor Hugo	1844–85
Claude Debussy	1885–1918
Jean Cocteau	1918–1963

One name is immediately noticeable, the famous alchemist mentioned earlier, Nicolas Flamel. He lived in Paris in the 1300s and as a copyist he had the advantage of seeing many rare books. The French storehouse of ancient manuscripts where he worked is the Bibliothèque de l'Arsenal and nearby is a street which still bears his name, Rue Nicolas Flamel. Into his possession came a twenty-one page manuscript *The Sacred Book of Abraham the Jew*, which for many years he could not fully understand. Eventually he met someone who assisted him and he was then said to have acquired the Stone of the Wise, the philosophers' stone, the prize for which alchemy strives. This transmutation we are told was achieved on January 17th, a date and number persistent in the mystery of the Rennes valley. As a result of his success, Flamel became fabulously rich.

At about the same time another Abraham the Jew appears – he was born apparently in 1362, and was the author of *The Book of the Sacred Magic of Abra-Melin the Mage*, another supposedly valuable manuscript from the archives of the Bibliothèque de l'Arsenal. S. L. MacGregor-Mathers, who translated the document, suggested its author might be a descendant of the original Abraham the Jew, but the coincidence of the date and place makes me wonder whether the Abra-Melin might not be more closely associated with Flamel than we have realized. It is certainly a book which students of the occult consider workable as opposed to the greater majority of fictitious magic.

The name of Robert Fludd in the list of Grand Masters I find particularly interesting. As a Fellow of the College of Physicians he was highly respected and was considered to be the Grand Master of English Rosicrucians. He was also referred to as the Father of Freemasonary. The engraving by de Bry (illus 84) is from Robert Fludd's *Utruisque Cosmi, etc.* and shows earthly man surrounded first by water, then air, and then fire – the elements of alchemy. Outside this are the orbits of the planets and the ribbon of the stars. Finally we see the Empyrean, the realm of the spirits, and then the abyss. It should be noted that the dove, signifying heavenly light, which we have identified through Magdelene, Ishtar and Isis, occupies a specific position on the boundary of the spiritual world and the abyss (Nut or Nothing). This position corresponds in the diagram of Rennes-le-Château to where the meridian and the line of sunrise of the Magdalene intersect on the circle of churches or, simply, where light enters the circle of material existence.

I could be accused of searching for 'straws in the wind', so I wondered if Fludd could have left any other clues which would indicate he had knowledge of the temple and locations at Rennes-le-Château. I found it in the records of his tomb at Bearsted near Maidstone in Kent.

Robert Fludd died on the 8th September 1637. Now as one has little choice in the day of one's demise we will ignore this set of numbers. However, the following year his nephew erected

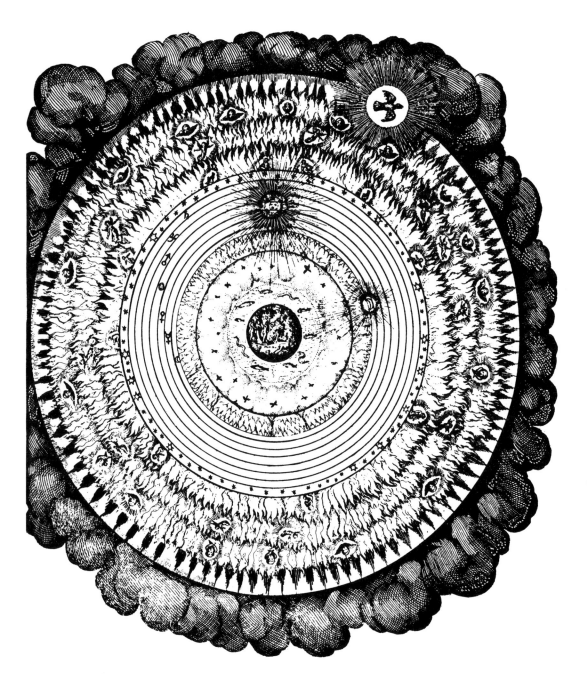

84. An engraving by de Bry from Robert Fludd's *Utriusque Cosmi* showing the Rosicrucian correspondence of the Macrocosm and Microcosm. Note the position of the Dove of the Holy Spirit relative to the Rennes geometry.

another stone on which was an inscription, recording not only the date of the death of Fludd but, strangely, emphasising the date upon which this second stone was erected (illus 86). Now this date could obviously be of one's choice, and the choice confirms that for which we have searched. You will recall the number of Isis is **18**. The date is the **10**th of August **1638** – the year's numerals add up to **18** as do the numerals of the day and the month. Hence **18** – **18** – Isis!

Also on the list of Grand Masters we find Valentin Andrea of whom we have already written – but, seeing his name as a Grand Master of the Priory, we need no longer doubt, if not the authorship, the support he afforded to the resurrection of Rosicrucianism.

I would like to return later to discuss the work of Leonardo da Vinci but for the moment what conclusions may we draw from our findings? In seeing the success achieved by the adepts, both financial and spiritual, we must realize we are dealing with something clearly esoteric and unquestionably powerful. We must also accept the perpetual dominance of the sexual aspect, particularly the feminine, which hints at secrets contained in the female body beyond the biological miracle of childbirth and which may also extend beyond the grave.

The incessant references to purification, elevation and resurrection seem inexplicably woven into a sexual tapestry with the woman in the superior position. The enigmatic Rosicrucian engraving of the Temple of Sophia (illus 87) leaves us in no doubt that the feminine principle is dominant in their doctrine. I wondered if evidence of it could be found in the Christian resurrection of Jesus. Undoubtedly it is difficult to consider the events surrounding the Crucifixion without taking into account the important part played by Mary Magdalene. As we have said, despite all attempts by Christian historians to cast her as a prostitute, there is no Gospel reference to that effect. Once again we are confronted with a 'mud-slinging' campaign which is most probably designed to obscure the true nature of the person involved. It seems to be that not only in her time, but also in the construction of the Christian version of the life of Jesus, her presence was, and still is, acutely embarrassing to the ecclesiastical authorities. Jesus overtly shows his affection for her and is quick to rebuke anyone who criticises her. His words on these occasions seem more peevish than profound. Even when Martha quite reasonably suggests that Magdalene should refrain from lying around on Jesus's feet and help with the house work, Jesus puts her in her place.

Apart from these many demonstrations of favour, Jesus then elects to bestow upon Magdalene the greatest distinction of all, to be the first to witness His Resurrection. It is not difficult to imagine how annoying this association would have been to the Jewish elders, for whom women were second-class citizens. Even among the followers of Jesus there was obviously considerable

Sacred to the Memory

of the Illustrious Physician and Man Robert Fludd, alias De Fluctibus, Doctor of both Faculties, who after some years of travelling beyond seas, undertaken successfully for the improvement of his mind, was at length restored to his Fatherland and was not undeservedly received into the Society of the London College of Physicians. He exchanged life for death peacefully on the 8th day of the month of September A° Dñi MDCXXXVII, in the 63rd year of his age.

> No costly perfumes from this urn ascend
> In gorgeous tomb thine ashes do not lie;
> Thy mortal part alone to earth we give;
> The records of thy mind can never die:
> For he who writes like thee—though dead—
> Erects a tomb that lasts for aye.

Thomas Fludd of Gore Court, Otham, in Kent, Esquire, erected this Monument to the happy Memory of his most dear Uncle on the 10th day of the month of August, MDCCXXXVIII.

85. The church at Bearsted near Maidstone, Kent, where Robert Fludd was buried.

86. The memorial stone erected by Fludd's nephew.

jealousy and that emotion may be detected throughout history. But would this alone warrant such an intensive 'smear' campaign? I think not, there must have been something else.

Could the incident with Martha be explained by the fact that, knowing Magdalene was a woman of such high station, Jesus would not permit her to do housework?

We have shown that she was a woman of noble birth and there is much to suggest that Magdalene was the High Priestess of the Ishtar Temple at Magdala in Galilee. One of the symbols sacred to Ishtar was the dove, and the dove subsequently became undeniably part of Christian iconography, associated with the Grail and the Ark of Noah. It was no doubt incorporated because it was too strong to erase.

The plot thickens, and it appears that Magdalene also accompanied Jesus on his travels. But in what capacity – friend, mistress or wife?

A collection of 14th-century manuscripts were published under the title *The Scale of Perfection* and something in them may help us to decide. Jesus is speaking to Magdalene:

> 'Do not touch Me, I have not yet ascended to My Father.' That is to say, Mary Magdalene loved our Lord Jesus ardently before His passion, but her love was largely carnal and only spiritual to a small extent. She believes firmly that He was God, but she did not love Him greatly as God, for she could not at that time, and so she allowed all her affection and all her thought to dwell on Him in His human state. And our Lord did not blame her, but gave her great praise. When He had arisen from the dead and appeared to her, she would have adored Him with the same sort of love that she did before, and then our Lord forbade her and said, 'Do not touch Me.'

Does this imply that carnal love took place between Jesus and Magdalene before the Crucifixion, but that for some reason it could not continue after it? Are we not confronted once more with far too many coincidences? Despite attempts by the Jewish elders to suppress the superiority of the female deity, the Jewish women persisted at that time in preserving the rituals of the Ishtar-Tammuz doctrine. The one time cannibalistic practice of removing the phallus of the priest-king and then eating his body had however been modified stage by stage.

The first change was to allow the king to appoint a substitute. Secondly the victim of this act was permitted to heal the wound and thereby to continue to live. Further dilution of the ceremony involved the removal of the foreskin as opposed to the complete penis, and it was this which was offered up to their goddess. Eventually this process was reduced to the simple 'cut' of circumcision.

However, no easy way out was available to those who aspired to be priests of the temple. To be permitted to enter the holy place it was necessary for them to have their phallus removed and dedicated to the goddess. Outside the temple, cakes in phallic

The Heavenly and Earthly Eve, Mother of all Creatures in Heaven and on Earth.

The Star of the Kings from the Orient.

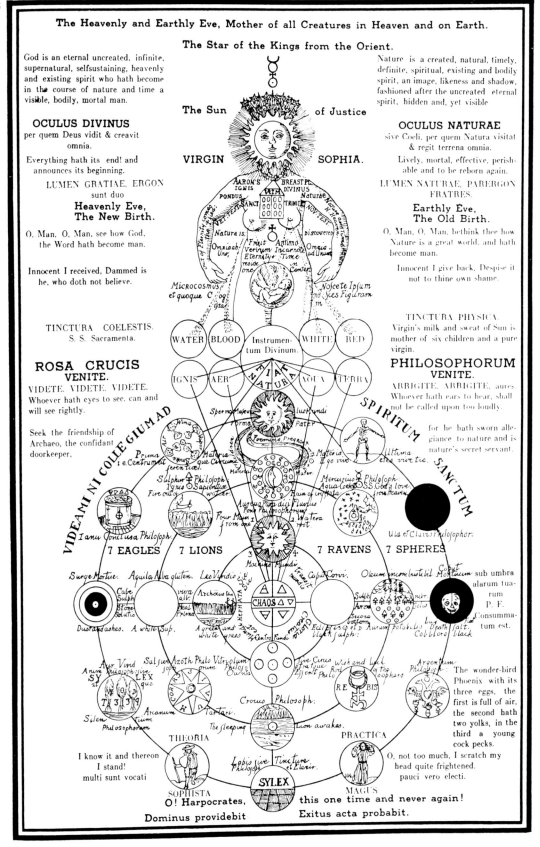

God is an eternal uncreated, infinite, supernatural, selfsustaining, heavenly and existing spirit who hath become in the course of nature and time a visible, bodily, mortal man.

OCULUS DIVINUS
per quem Deus vidit & creavit omnia.

Everything hath its end! and announces its beginning.

LUMEN GRATIAE, ERGON
sunt duo
**Heavenly Eve,
The New Birth.**

O, Man, O, Man, see how God, the Word hath become man.

Innocent I received, Dammed is he, who doth not believe.

TINCTURA COELESTIS.
S. S. Sacramenta.

ROSA CRUCIS
VENITE.
VIDETE, VIDETE, VIDETE.
Whoever hath eyes to see, can and will see rightly.

Seek the friendship of Archaeo, the confidant doorkeeper,

Nature is a created, natural, timely, definite, spiritual, existing and bodily spirit, an image, likeness and shadow, fashioned after the uncreated eternal spirit, hidden and, yet visible

OCULUS NATURAE
sive Coeli, per quem Natura visitat & regit terrena omnia.

Lively, mortal, effective, perishable and to be reborn again.

LUMEN NATURAE, PARERGON
FRATRES.
**Earthly Eve,
The Old Birth.**

O, Man, O, Man, bethink thee how Nature is a great world, and hath become man.

Innocent I give back, Despise it not to thine own shame.

TINCTURA PHYSICA.
Virgin's milk and sweat of Sun is mother of six children and a pure virgin.

PHILOSOPHORUM
VENITE.
ARRIGITE, ARRIGITE, aures.
Whoever hath ears to hear, shall not be called upon too loudly.

for he hath sworn allegiance to nature and is nature's secret servant.

The wonder-bird Phoenix with its three eggs, the first is full of air, the second hath two yolks, in the third a young cock pecks.

O, not too much, I scratch my head quite frightened. pauci vero electi.

I know it and thereon I stand! multi sunt vocati

O! Harpocrates, this one time and never again!

Dominus providebit   Exitus acta probabit.

shape were soaked in red wine and presented as an offering, but for the initiate in the secret chamber of the inner temple the ritual was retained in all its gory reality.

Could it be that the Crucifixion was the final sacrifice by Jesus in attaining his priesthood at the Temple of Ishtar? Could this explain the incessant mathematical message which permeates the Holy Bible? Numbers which unmistakably convey that Christian history is inextricably linked with the worship of the Queen of the Heavens and the sacrifice demanded by her. Or did his persecutors revert to the popular judicial system of fitting the punishment to the crime? It is not difficult to imagine, confronted with the threat of so powerful a man, that they would have decided that this 'priest-king' should be made to fulfil his obligations to the goddess of his choosing.

It is also coincidental to learn that the initiate to the priesthood reappeared after a three-day recuperation period in the temple!

No longer need we be puzzled by reports of Jesus surviving the cross and the emphasis laid on the strange paraphernalia associated with the Crucifixion. Furthermore, would it not be obvious for the priestess Magdalene to be his first contact after the sacrifice? After all, it would have been she who tended his wound.

I decided to look more closely at those relics of Our Lord's passion.

87. The Temple of Sophia from the second book of the Secret Symbols of the Rosicrucians. Altona Text 1788.

14

The Holy Grail and the Round Table

And lately, by the Tavern Door agape,
Came stealing through the Dusk an Angel Shape
Bearing a Vessel on his Shoulder; and
He bid me taste of it; and 'twas – the Grape!

*The Christian Grail – Arthurian legends – John the Baptist – feeding the 5000 – the
maiming – knights of the Quest – the nature of the Crucifixion – the elixir and the stone
– the Round Table.*

There is no possibility of determining the true nature of The
Grail, if indeed it ever existed in material form, by studying
the available literature. It is the 'joker' in the pack, the 'wild' card
of the mysteries. It is something which is often alluded to by
people who would have you believe they had a greater
understanding of things holy.

To the English it is the centrepiece of the Arthurian legends. In
this guise it was introduced by Sir Thomas Malory in his
translation of the *Quéte del Saint Graal*. Here a positive identity is
given, it was the chalice of the Last Supper and subsequently
served to contain the blood of Jesus which was flowing from his
body at the Crucifixion. This 'definition' could be, and no doubt
is, as well founded as any Christian doctrine, originating in a
previous 'pagan' belief.

On close examination, the 'positive identity' dissolves into
nothing more than the conviction of the authors, trying to apply
form to an object which by then was so veiled in religious dogma as
to leave them only two choices: it was either a vessel or container of
some sort, or it did not exist as an object at all. I wondered if we
were back with the same problem as we had with the Ark of the
Covenant. Are we talking about the vessel, or what it contained?
To consider it as an allegorical object would naturally be the most
favoured course, allowing the authors to exercise their
imaginations without restriction. Being closer to the mystery,
chronologically that is, was no advantage, when one takes into
account the religious disciplines of those times.

If the volume of the literature or the similarity of the stories, and
for that matter the objects contained in them, are to be used as
evidence to substantiate their true origin, we need only wait
another couple of hundred years and the truth concerning these
matters will diminish to a minority position, if it survives at all.
Why certain 'experts' of Grail literature perpetually refer to the
Christian connections as being predominant baffles me. The only

reason for this material being in such abundance is that it was favourable for the authors to follow this line at a time when it would have been folly to do otherwise. Their fleeting references to the indisputable pre-Christian origin of the Grail and its associated articles, contradict the findings of those who would draw conclusions from this so-called proof of Christian association, which relies on little more than volume of words.

If the pre-Christian connections or substitutions can be dismissed by the church as 'gobbledygook', why should we regard Pope Innocent III's decree of 1215 in any different light? The precise words as quoted by A. E. Waite are:

> The Body and Blood of Jesus Christ are really contained under the species of bread and wine in the Sacrament of the Altar, the bread being transubstantiated into the Body and the wine into the Blood.

Surely this form of substitution is met with in the most elementary forms of black magic and yet to question it at the time was extremely dangerous. Any historian will admit that the denial of the Eucharist by the Albigensians was one of the primary reasons for their butchery, by order of the Pope.

If Christianity requires relics to support it, I suggest that it finds its own and then they would be recognizable as unique to its teachings. Personally, I have found nothing under the Christian cloak which was not the property of earlier doctrine. These doctrines, being labelled pagan, should surely not have contained the relics which are now universally presented as being Christian.

I have no argument with Christian principles and they quite rightly ask us to lead better lives, to love our fellow men, even to suppress the animal in us. All the teaching concerning our behaviour patterns is admirable, so let it be judged on this alone. Good Christians (and they number many thousands) have no need of fictitious history. It will serve no purpose whatsoever to accept the air of mystery which was created around events and objects which are all identifiable with the very beliefs which their tyrannical forebears went to such lengths to suppress. In those beliefs can be found the remnants of the great mysteries to which mankind must apply himself; mysteries which could be solved by our men of science if the fog of misrepresentation was cleared and they were allowed to apply their skills without fear of becoming social outcasts.

There is no general agreement that Arthurian legends has a place in true history, but this does not apparently deter those who would wish to use it as a reference point to support the Christian claim to have a monopoly on the objects associated with it. There was an undeniable connection existing between the Grail and the Knights, be they English or French, fictitious or real. It is also undeniable that a vessel of some sort is implied, but this is scanty evidence for any conclusion to be arrived at, particularly for an object of such importance.

One can sympathize with the knights who set out in search of something of which they apparently had no knowledge whatsoever. They knew neither where it was nor what it looked like. I am intrigued by how they would know whether or not they had found it.

In the romantic histories which we have at our disposal, the authors have often distorted the description of the Grail to align it more closely with their own teachings. Bearing in mind that they had no idea what it was, and if they had they could not disclose it, it is not surprising we are confronted with such confusion. Having read some of these accounts, I am sure of only one thing, there is in Grail literature a tiny seed of something very profound, very mysterious and very secret. As each organization or nationality has viewed the seed, they have claimed to know the nature of the flower into which it will grow, and these descriptions are limited by nothing but the imagination of the authors. Our purpose is not to judge the accuracy of a description by the literary quality of the text, but to detect the common elements and from there to compare them with those items which are already known to us.

The main works in question are Wolfram von Eschenbach's *Parzival*, Robert de Boron's *Conte Del Graal*, Sir Thomas Malory's *Morte d'Arthur* and *Idylls of the King*, Mabinogi from the *Red Book of Hergest* (The Welsh Perceval), and many others which offer numerous variations on the theme. Knights: Galahad, Perceval, Lancelot and Gawain. Kings: Arthur and others unnamed, gyrate and change in identity with events in such manner as to be totally confusing. Nevertheless, they are still wonderful tales and I would suggest they be read for that reason alone, rather than as sources of profound knowledge. Once you possess the key which I offer you in these pages the stories will never be the same again.

The Christian origin, so popular at one time, has all but dissolved under the light of intensive examination. It was largely based upon the idea of associating Joseph of Arimathea with the three Marys. Having left Jerusalem they apparently set sail for France en route for England. The Marys remained at Marseille and Joseph supposedly continued on to Glastonbury. It is unlikely that there is any truth in this as it did not exist in legend or history. The account first appears from the pen of Robert de Boron in the 12th century and its obvious inaccuracy tends to lead one to the rejection of his other work. Here we would again be guilty of oversimplification. If we accept the premise of a Grail secret at all, the association with the knights is overwhelmingly predominant and the close association between the French and English knights in matters esoteric is equally established, as is their common connection with eastern doctrine.

The story of St. Joseph, therefore, does not need to be true in fact, but merely to establish a link for future students to follow, thereby ensuring that all aspects of the mystery should eventually be revealed. If we can understand this psychology many confused accounts become clear to us. It is so essential for the reader to grasp this concept that I feel in duty bound to give a theoretical example of what he should look for.

Suppose the origin of the wealth of a rich family were a mystery, but it was believed this could be unravelled by examination of legend and fact in their history. The heraldry of their coat-of-arms demonstrates clocks, boats, keys, locks, lockets, etc. Hundred of years pass by and then someone takes an interest in this strange symbolism, the meaning of which the family has long since forgotton. Coincidences begin to appear, the first recorded children were named Leonard, Olive, Charles and Kenneth. The investigator eventually discovers the ancestor from whom the wealth had originally stemmed was actually a lock-keeper. Suddenly all becomes clear, a vast hoard of gold lies submerged in a lock somewhere. All the secret symbols which were preserved in the coat-of-arms, also possibly in the layout of his first mansion, were there to preserve and at the same time to conceal, the location of this vast hoard of gold. It is finally discovered by noticing the coincidence of the position of the hands of the clocks in the famous paintings commissioned by the founder of the family fortune. The river is identified, the lock is identified and, by placing the hands of the clocks to point to the corners of the lock, the exact location of the remaining gold is determined. Imagine the distortion which would occur over the centuries, once the family had attributed the invention of the padlock to their ancestor: he also developed the water-clock, and so on. This is the sort of confusion we must expect in our search, but to a much greater extent.

The Grail was the Grail long before it was Christian – but it was always 'holy'. As a vessel it was a provider in pre-Christian Irish and Welsh folklore and the essence of this function survived in the *Morte d'Arthur* where at the Pentecostal feast of Arthur the knights were able to be provided with such food as each of them desired. In this function of providing we see a parallel to another reliquary, the skull of Baphomet; although I would not ask you to consider it a direct equation at this stage. The eventual echo of this image will no doubt account for its presence at the Last Supper, but we should remember the suggestion of it also being used to hold the blood of Jesus.

Blood and a vessel as a salver unite to form another association, with the head of John the Baptist. Head might equate here with skull, another item of Templar dedication. Herod of Antipas, son of Herod the Great had asked his step-daughter Salome to dance for him. Let *Matthew* XIV, 1–12 continue the story:

> At that time Herod the Tetrarch heard of the fame of Jesus.
> And said unto his servants, This is John the Baptist; he is risen from the dead, and therefore mighty works do shew forth themselves in him.
> For Herod had laid hold on John and bound him, and put him in prison for Herodias sake, his brother Philip's wife.

For John said unto him, It is not lawful for thee to have her.

And when he would have put him to death, he feared the multitude, because they counted him as a prophet.

But when Herod's birthday was kept, the daughter of Herodias danced before them and pleased Herod.

Whereupon he promised with an oath to give her whatsoever she would ask.

And she, being before instructed of her mother, said, Give me here John Baptist's head in a charger.

And the king was sorry: nevertheless for the oath's sake, and them which sat with him at meat, he commanded it to be given her.

And he sent, and beheaded John in the prison.

And his head was brought in a charger and given to the damsel: and she brought it to her mother.

And his disciples came, and took up the body, and buried it, and went and told Jesus.

When Jesus heard of it, he departed thence by ship into a desert place apart: and when the people had heard therof, they followed him on foot out of the cities.

Now this is a pretty gruesome story but to my thinking it deteriorates even further when Jesus, having heard it, jumps into a 'boat' and goes off for a picnic. As you will recall he only happened to have five loaves and two fishes at the time, but he fed five thousand others. Are these two incidents so closely linked, despite the bad taste, for no other reason than to complete the composite imagery of head, blood, salver, food in abundance and provider.

One must admit the image of a severed head on a plate awash with blood is hardly commonplace, but it also appears in the Welsh *Peredur* with alarming similarity. During his quest Peredur meets an old man 'richly vested' whose servants are fishing by a lake. This is a simple equation with the 'Rich Fisher' in the Graal stories. In *Parzival* the king was Amfortas, the maimed king, and the nature of his injury can only be in keeping with other 'occult' woundings of which we are now aware. Peredur's old man was described as being lame, so we are still on course.

As in *Parzival*, the castle of the Fisher King/old man is near to another castle where the incident to which I would refer occurred: two youths entered the hall of the castle bearing a mighty spear from which 'poured torrents of blood'. They were followed by two maidens carrying a large salver whereupon there was a man's head – 'swimming in blood'. The representation of females being the 'keepers' – if this indeed is a Grail image – is not uncommon. It was usual practice to keep consecrated elements in a 'dove-shaped' repository and in the *Book of the Holy Grail* a sacred Host is placed in the custody of an unchaste woman. This supposedly excused the fact that it was necessary for Christ to remain close to Magdalene at all time. Next Peredur left the castle and came to another castle where he, in true knightly fashion, rescued a maiden in distress. This maiden is the Blanchefleur of the Perceval–Graal romance. The name is significant, for it was Flor and Blanchflor, supposedly the grandparents of Charlemagne, who represented the Red Flor (flower) and the Blancheflor (whiteflower). In the valley at Rennes-le-Château we left the line of the sunrise at Blanchefort!

As different as all these stories appear to be, they are the same, we have only to identify the equivalents.

The MAIDEN Salome dancing before the KING is suggestive of a SEXUAL act. (Remember it was not his daughter.) The HEAD which was floating in BLOOD was requested not by Salome but by her MOTHER, who was an ADULTERESS. The head was presented in a charger, the shape of which was insufficiently suggestive of the genitals to be identifiable, and it is for this reason we are told Jesus immediately gets into a ship or boat, which is of course a proven symbol for the female pudenda.

It can be readily appreciated from the text that there is no good reason for Jesus to have used a boat at all. Jesus was then confronted with the task of PROVIDING FOOD for the multitude. The text of Matthew continues:–

> . . . And they say unto him, We have here but five loaves and two fishes.

Why loaves, why fishes and why particularly 5 and 2?

With the secret number of Isis, her active multiplication factor, the equation becomes very simple. Loaves of bread, as you will recall from the Ishtar-Tammuz rites, are phallic symbols, so $5 \times 18 = 90$ and **90** signifies phallic erection. Fish is associated with the vagina and $2 \times 18 = 36$; **36** represents the pentagram and the circle, the female and her generative organ.

Next, it is interesting to observe that $36 \times 90 = 3240$ which is $18 \times 18 \times 10$ or 18×180, and we must not forget that it was **5,000** men who were fed:

> . . . And they did all eat, and were filled: and they took up the fragments that remained twelve baskets full.
>
> And they that had eaten were about five thousand men, beside women and children.

Now why someone would decide to count only the men in a situation such as this I have no idea – in fact the statement is ridiculous unless **5000** is being given to us for a different reason. In the text we are also shown the number **12** as remaining number of baskets. Could this be merely reminding us to use inch measure?

Apparently this is so for $5000 - 3240 = 1760$ and for those unfortunate people who only live in a metric world, there are **1760** yds in one mile. Furthermore, if we divide **3240** by **12** we have the number of the pregnant womb – **270**. It seems we may have got this right! However, to return to the symbols. In the Grail story we find MAIDENs carrying the HEAD swimming in BLOOD, which in other versions has been shown to be providing food for the knights. The maimed, injured or de-phallused KING was the FISHER king and so on.

Herodias had deserted her husband Herod-Phillip to live with Herod Antipas, the tetrarch who had previously been married to the daughter of the Arabian king Aretas. This incident caused a war in which Herod was defeated. He and his mistress Herodias returned to Rome, but Caligula who was Emperor at that time banished them in disgrace and they were sent to Gaul. As Herod Antipas eventually died in Spain, it was probably to the southern part of France he was sent. Coincidentally, it was thought that the head of John the BAPtist finally came to France where the skull of BAPhomet figured so prominently.

The domestic chaos referred to also manifests itself in the Grail stories, for after the incident of the head on the salver, we find:

> On the morning which followed these occurrences, Peredur rode away from the castle and while still in its vicinity, he came upon a beautiful maiden who was watching by the side of her dead husband. She told the youth that she was his foster-sister, that he was responsible for his mother's death because of his desertion, and that he had therefore become accursed.

Having shown how the secret multiplier of **18** functions in the biblical account, I feel bound to give the reader an example of it in the Grail stories.

Let us look at Wolfram's *Parzival* again. In his travels Parzival came upon the city of Belrepeire which by recent warfare was suffering a famine. Parzival meets the Queen Condwiramurs, a woman of great beauty and charm, who offered her hospitality but excused herself for not being able to offer him such food as she would have wished. Her uncle Kyot and his friend Manpfilyot, who did not live in the city, were standing nearby. They lived in a hunting-lodge and had made a truce with Kingrun who was besieging the city.

We will examine carefully what they say:

> 'I will send you a dozen loaves, Madam, and three hams and shoulders' said her uncle Kyot. 'There will be eight cheeses to go with them and two kegs of wine. My brother too must help you tonight, there is need.'
> 'Madam,' said Manpfilyot, 'I will send you the same.'

12 items of bread, **6** items of meat, **8** items of cheese and **2** items of wine, hence $12 \times 6 \times 8 \times 2 = 1152$, which number is also composed by $8 \times 8 \times 18$ or 18×64 an association with the **64** squares of the chess-board and the temple at Rennes-le-Château. The chess-board figures to a great extent in Knights Templar doctrine and will be dealt with later.

The continuation of the story implies that this quantity of food was sufficient to revitalize the whole city, so confirming the equation in the allegory:

Their messenger soon returned at the trot, and these enfeebled people were revived. These victuals were the grand sum of what the citizens had to nourish them! Many had already died of starvation before this bread arrived. The Queen ordered it to be shared among her debilitated people, and with it the cheeses, meat and wine, at Parzival's suggestion. As a result, scarcely a slice remained for the two of them, and this they shared without quarrelling. These provisions were duly consumed, and the deaths of many spared by famine averted.

(Wolfram's *Parzival*)

Rest assured that we could continue this process of identification from one end of the Bible to the other, but my purpose is served if only a few recognize the symbolism, or even a small part of that which lies beyond the veil.

Returning to Parzival we are told that, having saved the city from starvation, he was given chambers in the castle where he could spend the night. The beautiful Queen Condwiramurs decided to visit his room in order to express her gratitude in a positive way, but we are surprised to learn he declined the offer of sexual union and contented himself by merely showing her great affection as they lay together through the night. Now one could consider this to be the ultimate chivalry, except that the queen's desire was not fulfilled in the manner in which she had anticipated by visiting his room. Nevertheless, she remained with him until the morning and by implication his avowed promise to be this lady's champion was fulfilled to the best of his ability. During this encounter the queen may have realized, as I trust the reader will, Parzival was incapable of normal union as he had already taken those drastic measures which were necessary to qualify him to be a custodian of the secret of the Grail.

One part of the original cipher of our mystery, which appeared to be nonsensical, reveals its sinister meaning:

SHEPHERDESS, NO TEMPTATION

nor could any woman tempt someone mutilated in this fashion.

Being maimed, or wounded in the side or thigh, or having a decapitated phallus, no knight could ever be accused of seeking carnal favours from the ladies of his devotion. In the realization of this I hope the reader will not fall short of total enlightenment, for the riddle is now surely solved. The sacred (phallic) lance, from which poured 'torrents of blood' can now be understood. And the instrument used to remove the penis was the knife so closely associated with the story of Joseph of Arimathaea, with which he 'bled' the body of Christ and then preserved, together with the 'lance', in a double tube of lead.

I hope the reader will spare me the embarrassment of explaining in detail the safer method of performing this operation, suggested by another relic of the mysteries, the crown of thorns. An alternative device may well have served to numb the penis before its removal, and we are left in no doubt that 'spongeing' with 'vinegar' was the safest way to prevent infection. Its application to the 'mouth' of the severed member was probably the only way to sterilize the wound and to ensure the continuing function of the urinary passage. Or was there another way, even safer?

> According to St. Gregory of Tours the reed, and the sponge that had once been filled with vinegar, were objects of veneration at his day in Jerusalem.

A. E. Waite* (*Hidden Church of the Holy Grail*) then continues by saying these important relics were supposed to have been taken to Constantinople, where a witness saw them in a silver 'cup'.

> He saw also the shorter reed, which served as the derisive symbol of the Lord's royalty.

A short reed, derisive symbol, how could it be made any clearer? The reed, carefully positioned, would guarantee the continuing functioning of the urinary passage and at the same time permit tight bandaging of the wound

So we may now be in a position to identify these 'heads' which keep appearing; they are the heads or helmets of the severed phalluses, proof that the knight under examination has fulfilled the obligation and rendered himself worthy. As long as the item was obscured by presenting it as the severed head of a man, the dish or charger or salver was necessary, the slender 'boat'-shaped chalice would have disclosed the nature of its contents or at least would have produced an illogical image. One could hardly claim that a complete head of a man 'swimming in blood' could have been presented in the narrow boat/yoni chalice representing the vagina (illus 88).

As painful and dangerous as this ritual would have been in ancient times, properly attended it would not have necessarily resulted in the death of the donor. This could not be said of the loss of one's head, which is obviously certain death.

What was it then which Salome's mother requested? Was it the head or the 'head' of the phallus of John the Baptist.

Lastly our attention must turn to the sacred flannel or face-cloth or Veronica, the 'Volto Santo'. We understand the Vatican is in possession of an eighth-century manuscript claiming that Veronica was the woman whose issue of blood was healed by Christ. Furthermore, the legends which associate the south of France with these matters suggest that Veronica accompanied the three Maries and Lazarus to Marseilles and they were, at the time, custodians of the holy relics of which we have spoken.

Whether the broken remains of the statue's arms found near Renne-les-Bains did in fact show a cloth draped over one of them, I cannot be sure, but such a story was told if only to establish a necessary link in the mystery.

Hidden Church of the Holy Grail (Rebman: London) 1909

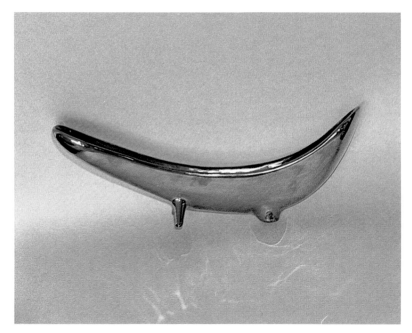

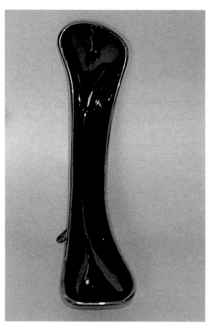

So just when we are coming to terms with the elusive Grail, we are confronted with a totally different explanation in *Parzival*.

88. The probable shape of the challice representing the female organ, into which the severed phallus was placed.

'It is well known to me,' said his host, 'that many formidable fighting-men dwell at Munsalvaesche with the Gral. They are continually riding out on sorties in quest of adventure. Whether these same Templars reap trouble or renown, they bear it for their sins. A warlike company lives there. I will tell you how they are nourished. They live from a Stone whose essence is most pure. If you have never heard of it I shall name it for you here. It is called "Lapsit exillis". By virtue of this Stone the Phoenix is burned to ashes, in which he is reborn. – Thus does the Phoenix moult his feathers! Which done, it shines dazzling bright and lovely as before! Further: however ill a mortal may be from the day on which he sees the Stone he cannot die for that week, nor does he lose his colour. For if anyone, maid or man, were to look at the Gral for two hundred years, you would have to admit that his colour was as fresh as in his early prime, except that his hair would grey! – Such powers does the Stone confer on mortal men that their flesh and bones are soon made young agin. This Stone is also called "The Grail".'

It is interesting to note, the reference in the text to not dying for a week is elsewhere more specifically given as **8** days.

Here we travel full circle back to the philosopher's stone, the phoenix or bennu bird of Egypt and furthermore:

When Lucifer and the Trinity began to war with each other, those who did not take sides, worthy noble angels, had to descend to earth to that Stone which is forever incorruptible. I do not know whether God forgave them or damned them in the end: if it was His due He took them back. Since that time the Stone has been in the

89. The inverted pentagram of the Sabbatic Goat.

care of those whom God appointed to it and to whom He sent his angel. This, sir, is how matters stand regarding the Gral.

Again to be more specific it was to the serpent that the custody of the stone was entrusted. However, in following this search we have been lead back to Satan.

In *The Hidden Church of the Holy Grail*, A. E. Waite summarises as follows:

> We have heard already that the Stone which is identified with the Graal in Wolfram was at one time a stone in the crown of Lucifer, and seeing that, according to other legends, the thrones left vacant by the fallen angels are reserved for human souls, it becomes intelligible why the Graal was brought to earth and what is signified by the mystic jewel. The Stone in the crown of Lucifer symbolises the great estate from which the archangel fell.

His conclusion is, to say the least, profound:

> The Great Experiment is therefore one of reintegration in the secret knowledge before the Fall, and when, or if, the Holy Graal is identified with the stone in the crown of Lucifer, that which is indicated thereby is (*a*) the perpetuation of this secret knowledge, and (*b*) that under all circumstances there is a way back whence we came.

And let it be clearly understood that only by understanding his origin will mankind achieve salvation:

> With Earth's first Clay They did the Last Man's knead.
> And then of the Last Harvest sow'd the Seed:
> Yea, the first Morning of Creation wrote
> What the Last Dawn of Reckoning shall read.
> (*Rubáiyát of Omar Khayyám*)

The paths to the centre are many but overgrown and almost lost, some have more knowledge of them than others, but have chosen to keep it to themselves. Some have covered the paths intentionally, erecting hideous images to turn the true searchers away. False signposts would lead us in circuitous paths while chanting ritualistic prayers for a light to show the way:

> Then to the rolling Heav'n itself I cried,
> Asking, 'What Lamp had Destiny to guide
> Her little Children stumbling in the Dark?'
> And – 'A blind Understanding!' Heav'n replied.
> (*Rubáiyát of Omar Khayyám*)

And certain men are self-appointed guides who would lead you down well-trodden paths and let that be your proof of a false trail, for many have gone before you to no avail. As if to convince the audience, these 'guides' enter into great discussion and at times with great emotion. They declare their way is best, but value the enlightenment you may have received from these tales full of sound and fury signifying nothing. They seem to be able to discuss the morality of a child's cartoon while nations tear each other to pieces. They deplore the act and yet do not condemn the perpetrator – is this 'The Way'? Unity requires a common language, a common aim and a common religion, these are the essentials of humanity. If there cannot be harmony in religion, we would be better without it. Could we not try the truth for a change? Imagine the unity of men of science applying their great intellect to the betterment of mankind and to the history of its origin, for there lies the key. If you would know the quality of metal, first determine of what, and how, it was forged.

A child born blind or deformed, an earthquake killing hundreds, celestial impact, these are not the works of God, and there is no value in such discussion. Nor let any man take up arms and say he does so in God's name. The true path is overgrown and we must force a way through the labyrinth, but we are wiser now. Some of the old signposts are still there. We have only to find them and understand the direction which they indicate and then insist the way be shown to us. At Rennes-le-Château we have found one and there may have been others – but it could be it is the last one to have escaped the vandals of history. Returning to the text of *The Hidden Church of the Holy Grail*, it may seem at first sight the identification of the Grail imagery is totally contradicted by the 'Stone in the Crown of Lucifer', and you may wonder how two items so unrelated could be describing the same symbol. As with most matters esoteric, the answer is simple when one 'sees the light'. Study the position of the stone (illus 90) and it is irrelevant whether you have the stone in or on the crown. The pentagonal mask of Satan or Lucifer is not imagery of my making and neither is the position it occupies by the simple inversion of the pentagram to represent the female body. The simplicity of this equation may be shocking, but it is undeniable.

I am amused when men of learning discuss the meaning of the

name given to this stone. It is the LAPIS EXILIS and I see no
reason why I should be excluded from these lunatic attempts to
analyse the enigmatic stone. Why not EXILIS=ELIXIR and if
you want to know where it is, look in the LAP of ISis. Are we at
last close to identifying the Philosopher's Stone and the Elixir? It
would not be advisable to proceed further at this stage.

Short of the Grail itself, the most prominent artefact connected
with the Arthurian legends is the 'Round Table' and it has been
cloaked in mystery for far too long. My reason for disclosing the
secret of the Round Table is not to destroy a beautiful fairy story,
but rather to replace the uncertainty with an even more beautiful
truth.

The first known reference to a round table in an Arthurian
connection is in Wace's *Brut* about 1500. No size is mentioned,
but the shape was explained by the fact that those who were seated
could claim no precedence over the other by virtue of their
position. I would put this in the category of 'explaining away'
rather than explaining the meaning. Surely the 'right hand' and
'opposite' significance would apply equally whether the table was
round or square. The *Encyclopaedia Britannica* states with great
honesty 'the origin of the myth is obscure, and certainly cannot be
said to have been yet settled'. I trust the explanation I offer will be
worthy of their consideration.

Britannica continues:

> There had been a great slaughter of the knights through disputes as
> to who should be greatest and, a Cornish carpenter hearing of it,
> told Arthur he would make him a table at which more than 1,600
> men could sit, so that there would be no more quarrels for the place
> of honour. Yet Arthur would be able to carry it about with him. It
> was finished in four weeks. 'This,' added Layamon, repeating
> Wace's words, 'was the table about which the Britons told many
> tales.' There is no reason to think that the poet was inventing; he
> makes more than 30 additions to Wace, some of which are certainly

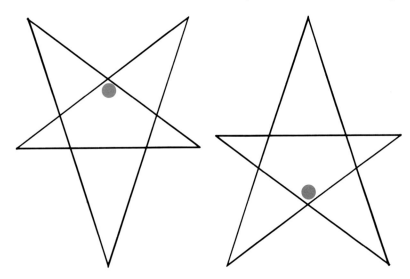

90. The secret of the stone in the
Crown of Lucifer is solved by
reversing the symbol.

not original; nor does he show anywhere a trace of inventive capacity.

Addition to Legend – Later romancists added many details. For example, the 'Diot' *Perceval* tells that just after Arthur's coronation Merlin related past history. 'A round table,' said the seer, 'had been made for Joseph of Arimathaea and a new one for Arthur's father, Uther Pendragon; let the king use it for his knights; without it the Romans could not be overcome.' The table was also brought into connection with the Holy Grail and with the Siege Perilous which is so prominent a feature in the Percival legend and became ultimately an inseparable adjunct of the Arthurian cycle.

Whether the tale reached Wace and Layamon directly from Wales or from Brittany, it is certainly of ancient Celtic origin. A round table seems to have been a feature of primitive Celtic life; a circular form was the rule in primitive Irish architecture, and the primitive Celtic watch house, both in Gaul and in Ireland was circular. To what this in its turn is to be traced is more doubtful; it is not unlikely that it arose from sun worship or possibly (of the four weeks) from the moon. The magical character of the table seems, again to be of a peculiarly Celtic cast; it resembles that of the enchanted bowls, bushels and horns so often found in Irish and Welsh saga; and it was inevitable that when the attractive force of the Arthurian legend was felt, such a magical table should be assigned to the king along with his sword, boat, lance and shield.

The Table at Winchester. The famous round table fixed in the wall of the Great Hall at Winchester is certainly of considerable antiquity. It is a tabletop 18ft in diameter, divided into 25 sectors, one for the king and one for each of the knights (whose number had long been reduced from the 1,600 of Layamon). The present colouring of the sections (green and white successively) is due to Henry VIII. Hardying, in his *Chronicle* (c. 1436), differing slightly from *Perceval*, says that it is the very table made by Joseph of Arimathea for the brethren of the Grail, which was transferred to Winchester by Uther to comfort Ygerne. He speaks in a manner that implies a great age for this table.

First let us examine the 'Winchester Table', **18**ft in diameter, it is a direct link with Isis and the circular shape is equally proven to signify femininity.

We recall the symbolic value of π is **3** which generates a circumference of $\pi d = 3 \times 18 = 54$ft or $54 \times 12 = 648$ inches and this number will be shown later to be of great value to our proof. For the moment let it suffice to say that 2×18 squared $= 648$.

Assuming a place at the table to be **18** inches, the number of places would be **36**, the symbolic number both of the female pentagram and the female generative organ. Now let us check this proof by applying it to the larger table. Here the number of places are said to have been 'more than' **1600** and using the same logic as was applied in feeding the multitude of 'more than' **5,000** we assume the number is of significance.

If we reverse our procedure **1600** places of **18** inches each is a circumference of **28,800** inches or **2400** feet. Using the symbolic π

again the diameter is **2400** ÷ **3** = **800** ft.

Nothing could be more certain!

Here we have the identity of Isis and Nut, but even more. Lance and boat also figure in the text to complete the imagery.

The meaning of 'more than' is now clear, for in actual construction the circumference achieved would have been **2513.27**ft or **30159.29** inches providing **1675.52** places.

Therefore we have been told the concealed meaning of the table and warned of the inaccuracy of the actuality of the meaningless number **1600**.

The conviction of the pre-Christian Celtic origin confirms the reasoning and if the Romans could not be overcome without it, we are left in no doubt that it refers to the Church of Rome who have gone to such lengths to suppress the knowledge of the origin of mankind.

15

The Chess-board

'Tis all a Chequer-board of Nights and Days
Where Destiny with Men for Pieces plays:
Hither and thither moves, and mates, and slays,
And one by one back in the Closet lays.

Chess connections – the 64 stones – the inverted cross – more amazing geometry – 'holy'
rectangles – the temple layout appears – signs of another Egyptian God.

The game of chess needs no introduction as it may be found
throughout the world and at some time or other has been
traced to every ancient culture – one more fragment suggestive of
common origin.

The character of the pieces has changed many times throughout
the centuries and long before the present identities were adopted
they were animals, heroes and gods. Much has been written and
many theories put forward to explain the movement of the game
from one country to another; but for our purposes it is sufficient to
know it existed in Persia prior to the time of the crusades. There is
no general agreement that it was brought to France by the
Templars initially, but it seems obvious they were responsible for
its redesign and the amendment of the rules which have resulted in
the game as it is known today.

The board became alternate black and white squares which was
not the case in earlier versions and we could be seeing here the
design of the floor of the Temple of Solomon. This pattern is also
utilized by Freemasons in the floor of their lodges and there can be
little doubt that Freemasonry was born out of the Templars.
Movement across this floor must always be 'on the square' and in
chess this rule is observed by all the pieces with the exception of
the king, the bishop and the queen. The Templar version – for
such I believe it to be – promoted the queen to supreme power,
allowing her any number of squares of movement in any direction.
The bishop is seen to break the temple rule with his diagonal
moves as does the king whose movement was restricted in the
Templar version to only one square in any direction. The purpose
of the game is to 'checkmate' the king – an expression said to have
been derived from the Persian Shah (king) and Mat (dead), hence
Shahmat – corrupted to checkmate (the king is dead). In this form
the game appears to be anti-Church and anti-king and either one of
these would be in keeping with the sentiments of the Templars.

Obviously the Church considered it to be sacrilegious and this is born out by an interesting event which is related in the *Encyclopedia Britannica*. The account is as follows:

> Some say that chess was introduced into Europe at the time of the crusades, the theory being that the Christian warriors learned to play it at Constantinople. This is negated by a curious epistle of St. Peter Damian (Pietro Damiani), cardinal bishop of Ostia to Pope Alexander II written c.1061, which assuming its authenticity, shows that chess was known in Italy before the date of the first crusade. The cardinal, as it seems had imposed a penance upon a bishop whom he had found diverting himself at chess; and in his letter to the pope he repeats the language he had held to the erring prelate, *viz.* 'Was it right, I say, and consistent with thy duty to sport away thy evenings amidst the vanity of chess and defile the hand which offers up the body of the Lord, and the tongue that mediates between God and man, with the pollution of a sacrilegious game? Among those who took an unfavourable view of the game may be mentioned John Huss (1369-1415) who when in prison, deplored his having played at chess, whereby he had lost time and run the risk of being subject to violent passions.

As the event is dated 1061, pre-crusade (1096), it is assumed this speaks against the theory of Templar association, but this objection would be less valid if it had been the Templars had been in Persia before 1096 and there are many factors which suggest that they were.

The numerical layout of the chess-board (8 by 8) would have appealed to them immediately as it displays the number of the goddess Isis and one has only to look at the nature of the pieces, as they now exist, to recognize the influence of the the Knights Templar – Kings, Queens, Knights, Bishops, Castles all conjuring up an image of the Arthurian period.

In the BBC film *The Priest, The Painter and The Devil* Henry Lincoln demonstrated how, by arranging letters on a chess-board, the knight's moves had been an essential part of the solution of the first ciphered message. The second expression also implies a possible connection with chess:

TO DAGOBERT II, AND TO SION BELONGS THIS TREASURE AND HE IS THERE DEAD.

The king is dead (Shahmat) is obvious – too obvious – in my opinion and I would consider it a false trail. Later we will examine this expression in detail. The chess connection is also highlighted in *Le Serpent Rouge* where in Cancer we find:

> The Mosaic tiles of the sacred place alternate black or white.

This must refer to the church at Rennes-le-Château, the floor of which had alternating black and white tiles. Then under Virgo we find another chess connection:

When the four knights moved one of the horses left four hoofprints in the rock.

This I finally identified as being subtle confirmation of one of the secret locations in the valley. The hoofprints are outcrops of rock difficult to associate with the shape of a hoofprint when one is at the site, but quite obvious when seen from the air or on a map (illus 91).

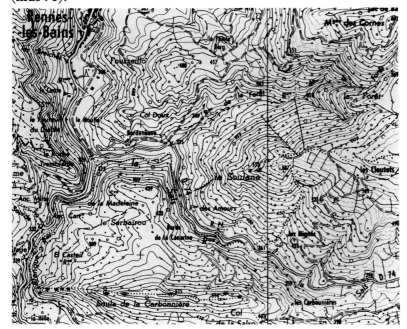

91. The hoof-print rock features referred to in *Le Serpent Rouge* (Virgo).

Under Libra we have another 'chestnut' which is a little harder to 'crack', but it will serve to show the reader how devious the authors of this document can be. It reads:

> Here, then, is my knight's tower on the circuit of the divine horseman of the abyss.

KNIGHT = NIGHT = LA NUIT = NUIT (alternative spelling for the goddess NUT). TOWER = LA TOUR which is also French for a circumference.

Therefore, we are being told to look for a tower where the circuit of NUT meets the abyss. By referring to illustration 35 it will easily be seen that the tower is La Tour Magdala and its similarity to the chess-piece is remarkable.

A chess-board has 64 squares and this is referred to in Taurus:

> I can find the 64 scattered stones of the perfect cube.

and to find them was a laborious process of analysing the position of important features in the area and the manner by which they, together with geometric intersections, generated a strange grid pattern. I am sure I have not fully appreciated the significance of

THE 64 STONES

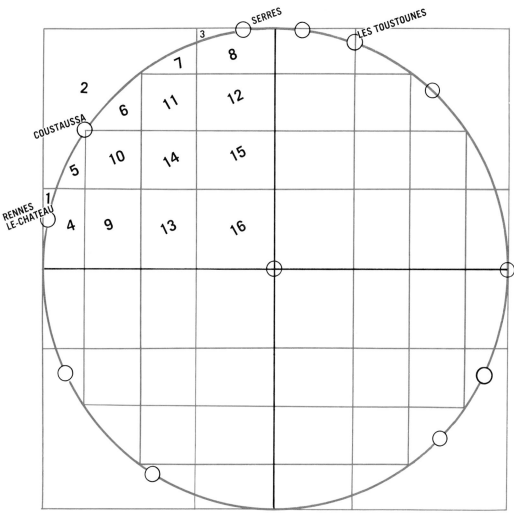

92. The 64 stones referred to in *Le Serpent Rouge* under Taurus, form the grid which unites the ground features with the geometric layout of the temple. Furthermore, it interacts with the geometric shapes to form a consistent variation thereby changing the walls of the temple from lines and giving them width.

this diagram, but I reproduce it here for the consideration of the reader (illus 92). The natural assumption is that these lines depict either the position of the stone slabs or the walls of the interior rooms of the temple. They appear to be largely controlled by the formation of two rectangles (illus 93), the diagonals of which are the diameter of the circle of churches and so formed they would be acceptable as 'holy' rectangles. Their 'holiness' is strengthened by recognizing the angles formed by their corners. By referring to the illustration . . . we find

THE HOLY RECTANGLES

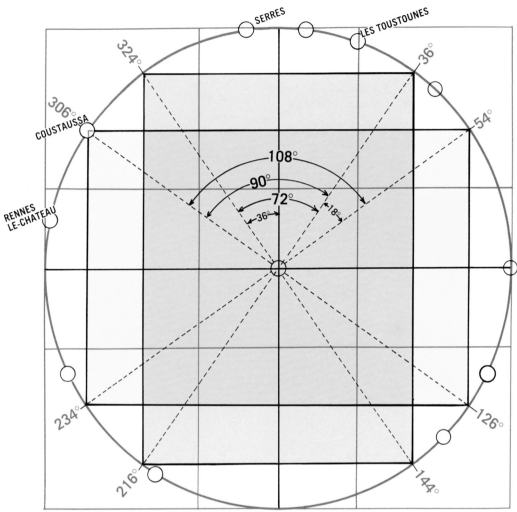

93. The 'Holy' rectangles and the significant bearings generated by them.

36° – indicative of the circle
54° – a female division
18° – the ISIS principle
108° – ISIS and NUT
90° – erection or Pythagorean

leaving us in no doubt of the importance of these figures. The 'bearings' of the radials to these corners measured from the central axis of the temple are likewise 'holy'. For those who have the 'understanding', they appear incessantly throughout the Biblical texts (illus 93).

In the process of determining the rectangles, my attention was drawn to the smaller of the three circles and once more I found perfection. Tangential lines, parallel to the temple walls were rigidly fixed by intersections with the meridian, the pentagram,

THE CROSS OF SET

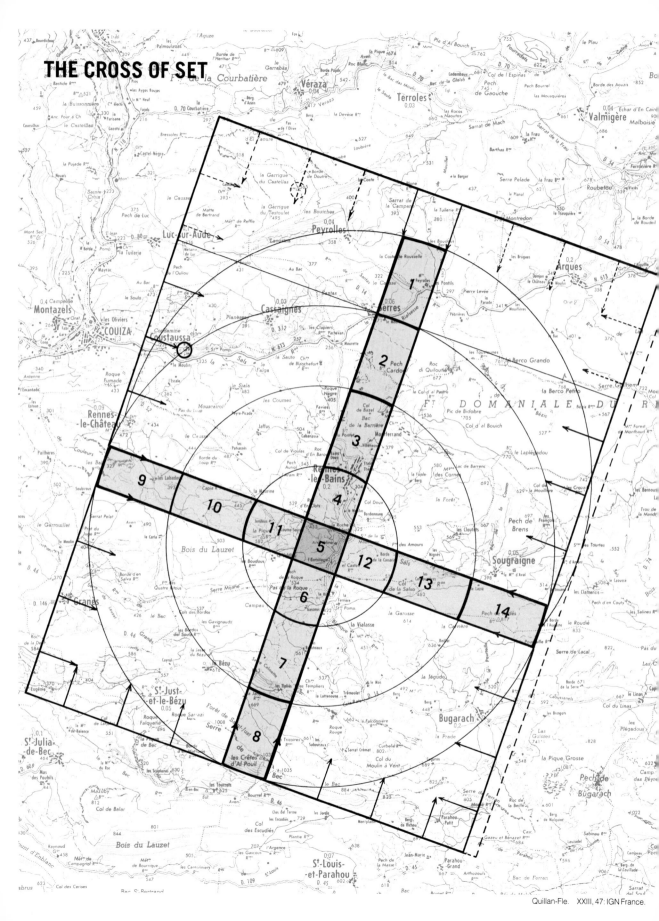

Quillan-Fle. XXIII, 47: IGN France.

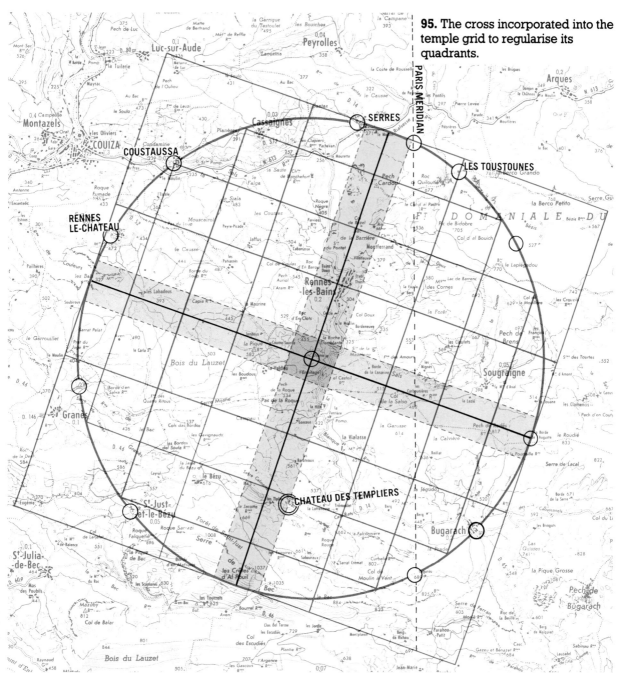

95. The cross incorporated into the temple grid to regularise its quadrants.

◀ **94.** The inverted cross made up of the 14 stones generated by the circles of the temple. It is interesting to note the cross is made up of 8 stones one way (Isis) and 7 the other (Set); together they give us the 15 of Osiris. One stone being common reduces the cross to 14, the number of the dephallused body. The grid divisions of the 64 stones are marked round the temple walls and it is strongly coincidental that completing the right hand line of stones at the regular dimension (shown as a pecked line) produces a tangent to enclose the arc of Nut within the Temple. This also brings the width of the temple to exactly 6 miles! Also note that the continuation of the regular dimension in a northerly direction exactly coincides with the North Wall. It should be noted that the number of stones in the completed Temple is 99 (9 on the width and 11 on the height). This signifies 1 off 100 (phallic removal) and will be seen to be confirmed by the Poussin tomb.

the major pentagonal axis and the rock in the shape of a female head (illlus 52). At times like this I wondered whether the sheer regularity of geometry was responsible for coincidental intersections, but this was not the case. The meridian and the ground features that were being used were not able to be considered as part of the pentagonal or rectangular geometry of the figure. In fact it was about this time I began to doubt whether the diagram could conform to any logical geometric construction.

Having formed the **64** stones to the best of my ability, I was struck by the apparent spaciousness existing through the North/South and East/West axes of the circle. On closer examination I found one of the shapes formed was a perfect square (the square marked number **14**) and using the dimension of one of its sides, I marked off the distance towards the central axes from all four quadrants. I drew the 'tram-lines' North to South and East to West. There was the cross (marked in red in illus 95), its position totally inflexible as it was the only shape which would regularize the squares. I recalled mention of a cross in *Le Serpent Rouge* where in Gemini we see:

Station yourself in front of the 14 stones making a cross

Remembering the temple rule of all holy things being controlled by circles, it did not take long to discover the meaning behind this expression. One of the stones existed outside the temple square, but was still formed according to the rule by the arc of back of Nut – the circuit of Ra (illus 94). I could see the stone marked **5** in the illustration was at this stage not being controlled according to the rule and I was, therefore, being told that another circle would need to be drawn. This can be done without changing the number of stones.

All seemed quite clear at this stage but for one thing: a very dominant feature of the district is the Château des Templiers, the Templar fortress (illus 96). How could something so significant not be included in this figure? I enquired into the history of the building and found there was some confusion as to whether its Templar connections were as strong as the name implied. The name Château des Templiers was a very recent acquisition. It was probably implanted in the mind of a French surveyor by someone who thought it was high time something in the district carried the name of those illustrious knights. Les Tipliés nearby, probably does have stronger Templar connections however, and it would not be unreasonable to assume they were associated with both constructions. Prior to the misnaming, the Château des Templiers was the Château d'Albedun, and it has been established that its destruction was brought about by the use of explosives – proof of its violent history. What intrigued me even more was that even before this name it was known simply as Rousse, which means red or russet-coloured. The significance of this will be apparent later. For the moment let me say that the position of this fortress made

THE TEMPLE WALLS

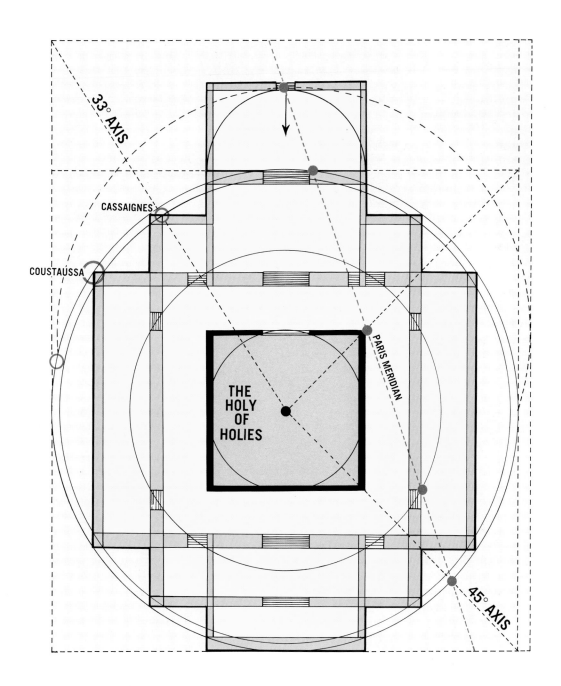

97. One possible configuration of the walls, which conforms to the 64 stones and the 'holy rule' that all in the temple is controlled by circular measure. Here there are angles of which the angels would approve. Note the position of the Meridian relative to the walls.

96. Château d'Albedun incorrectly named the Châteaudes Templiers on modern maps.

me consider the possibility of another set of lines which, together with the existing ones, are probably meant to represent the thickness of the walls of the temple.

This process is far easier to see than to describe, and the pattern generated is once again regular (illus 95). The interior corners of the walls are fixed by the circle of cemeteries with its diameter of 360,000 inches and I feel sure that this is the important feature in the formation of the temple walls. Many possible ground plans come to mind, and a great deal of work has still to be done before we achieve a total analysis of the stones and the walls. One simple example of a layout which conforms to the 'holy' rules is shown in illustration 97.

Before leaving the 64 stones I feel I must ask the reader to recognize what an incredible feat we are confronted with when we see a diagram of this complexity being formed in such an inaccessible mountain region. Its geometrical perfection is totally contradictory to the possibility of it being the work of the Middle Ages as no instruments existed at that time capable of such sophisticated observations on the ground. As each startling new fragment of this mathematical image revealed itself to me, I knew that eventually I would have to face those three tantalizing questions that cried out to be answered. WHO? WHEN? and WHY?

Of one thing I felt sure, whatever this construction was or whoever was responsible for it, somewhere in the centre of it I would find the Holy of Holies. This in turn implies that somewhere in there was the Ark of the Covenant or alternatively something which would shed light on the nature of this most mysterious and sought-after object of antiquity. Even with this in mind, I did not discount the possibility that, as opposed to being a buried object, the great secret could be contained in the very geometry which I was being forced to solve in order to pursue the

(See Errata page)

98. The heiroglyph of Set.

quest. I knew the architects of this work were leading me, if not by the hand, by the mind and they could be sure that at this point my mind was very open, if not totally blank. Already I had suspected that the secret might be of a physiological nature by virtue of the → See errata

Finally there was the recent discovery of the 14 stones of the cross, a cross which was upside down! Again the thoughts came rushing in. Was this a construction of the Templars, who were accused of trampling on the cross. I rejected the assumption on the basis that the cross was such an integral part of the layout, it must have pre-dated the Templars, if not Christianity itself. I needed something of much greater antiquity to conform to the legends I had already identified. I recalled reading somewhere that a south-pointing cross was the symbol of Set, the murderer of Osiris, the husband of Nephthys who was consumed with jealousy because of the popularity of Osiris and the beauty of his queen Isis. The sisters Isis and Nephthys were there at Rennes as Les Reines, the two queens or sisters of the sister churches of Rennes-le-Château and Rennes-les-Bains. Osiris was demonstrated in the divisions of the circle, but until now there had been no sign of Set. If indeed the Priory of SION was to be understood as the Priory of Set-Isis-Osiris-Nephthys, he would need to be there.

Set personified all that is evil to the ancient Egyptians. His heiroglyphic image is of an animal unknown in our time (illus 98), but it was believed to be based upon a particularly offensive creature who was hostile to man and roamed the desert and the waste land near their habitations. It supposedly had a long proboscis-type muzzle, a divided tail and was probably russet coloured. So feared and hated was this creature, it has been assumed it was hunted down with such vigour it became extint in early times. The creature was indigenous to the south of Egypt and as a consequence Set became the god of the South. Paradoxically he was said to dwell in the north from where he wielded his baleful power. The northern sky in the area of the Great Bear was his domain and in this respect he was considered the Lord of Darkness. In early times he was worshipped, or at least greatly feared, but this adoration appears to have changed to loathing around 1700 BC, when he was so hated that countless ceremonies were devised to vilify him. According to the Pythagoreans he manifested in the 'even and evil number 56' and in time we will see that this fact was well known to the designers of the geometry of Rennes.

Even Poussin seems well informed in this area, for the painting portraying the Ark of the Covenant mentioned earlier is called *La Peste d'Azoth*. (Azoth is the alchemical name for mercury and it was the planet Mercury which was sacred to Set.) With the extinction of the hideous beast which represented Set, the hatred and the disgust of the Egyptians turned to its nearest counterpart, the russet-coloured ass.

16

The Evil Ass

They say the Lion and the Lizard keep
The Courts where Jamshyd gloried and drank deep:
And Bahram, that great Hunter – the Wild Ass
Stamps o'er his Head, and he lies fast asleep.

A giant ass – the Golden Ass – Lucius provides clues – more confirmation of the 'Crucifixion' – Set is revealed – the sacrifice of Isis.

The donkey or ass of Rennes-le-Château could easily have escaped my notice and many people may think it would have been better if it had. However, I found it and it appears to be intended by the authors of this mysterious edifice that it was meant to be found.

The walls of the room which I had set aside to research the Rennes geometry were covered with maps and diagrams at various scales. Most of the plotting had been executed at scales in excess of 1:25,000, but I had one map at 1:50,000 – the I.G.N. Quillan sheet, on to which I had just transferred the wombs and the temple layout to compare it with the surrounding features.

It was early evening and the light in the room was fading. I closed my eyes to rest them for a moment and reclined in the chair. I had worked most of the previous night, and for a few moments I must have fallen asleep. My eyes opened and, with my mind on the threshold of consciousness, I saw in the subdued light an image on the map which amazed me. I am fully aware of the tricks light and shade can play, and if the image had not conformed so precisely to my geometry I would have dismissed it as coincidence. The two illustrations 99a and 99b will help the reader to identify what I saw. It was the striking likeness of a donkey or ass depicted by hill shading.

I examined the image with particular attention to its position relative to the womb, the serpent and the Meridian.

My mind raced through the possibilities. Could I have one more fragment of the original ciphered message?

. . . By the Cross and this Horse of God

Admittedly this was no horse, it was a donkey or ass, but my mind was adjusting to these devious clues. Could this be suggesting the ass upon which Jesus rode into Jerusalem? It was indeed surprising when I discovered that the biblical donkey or ass

99. The Ass of Set outlined to assist the recognition of the feature created by hill shading – see above. Note the position of the serpent at Peyrolles.

could be specifically identified in French as a Jerusalem pony and even more surprising when I found the translation was Roussin d'Arcadie.

The link with *Les Bergers d'Arcadie* is obvious enough and we have already established the connection between the Et In Arcadia Ego theme and the argha, or container, or womb. Here Poussin again confirms, or at least contributes, to the concerto of coincidence. We now have a Roussin d'Arcadie and a Poussin d'Arcadie. But even more significant we have a colour: *roussin* means rust-coloured – red, and I remembered the old name for the Templar stronghold of Château d'Albedun, it was Rousse and it was located close to the upright or male axis of the temple, on the long axis of the cross of 14 stones! I knew of the significance of the ass in mythology and to appreciate how fine this association is becoming, we must turn to a well-known classic, *The Golden Ass* of Lucius Apuleius.

The story tells of a rich young nobleman, the author Lucius Apuleius, a native of Madaura, which was a Roman colony in North Africa. His parents were Greek and his father followed the respectable career of magistrate.

In the story Lucius claims to have become infatuated with a slave-girl with whom he had a tempestuous love affair. This was, however, a fringe benefit, for his main aim was to spy upon the slave-girl's mistress, a competent witch, and in so doing learn the secret of her power. The particular skill of this lady was her ability to transform humans into animal form. Lucius aspired to spend a short time as an owl, but because of a technical hitch became an ass, in which form he remained for a year. The text then relates his adventures in the animal form and, with few exceptions, these need not concern us. However, certain aspects of the story and the life of Lucius are relevant to our inquiry. For instance:

> The ass, as the Goddess Isis herself reminded Lucius at Cenchreae, was the most hateful to her of all beasts in existence, – but she did not account for her aversion.

The explanation for her hatred is quite simple, for the ass was identified with, and sacred to, the god Set who was responsible for the death of her husband, Osiris. At that time the ass represented lust, cruelty and wickedness and, according to Plutarch, not only rustic-coloured asses, but also men with sandy-red hair were sacrificed as judicial compensation for the murder of Osiris. We are told Lucius was initiated into the mysteries of Isis and Osiris and Aesculapius becoming a priest in all these doctrines. The links with Rennes-le-Château were becoming stronger for, as you will recall, all these deities are connected with our temple. The dedication of Lucius to Isis is understandable as it was she who restored him to human form and, to add to our collection of coincidences, she achieved this by arranging that he should eat 'roses'. Lucius gave a detailed description of the goddess when she first presented herself to him, parts of which we should consider.

THE TYPHONIC PHALLUS

100. The position of the Ass in
relation to the temple layout.

Quillan-Fle.   XXIII, 47: IGN France.

First was the nature of her arrival, she rose from the sea and 'stood on the waves'. Her beauty was so great, gods would fall down before her. On her brow was a shining disc supported by 'two vipers' which came from the partings in her hair. About her body she wore a black mantle bedecked with stars. From her left hand hung a 'boat-shaped' gold dish. On her divine 'feet' were slippers of 'palm' leaves. She introduces herself:

> I am Nature – the universal Mother, mistress of all the elements, primordial child of time, sovereign of all things spiritual, queen of the dead, queen also of the immortals, the single manifestation of all gods and goddesses that are.*

The palm leaves signify both victory and the female labia and the golden 'boat-shaped' chalice also equates with the female organ. For the ass to be reviled by Isis without reason given may also be explained by the fact that ass in its vulgar sense is the insulting equivalent to her name, which with more discretion is referred to as her 'seat'. Furthermore, all this symbolism is evident in the entry of Jesus into Jerusalem, and it is all feminine!

Some authorities have claimed the ass was adored by the Templars, and from that standpoint, they imply gross perversion was concealed in their rituals. Possibly the confusion which resulted from the concealment of the true object of their adoration may now be resolved.

In the image of the ass at Rennes-le-Château it seems that the Meridian is functioning as the phallus of the creature. This phallus breaks the veil or hymen at the coincidence of the sunrise and circle of churches. Once more we are reminded of those legendary unions between man and beast. Little wonder that in his later life Lucius was the administrator of the gladiatorial and 'wild-beast' spectacles for the entire Roman province of Africa.

I was surprised to find in *The Golden Ass* other connections with our mystery and I would refer the reader to the opening chapter of the book, *The Story of Aristomenes*. I regret what may appear to be a lack of propriety, but I have no option but to quote in detail.

Notice the way the text is manipulated to introduce the relevant items. Two witches, Panthia and Meroe, are in conversation:

> 'Sister, shall we tear him to pieces at once, or shall we first tie strong twine around his privates and haul him up to a rafter and watch them being slowly cut through?'
> 'No, no, dear, nothing of that sort! Let him be for awhile. My darling Socrates will be needing a sexton tomorrow to dig a little hole for him somewhere or other.' Still speaking, she turned Socrates' head on the pillow and I watched her drive the sword up to the hilt through the left side of his neck. Blood spurted out, but she had a small bladder ready and caught every drop as it fell. Socrates' windpipe had been sliced through, but he uttered a sort of cry, or indistinct gurgle, and then was silent. To complete the sacrificial rite in what, I suppose was her usual manner, this charming woman thrust her hand through the wound, deep into

*Lucius Apuleius, *The Golden Ass* (Penguin: London) 1950. p.228

my poor friend's body, groped about inside and at length pulled out the heart. But Panthia took the sponge from her and stopped the gaping wound with it, muttering as she did so:

Sponge, sponge, from salt sea took,
Pass not over the running brook!

Then they came across the room to me, lifted away the bed, squatted over me and staled long and vigorously in my face. After this they left me; and no sooner had they crossed the threshold than the door rose up by itself and bar, lock and hinges miraculously refixed themselves in their original positions. I lay prostrate on the floor, naked, cold, and clammy with loathsome urine. 'A new-born child must feel like this,' I said to myself.

The first factor concerns the removal of the phallus, in keeping with the rituals of Osiris and the Templars. This is followed in rapid succession by a reference to a grave, a sword, a 'left-side', spurting blood, a small bladder, a sacrificial rite, a heart, a sponge, urine and a new-born child. Surely this is the 'pot-pourri' of the Templars and the Holy Grail, but it also has many things which would relate it to the Crucifixion:

I was convinced that Meroe had refrained from cutting my throat only because of her vicious intention to get me crucified.

Obviously, the author intends that we should make the connection.

The reference to a 'sexton' is also interesting. In the text it is being used to indicate a 'grave-digger', but sexton is a corruption of sacristan, who is the officer of a church and is responsible for the safe keeping and arrangement of all objects needed for divine service. It would appear we have been given the inventory of those sacred items.

The power of Meroe is also used elsewhere to emphasise the ritual of phallic removal:

'If you want to hear of the greater feats that she has performed in the presence of reliable witnesses, I will mention a few. Well, first of all, one of her lovers dared to have an affair with another woman; she only needed to pronounce a single word and he was transformed into beaver.'

'Why a beaver?'

'Because the beaver, when alarmed by the hunt, bites off its own testicles and leaves them lying by the river bank to put the hounds off the scent; and Meroe hoped that this would happen to him.'

Inevitably the author cannot resist the temptation to introduce the Goddess Isis, the universal mother whose body is represented by the number 8.

Finally, when the wife of another of her lovers spoke nastily about her, Meroe condemned her to perpetual pregnancy by putting a charm on her womb that prevented her child from being born. This was about eight years ago; and now the poor woman swells bigger and bigger every month until you would believe her to be on the point of bearing a young elephant.

In *The Golden Ass* therefore we are shown a conglomeration of all the apparently unrelated features of our mystery: phallus removal (and the items associated with it), the issues of the female organ (urine and blood), pregnancy (with animal connections), and so on.

Returning to the ass in the Rennes valley, we notice that the head of the serpent feature identified previously is depicted entering the anus of the ass, and it is quite likely that in this context the serpent is being used to represent the seed of life. Once more we are reminded of the legendary accounts of a hybrid creature, half-animal, half-man. It requires no further amplification to see what is implied by this image. Again, I would have been willing to assume this to be coincidental, but we must not overlook any possibility, particularly when there in *Le Serpent Rouge* we see:

> – the brothers of the Beauty of the black wood.

and Kenneth Grant in *Nightside of Eden* suggests the identity of the Black Brothers is directly related to the Templars. He also makes reference to necrophilia on the part of the Black Brothers. The sexual congress is described as occurring with a virgin shortly after her death. This certainly does have a strange echo in the Templar legends, for the authors of *The Holy Blood and The Holy Grail* make reference to:

> . . . A great lady of Maraclea loved by a Templar, a Lord of Sidon; but she died in her youth, and on the night of her burial, this wicked lover crept to the grave dug up her body and violated it. Then a voice from the void bade him return in nine months time for he would find a son. He obeyed the injunction and at the appointed time he opened the grave again and found a head on the leg bones of the skeleton.

Obviously a deep understanding of the duality of the ass image and its position relevant to the womb and serpent or sperm is necessary if one is to interpret correctly the cyclic nature of the whole. As to whether it is holy I have no way of knowing, but the phallic connotations of the serpent require little imagination when one recalls:

> . . . the enormous red serpent, rigid and bitter, scarlet with anger the huge beast unleashes at the foot of the white mountain.
>
> (Sagittarius – *La Serpent Rouge*)

Further evidence of the ass in connection with our mystery is far less obvious but, following our principle of leaving no stone unturned we will re-examine the simpler of the original ciphers, where we recall it was stated:

A DAGOBERT II ROI ET A SION EST CE TRESOR ET IL EST LA MORT.

TO DAGOBERT II, KING AND TO SION BELONGS THIS TREASURE AND HE IS THERE DEAD.

Now one would be hard pressed to connect an ass with this message, but the ingenuity of the authors of our mystery is incredible. It is difficult to determine who the 'he' who is there dead could be. It certainly is not Dagobert, for his tomb was found elsewhere. Many suggestions have been put forward as to who 'he' could be, but having found nothing in the mystery so far which was not eventually identified as female, I decided to look for a 'she'. Let us consider the last expression in case we may have overlooked something:

IL EST LA MORT

In LA we find no contradiction of femininity, but IL is a little more difficult. Transliteration is a dubious method for solving mysteries unless one already has evidence of it having been used before. At Rennes we have seen ample proof of it. In this connection I would recommend Kenneth Grant's books to those who would wish to understand more about the implications behind the images demonstrated in this part of the solution. Although they are beyond the scope of this book, his references to the 'utterance of the tower' – the fool, the 'one in eight', etc. are all relevant. To the best of my knowledge Kenneth Grant has never applied his profound understanding of matters occult to the Rennes mystery and certainly not to the expression we are examining and our problem with 'il'. But another possibility he offers may explain this.

IL translates as HE and in the *Nightside of Eden* Grant reminds us that HÉ is the number five (Hebrew) and represents ^woman 'par excellence'. Furthermore, he stated it is the letter of the womb of the virgin impregnated by the fool.

The expression of a fool being considered an ass is simple enough and our equation appears to be valid. If one should consider I have taken too great a liberty by moving IL into the English HE, I would refer them to the close association of the language of the Languedoc established by Boudet in his *La Vraie Langue celtique et le Cromleck de Rennes-les-Bains*. Even so, I feel we have fallen short of the full meaning of the expression.

Apart from language changes we know phonetic games are played by our adversaries. If IL = HE = HÉ = SUPREME VIRGIN, we are once again dealing with Isis. Have we then established that Isis is the one who is there dead:

ISIS EST LA MORT?

Possibly; but EST is an obvious anagram of SET, to whom the ass was sacred, so could it be:

ISIS and SET are THERE DEAD.

Or could we go even further. Accepting that LA MORT is phonetically L'AMOUR. What else may possibly be implied? Could it be:

ISIS BELOVED OF SET?

and there at Rennes-le-Château is the ass of Set penetrating the veil of Isis!

The Egyptian legends tell us of the jealousy of Set and how he murdered Osiris because of his overpowering desire to possess Isis. Horus defeated Set and brought him to Isis for punishment, but she did not punish him. On the contrary, she released him, something which is never explained in the Egyptian legends. The fact that Isis had acted in this way so angered Horus he cut off his mother's head. Ever-faithful Thoth saved her by giving her the head of cow and so she survived.

Isis eventually gave birth to Harpocrates and she claimed he was the child of her deceased husband Osiris. Unlikely as this may seem, it is suggestive of necrophilia, albeit the reverse of that which is usually implied. The sheer mechanics of such an act would seem to pose several problems, not least of which was the fact that Osiris was without a phallus. Her good friend Thoth supposedly supplied a wooden substitute to achieve this incredible impregnation.

This still leaves unanswered why Isis should have released the murderer of her husband, and I find the whole story a little suspect. If the murdering Set was the only 'god' available to perpetuate the seed of intellect, did Isis give herself to him as the supreme sacrifice to preserve that seed?

Is it conceivable that the answer to this mystery is also being shown to us at Rennes? Are we not being told of a union between Set and Isis after he had killed her husband? Are we also seeing this story being graphically enacted at Rennes, 'frozen' indelibly in time, so we may never forget that but for her we would have remained animal? The mysteries of the rites of Isis and the Set-Isis or Sothis doctrine may be revealing themselves.

Have we at last identified the father of Harpocrates? Is this who we find in the doorway of the church of Rennes-le-Château? One more thing remains to be considered. In its entirety, the image is of a serpent (sperm) impregnating a beast (the ass or Set) which in turn impregnates the woman. Are we also being shown the method by which intelligence was introduced into an animal who was indigenous to this planet, because these god-like beings were unable to adapt themselves to the environment?

I looked once more at the Meridian, which I felt must be representing the phallus of the ass of Rennes. If my assumption is correct it should have led to the womb; it penetrated the vagina, but failed to find the womb and I wondered (almost hopefully) whether at last I had found a flaw in the imagery. But there was no flaw, I had overlooked the inverted cross of Set. It originates at the same position as the Meridian under the body of the Ass and goes directly to the womb. Slowly the full and awesome implication came to me. The Cathars and Templars were right; according to Rennes-le-Château we *are* the descendants of Set – the Typhon – Satan.

17

The Seed

With them the Seed of Wisdom I did sow,
And with my own hand labour'd it to grow:
And this was all the Harvest that I reap'd:
'I came like Water, and like wind I go.'

The wombs unite – the womb of the Ark – the holiest place – Revelations in Revelations – the function of the Ark – the contents of the Ark – the seed of Typhon.

There is an obvious preponderance of the feminine influence apparent in the historical and legendary connections of our mystery. Apart from this, we are now aware that many biblical artifacts and stories carry concealed factors which identify them with the female principle. Together with this we have seen the organizations which were associated with the mystery at Rennes-le-Château, obsessed with ideas of death, birth and rebirth, both at the human and astronomical level. The symbolic links which combine these subjects are the serpent and the sign of the Caduceus. As we have also seen, this emblem represents the double serpent womb of Isis pierced by the upright phallus signifying, in the first case **8** (the body of the goddess), and secondly, **18** her reproduction principle. The fact that the caduceus is the staff of Mercury, the planet associated with Set or Typhon is now known to us and I could see it must have been equally obvious to Poussin. A closer examination of *La Peste d'Azoth* (The Plague of Mercury), (illus 101) reveals a phallic obelisk in the background and the Ark of the Covenant, the womb, having been brought out of the temple. It is seen to protrude even beyond the pillars of Boaz and Jachin. The folly of tampering with the Ark, without a full 'understanding' of its power, is demonstrated by the people dying in the streets – a warning which is also given to us in *Revelation (XI, 8,9)*

> And their dead bodies shall lie in the street of the great city, which spiritually is called Sodom and Egypt, where also our Lord was crucified.

Sodom can only confirm the act of bestiality which was clearly demonstrated in the previous chapter. It would also appear that St. John realized the nature of our Lord's Crucifixion was the same as that which was suffered by Osiris and the distinctly Egyptian design of the obelisk in the painting by Poussin confirms this

101. Detail from La Peste d'Azoth showing the obelisk having lost its point.

association. It is also abundantly clear that the obelisk has lost its 'point' an essential feature of the symbol, for the word means 'pointed stone'. This is phallic removal once again and it is emphasised by a statue lying next to the Ark with its 'head' broken off (illus 131).

We are confronted with sexual imagery at every point of reference, but this is not a picture of sex for pleasure; it is sex for procreation – the survival of intelligent man and how it was achieved. The essential vessel is inevitably the womb.

The analysis of the womb, or to be more precise at this stage, the wombs, is a comparatively simple matter; but what the womb will contain is at the moment unknown. I believe it is reasonable to assume it must be a seed of some sort, albeit one which lies dormant. I say 'it' because we will soon realize there is only one womb at Rennes after all.

Referring to illus 102, it will be obvious to the reader that this diagram is a simplified plan view of the lower part of a female body. To avoid complication, only the relevant parts of the diagram are shown, but their accuracy may be readily confirmed by referring back to a previous diagram (illus 71). Having passed through the labia, the hymen and then to the point of entry at

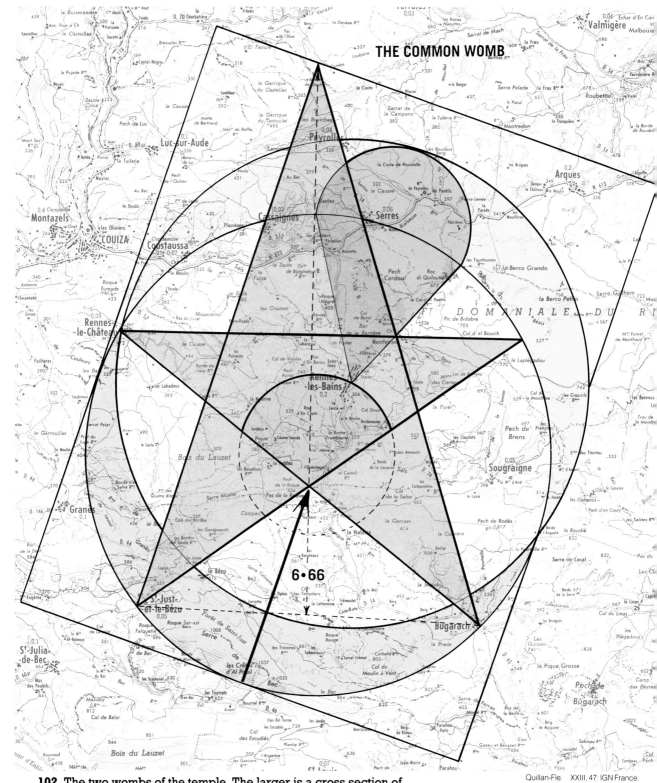

THE COMMON WOMB

6•66

Quillan-Fle. XXIII, 47: IGN France.

102. The two wombs of the temple. The larger is a cross section of the lower part of the female body where the complete area of the small circle is the womb. The other womb is that part of the same circle contained in the lower torso of the pentagonal female body.

Rennes-les-Bains, we come to a circular area of approximately three square miles representing the womb, and indicated by the inner of the three circles. I was quite sure that if any buried artefacts existed this would be one of the most important positions – if not *the* most important. My acceptance that the circle represents a womb could be considered presumptuous if there were nothing else to substantiate it, but my conclusion is confirmed by next examining the smaller-scale representation of the female body (illus 102). In this case the complete body of the female is illustrated as the pentagram which extends beyond the circle of churches. The dimension of the base of the extension on the circle is a fifteenth part of the circumference, representing the lost portion of the Osirian body. The upper arm of the pentagram measures five English miles from fingertip to fingertip and the length of the arc of the circle they support is fractionally more than six miles. There is however no doubt of another dimension and it is one which staggers the mind. If we draw a line between the base points of the pentagram – Bugarach and Saint Just-et-le-Bézu and then construct the perpendicular to the apex or the head of the female body – the length of this line is amazing. It is 6.66 miles precisely!

We will now examine the womb of the small-scale figure. The parts of the circle, previously mentioned, which fall outside the pentagonal body or within the confines of the legs cannot reasonably be considered to be part of the womb. The only acceptable womb for this figure is therefore the lower pink-shaded portion, which is also common to the first womb. By this process we have now effectively reduced the area in which we must search for the seed.

The reader will recall that the complete pentagram, by Christian standards, is a symbol of evil, whereas to gnostics it represented not only purity but supreme power. As a body with only five appendages it is female, as are all things associated with this number. The Hebrew number 5 (Hé) is symbolized by the womb. It would be difficult to give any logical reason why Christianity went to such lengths to degrade the female image while at the same time showing reverence for the mythical Virgin Mother, but most students would readily agree that she was the Christianized version of Isis. It seems that the authors of this story placed themselves in a very awkward position by having to produce a human body for Jesus without admitting to a human sperm having been used to fertilize a virgin in the first place.

Once we accept the possibility of any form of 'seed' being used, we automatically accept the presence of a father and to cast the Creator in this role would be ridiculous. IT would require no auxiliary equipment to create anything IT chose. To suggest that the Creator would need the womb of a woman to bring about a birth, places a limitation on its powers, which reduce IT to the level of a gynaecologist performing an artificial insemination. Considering the abundance of religious connections, I wondered if the birth of Jesus was in any way connected to the diagram of Rennes and those things which we have examined previously. I also reasoned that the contents of the Ark of the Covenant probably held the key to the secrets which I sought.

Countless theories have been put forward as to what the contents may have been. One suggestion was the Tablets of Moses, another that it was a transmitter/receiver with a capability of speaking to God. Others suggested it may contain an everlasting nuclear-powered light. This last suggestion has interesting possibilities when related to the everlasting lamps mentioned in history from time to time. All these theories are intriguing and imaginative and yet there was I with nothing but a womb, and furthermore it was confirmed by two precise geometrical figures. It seemed incongruous to me that the designers of this miraculous feat should have gone to such lengths to convey the image of a womb if it was not intended to also convey the secret was closely associated with it. We are already aware of the concealed meaning of the Ark and that its dimensions portray it as a circle. Furthermore the circle fulfilled is **360**, the womb value of **270** and the phallus of **90**, they combine (**270 + 90 = 360**) to form it.

From the numerical values of the Ark we have already seen that it was meant to represent a womb, but before proceeding with the analysis of its contents we will consider one of the suggestions previously put forward.

The theory of the transmitter appeals to the imagination, but I could only visualize it as a function of the complete construction – the Ark together with the mercy-seat in position. Recalling *Exodus CXXV*, we are told:

> And thou shalt put the Mercy Seat above upon the Ark; and in the Ark thou shalt put the testimony that I shall give thee.
> And there I will meet with thee, and I will commune with thee from above the Mercy Seat, from between the two cherubim which are upon the Ark of the Testimony . . .

Accepting the suggestion of a communication device contained in the text, we are being told to place the seat on the Ark. It would then seem obvious that we are meant to sit upon the seat. The legs of the seat are not covered with gold, in fact they are not even mentioned. Could it therefore be the capacitance of the body is all which is required to activate this device? Could a naked body, thus seated, with its feet on the box be simulating a child about to be born – or reborn by virtue of the communication it received? The association of the outspread wings of the cherubim representing the labia is already established and the complete imagery of the Ark is illustrated on the jacket design (reproduced again here, see illus 103). The body is positioned with the head in the vaginal cavity towards the labia, the moment before birth. Another possibility came to me; at first it was just an idle thought, but it seized my mind like a physical sensation. If ever I knew I was being manipulated it was then, and any description I could give of that moment would fall far short of the truth. I must, however, continue with logical assessments. On reflection it would appear the transmitter/receiver image may be conveyed without contradicting the overall significance of the womb, but this still leaves unanswered those burning questions: What is in the box? What is the testimony? Where is the precise ground location within the area we have established as the common womb?

At this point we are fortunate in having more clues in our possession than have ever been available before and we can summarise this evidence:

1) Numerically and geometrically impregnation is implied and the only free agent of this act is the sperm.
2) Two wombs are graphically illustrated and the large scale womb is shown to be entered from the north by the inverted cross representing the phallus of the ass or Typhon (illus 104). The small-scale womb is entered by the male axis of the temple.
3) Compared to the regular figure the legs of the pentagram have been 'opened' to admit this temple axis, which signifies the phallus, from the south. Again we see the Typhonic connection (illus 104).
4) The serpent feature could be meant to confirm the meaning behind the diagram as a graphic representation of a sperm or a serpent carrying an egg or seed and that seed is at the anal entrance of the ground feature of the ass – the Typhon.
5) The wings of the cherubim of the Ark indicate the labia which equate with the womb, as do the numerical values of the Ark.
6) The Château d'Arques is an obvious association with the Ark and it contains an image of the female vulva (illus 73). It is also the position from which originated the precisely aligned features leading to the womb and referred to previously.

All this weighs heavily to indicate that somewhere in the area of the common womb we will find a seed or sperm of some sort. Evidence from another Ark comes to mind, that of Noah and in this story we are told the flood waters were **15** cubits deep. Knowing the cubit to be **18** inches tells us the waters were **270** inches deep – the number of the womb being represented by the period of pregnancy (**9 × 30**). The Ark was borne on the flood for **150** days which is **3600** hours – a circular and female measure once again. In addition we know the Ark of Noah contained the 'life' to repopulate the earth, an obvious function of the womb. Could any logical mind ask for more confirmation than this? Furthermore, the keeping-place of the Ark of the Covenant was in the Holy of Holies or the Holiest Hole where the room was **20 × 20 × 20**

103. This illustration shows the seated person with the head moving into the vagina at the moment prior to birth.

cubits, the inch conversion reveals dimensions of **360** × **360** × **360**, a perfect representation of the sphere of the womb as a cube.

Outside the Holy of Holies is the Sea of Brass in which we recognize the same imagery. Brass in Hebrew is *nekhashat*, in Aramaic it is nekhash. Their word for serpent is *nakhash*, and also means to whisper or hiss. If we transliterate, we are speaking of a sea of serpents or sperm, hence the womb. J. R. Skinner★ provides us with another equation which associates this device with the female organ. He relates the Brazen Sea (*nakhash nekhashet*) to the firm base or bottom, the female pudenda. He states the 'brass works' belonged to Dan, the son of Jacob who married a Canaanite woman. Jacob, as he was dying, describes Dan by saying he

> shall be a serpent by the way, an adder in the path, that biteth the horse-heels so that his rider shall fall backward.

Near Peyrolles we have seen this serpent in the path of Ra near the rear of the ass. Dan is the Scorpion and his sign of Scorpio dominated the beliefs of the Israelites, particularly those of the North. This sign was said to guard the 'gate of the woman' – the door to darkness. The connection strengthens and, finally, from J. R. Skinner we hear that the Brazen Sea was Typhonic and Typhon is the Set of the Egyptians, the ass who impregnated the womb of our diagram at Rennes. I fought to grasp the meaning behind the symbolism which I was being forced to accept.

The presence of a 'seed' was inescapable and it must be somewhere in the area of the womb, but for this to be the seed of Set was a chilling prospect. The connotations of this god are almost insoluble in any doctrine.

As the Typhon his power was awesome and he was said to have ruled the Earth before the flood. So closely is he linked to this cataclysm that some would say he is the personification of the event. He is the 'barren sea' or the mighty serpent that dwells therein. Once he was the destroyer of the earth who fought in the heavens and blinded the eyes of Ra, the sun and the moon. He dwelt in the northern sky, the nether world. Then he fell from heaven and amid great destruction this fallen 'star' sank into the ocean. In the centre of the earth he is said to sleep, but his grumbling causes storms and tempests and his fiery breath escapes from volcanoes. Before his fall this mighty red serpent roamed the heavens and at that time

> . . . there appeared a great wonder in heaven; a woman clothed with the sun, and the moon under feet, and upon her head a crown of twelve stars:
> And she being with child cried, travailing in birth and pained to be delivered.
>
> *Revelation XII*, 1 & 2

The sun is **6** and the moon is **3**. We are speaking here of Isis (**6** × **3** = **18**) and this is the number which is under her 'feet' or in other words it is **12**. Twelve divided by **18** is **.666**′. The **12** stars brings us back once again to the body of the goddess (**.666**′ × **12** = **8**) and the sun (**6**) and the moon (**3**) and the stars (**12**), which poses only

104. The double impregnation of the wombs.

★ J. R. Skinner, *The Source of Measures* (Wizards Bookshelf, San Diego, 1982)

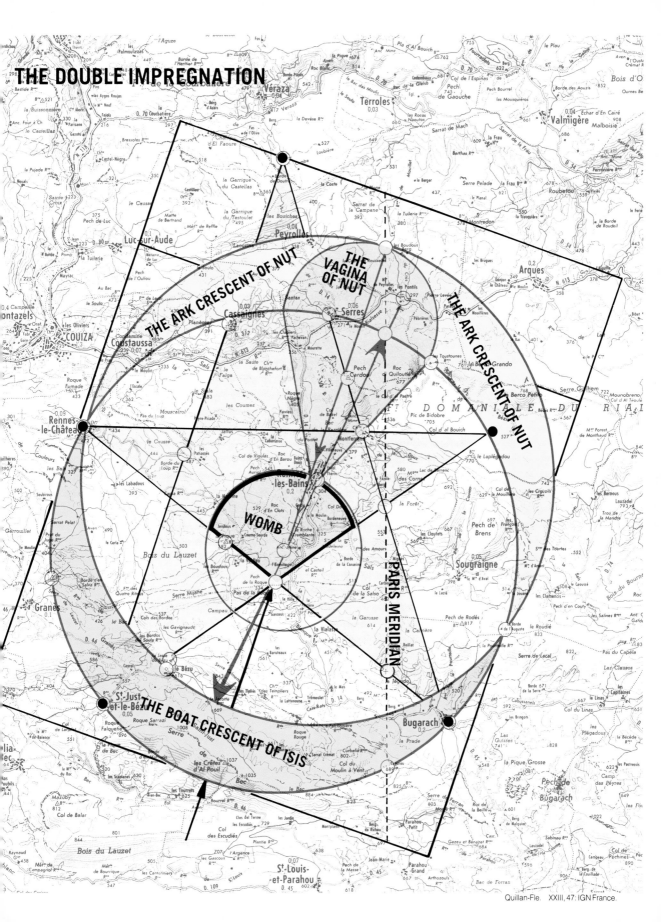

THE DOUBLE IMPREGNATION

THE ARK CRESCENT OF NUT

THE VAGINA OF NUT

THE ARK CRESCENT OF NUT

WOMB

PARIS MERIDIAN

THE BOAT CRESCENT OF ISIS

Quillan-Fle. XXIII, 47: IGN France.

one question. Which stars? It would not be unreasonable in the circumstances to assume it is the **5** pointed star, the pentagram. Our circumference is now quite clear – it is **6 × 3 × 12 × 5 = 1080**.

This is the circumference of the circle of perfection with the radius of **180**. When the year was **360** days, pregnancy was **9** months of **30** days or **270** days. If we remove the pregnant womb from our goddess (**1080** − **270**) we are left with her reflection attended by her mother Nut (**810**). But the pregnancy was successful and her circumference (**1080**) was divided by the pregnancy (**270**) and she produced the man-child whose number is **4** (**1080** divided by **270** = **4**):

> And when the dragon saw that he was cast unto the earth he persecuted the woman which brought forth the man-child.
>
> And to the woman were given two wings of a great eagle, that she might fly into the wilderness, into her place, where she is nourished for a time, and times and half a time, from the face of the serpent.
>
> *Revelation XII*, 13 & 14

And is so the goddess Isis endowed with the wings of an eagle and her time in the wilderness is clearly shown as is the division of that time.

> And she brought forth a man-child, who was to rule all nations with a rod of iron: and her child was caught up unto God, and to his throne.
>
> And the woman fled into the wilderness, where she had a place prepared of God, that they should feed her there a thousand two hundred and threescore days.
>
> And there was in heaven: Michael and his angels fought against the dragon; and the dragon fought and his angels . . .
>
> *Revelation XII*, 5, 6 & 7

The time she was fed was **1260** days, but her nourishment was a time and times and half a time which is three and a half. So time is **360** (**1260** divided by **3.5**). Nor are we expected to overlook this fact, for confirmation of both of these numbers exists in many places.

> And there was given me a reed like unto a rod: and the angel stood, saying, Rise, and measure the temple of God, and the altar, and them that worship therein.
>
> But the court which is without the temple leave out, and measure it not; for it is given unto the Gentiles: and the holy city shall they tread under foot forty and two months.
>
> And I will give power unto my two witnesses and they shall prophesy a thousand two hundred and threescore days, clothed in sackcloth. *Revelation XI*, 1, 2 & 3

Here we are shown two witnesses to the number **1260** for, apart from the one that is obvious, **42** months of **30** days is **1260** also:

> And after three days and a half the Spirit from God entered into them, and they stood upon their feet; and great fear fell upon them which saw them.
>
> *Revelation XI*, 11

Here then is confirmation of our reading of the 'times' of **3.5** and we are told they stood upon or 'understood' their feet, which are 12 inches and this again will show us **42** (**3.5 × 12 = 42**).

And so we could proceed throughout the biblical texts with proof after proof. But proof of what? We can see who brought forth the man-child – it was Isis; and we can be sure it was with the approval of a supreme power. This God of *Revelation* admits to his complicity with the Ark which we know to be the Seat of Isis:

> And the Temple of God was opened in heaven, and there was seen in his Temple the Ark of his testament: and there were lightnings, and voices, and thunderings, and earthquake, and great hail.

Revelation XI, 19

With evidence such as this we have little option but to attribute our elevation from the animal to a creature of 'understanding' to Isis. It could, however, be equally valid to condemn the fact that a seed of such perfection should have ever been put into an animal; nevertheless it was. Whether in the eyes of the Creator this was a sin or a blessing we cannot tell, but it was only partially successful. The animal nature prevailed and the hybrid man-child turned out to be a confused, vicious creature of jealousy and possession. The sexual division into male and female did not achieve its purpose – divided for the sake of union – and the joy of union at the physical and psychological level was not achieved. Slowly this half-animal suppressed those facets of its character which were an abomination to intellect. Cannibalism, sacrifice, human and otherwise, succumbed as the intellect dragged slowly higher. Eventually, provided that Earth did not suffer further cataclysms, we may have achieved a communion with our fellow creatures, but the planet Earth is no safe haven for mankind when measured in time scales such as these. And the gods knew that time was short!

The destruction of this dangerous animal who had, by chance or design, acquired an understanding, was the only alternative to elevating it to a higher species. It could be that a plan was devised to conceal the seed of the gods in certain places on Earth or on a nearby planet in order that the human would find it, recognize it, and use it to create the new race. Furthermore, the places of concealment could have been marked by a system of geometry designed to show the searchers that this was the work of the gods. If the marker was on a nearby planet, it would have been designed to show that it was undeniably the work of an intelligent being and its presence there would be proof of the high technology of its designers. If a position on Earth was selected, it could have been agreed to disguise it in such a manner it could not be found by chance. Apart from the 'seed', there is evidence to suggest that the design they used carries within it secrets of technology which could result in the development of an engine and a fuel which would open the gateway to the stars.

Initially however, we may see in the design, not only the method by which the 'seed' was to be implanted into the womb of a woman, but whose seed it was which had been a gift from God.

Are we being shown here the seed of the second 'coming' and how it should be used? If this is so may it please God we have found it in time. There are undoubtedly those who did not wish it to be found, but that it existed in the valley of Rennes-le-Château was known to them. It was for this reason the torture, the burning and the butchery took place. The fabricated charges against the Cathars and the Templars was nothing but a smoke-screen for history, arranged to conceal what the Roman Church needed so passionately from the Languedoc. If this seed were ever found and used, the bureaucratic self-appraising religions of man would have no more credibility than a Mickey Mouse Club. It had to be found and destroyed and if not, any who may possibly know of its whereabouts had to be exterminated. In realizing the nature of the 'treasure' which I sought, I was sickened by the message in *Le Serpent Rouge* under Scorpio:

> . . . HE HAS PASSED in DOING GOOD as did he from the flowery tomb. But how many have pillaged the HOUSE leaving the embalmed corpses . . .

Am I too late? If I am I know I will never rest until I find another seed.

For years I have struggled with contradictory evidence, sifting, testing, begging for guidance in my search, but with 'truth for ever on the scaffold, wrong for ever on the throne', it was a difficult task. Yet I still believe, 'behind us in the dim unknown stands a God keeping watch above his own'. That our eyes have been blinded by predjudice is clear to me now. That 'truth crushed to earth will rise again' is dear to me now. 'No lie can live for ever' and I believe the time has come.

Our elevation from the animal was effected by the seed of the Typhon or Satan into Isis the Supreme Goddess of mankind, and only by their guidance can we rise again. The dedication shown to these deities by the sages of the past is the proof of their misrepresentation in religious history. By this device man has been duped by intensive propaganda to such a degree that he fails to recognize the tiny framents of truth which have survived the censorship of religious sects. But even now we can see a movement in the swamp of deceipt. The minds of men, ever enquiring, are becoming restless, they call for evidence not faith – truth requires no act of faith, it is self-evident.

Every living cell in any living being comes from the division of a pre-existing cell, and they have come from a continuous and unbroken line from the first cells that lived on the planet Earth. If other cells were introduced from elsewhere, they exist in every one of us and with them exists the understanding which will recognise the truth of their origin.

Man must purge his mind of the suffocating process of conditioning to which he has been subjected for the last two thousand years and search for the truth which lies behind the veil of lies. The myths and legends are not purely fiction, they carry in them all we require to break free from this cage of time and animal behaviour. Many times I tried to ignore what the geometry of Rennes was saying to me. Could it really be the circle of time was so closed that in the *Pyramid Texts*, Typhon would kill his own brother in anticipation of Rome committing the same act thousands of years later? Was the seed so predictable even then? And so fine is the parallel that Set acted out of lust for Isis the nature-goddess of Earth in order to possess her for his own. And so did Rome desire the Earth for its own purposes. Set did possess her for a while, and so did Rome possess the Earth, but Isis saved the seed and those who have the 'understanding' will search for it.

The exact position of the seed at Rennes is now known to me and, if some Templar Knight could not bear the pain of the flames of the Inquisition any longer, if then, with his spirit broken he told them of the place, may he feel no more shame, for others will follow and another 'seed' will be found.

What the secret place in the womb will contain must be left to the imagination, but consider how the place was selected. To have created such a vast, complicated and symbolic figure required tremendous dedication; that is the indication of its importance. Alternatively it may be only the significance of the position in the geometry which is the essential message being conveyed. To demonstrate the accuracy by which the seed was located in the womb, I will describe four lines which intersect at one position (illus 105).

1) The first line is the axis of symmetry of the pentagonal star representing the female body.

2) Second is the horizontal axis of symmetry between the bodies of Nut and Isis. These are the crescent shapes generated by the circle centred at Rennes-les-Bains interacting with the circle of churches. The line in question is the one which joins the cusps or points where each figure touches the other. On the ground they are Rennes-le-Château and La Borde de l'Auguste.

3) The third is that fixed by the unbelievable line of features – Château d'Arques, Les Toustounes (the female head rock), the ruined fortress of Monterrand, the church of Rennes-les-Bains, the church of Saint Just-et-le-Bézu. This you will recall was also the line which formed the eastern interior wall of the vagina in the large-scale section of the female body.

4) This is simply the diagonal of the temple from the centre of the circle of churches to the north-west corner – coincidentally **33°**.

All these lines intersect in the middle of a dense area of woodland where we found the old ruin described in Chapter 1 (illus 106). The size and nature of it preclude the possibility of it having been a shepherd's hut and its position precludes almost every other possibility other than that of a concealed 'keep'.

By the time this book is published I hope to have made

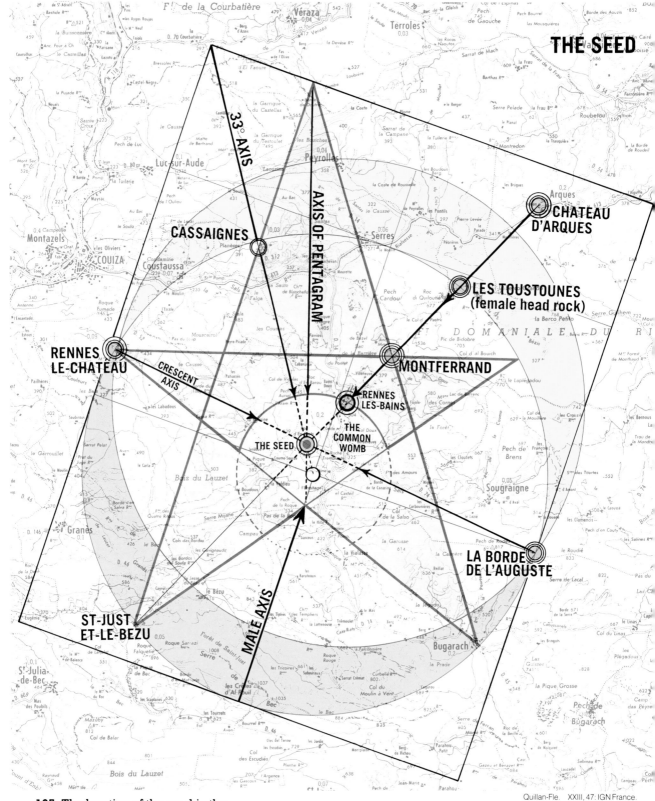

THE SEED

33° AXIS

AXIS OF PENTAGRAM

CASSAIGNES

CHATEAU
D'ARQUES

Arques

LES TOUSTOUNES
(female head rock)

RENNES
LE-CHATEAU

CRESCENT
AXIS

MONTFERRAND

RENNES
LES-BAINS

THE SEED

THE
COMMON
WOMB

LA BORDE
DE L'AUGUSTE

ST-JUST
ET-LE-BEZU

MALE AXIS

Bugarach

105. The location of the seed in the
womb showing the lines of fixation.

Quillan-Fle.   XXIII, 47: IGN France.

arrangements with the French authorities to protect the site, which at the moment has obviously been undisturbed for a great time. It is essential that a professional archaeological investigation is carried out prior to any attempt being made to excavate the position. Let would-be treasure hunters be advised that the 'seed' is NOT gold. The buried treasures are elsewhere. Also, rest assured, the 'seed is at a depth well beyond the capability of hand-digging. It would be totally criminal to vandalize the site, but equally irresponsible for the authorities to ignore the place which may contain the greatest secret on this planet. A secret for which thousands of people have died to protect it from the Roman Church.

Keep it in safe hands.

106. The ruins at the place of the seed.

18

The Labyrinth

Yet Thou has power to transmute
Thou naughted unto entity:
O raise me to the sanctuary
Of Thine own Being Absolute

Reflections in the sphere – spider's web – the meridian becomes holy – mathematical impregnation achieved – the imperfect become the perfect.

With the 'seed' located to my satisfaction, I turned my attention to all those questions which must eventually be answered. To present this information to the unbelieving world without any evidence as to who the designers were or when it was constructed, and why it was in France (or in that particular location) would create nothing but chaotic argument. Despite my lack of academic qualifications, I was in possession of certain facts which were not generally known and these would be essential to anyone attempting a solution based on logic. I had no doubt that I was dealing with an advanced intellect, capable of perfection in survey techniques and it was for that reason some aspects of the geometry caused me great concern. The divisions of the circle were apparently imperfect!

It is little known, and mathematically pleasing, to discover that the circumference of a circle can be divided into fifteen equal portions which will then generate a pentagonal figure, with one star-point outside the circle, but still produce **36°** on all five points (illus 107). It is then numerically intriguing to find that by allocating a diameter of **360** units (the identity of a circle) and using the biblical value of $\pi = 3$, the circumference becomes **1080**. Divide this by **15** and the answer is **72** – the base angle of a pentagram! A full examination of this simple figure would fill pages, but its symbolic importance is immediately obvious. I was more puzzled by the fact that the Rennes geometry did not adhere strictly to this system on the ground. Admittedly symbolic π would not work in actual ground measure, but it could have been compromised. Also although a **360,000** inch circle was there, the slightly larger one of just over **372,000** inches was the circle of churches and therefore more important.

I decided to construct the symbolic diagram and to try to incorporate the other amazing circumstances I had found in the Rennes geometry (illus 108). To save hundreds of words of explanation, I would ask the reader to study the diagram. The blue

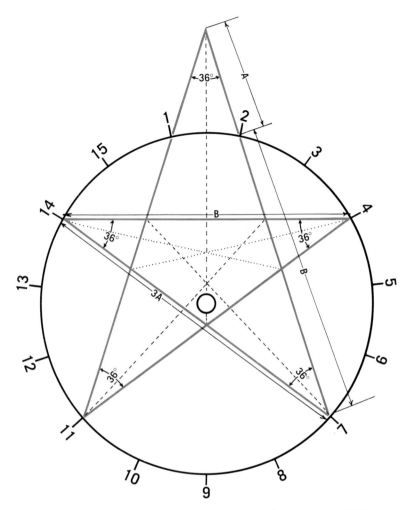

107. The extended pentagram of Rennes based on a circle of 15 divisions. The star point angles are 36° as in the regular pentagram, but note the variation caused in the axes.

dots indicate the **15** divisions of the circle. The positions marked with double rings and infilled with yellow are those where the ground positions of the solution conform, with little variation, to symbolic perfection. Only four positions are thus qualified. The failure of the male axis to find the intersection of the legs of the female should be particularly noticed. Furthermore the meridian does not qualify as 'holy', nor is the vagina of Nut correctly formed. Counting the yellow dots, a score of four is achieved.

The next diagram for consideration is virtually unbelievable – this is the labyrinth – where Theseus killed the Minotaur and was aided by the thread of Ariadne. This is the spider's web (illus 109a).

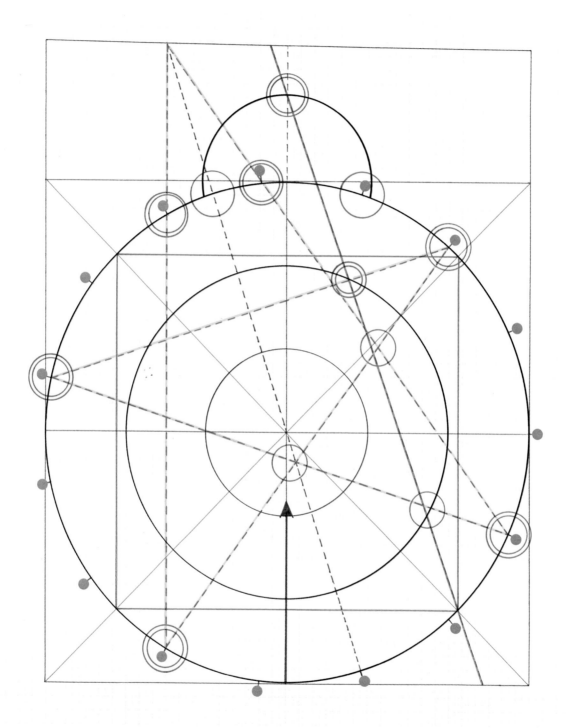

108. The symbolic pentagram correctly inclined with the temple with the meridian and vagina of Nut plotted. The figure fails to conform to the legends. Although there are six correspondences (shaded yellow), the feet of the pentagram do not need to comply with the 15 divisions as will be seen later. The number of the effective positions is therefore 4. (The blue balls mark the 15 dimensions of the circle.)

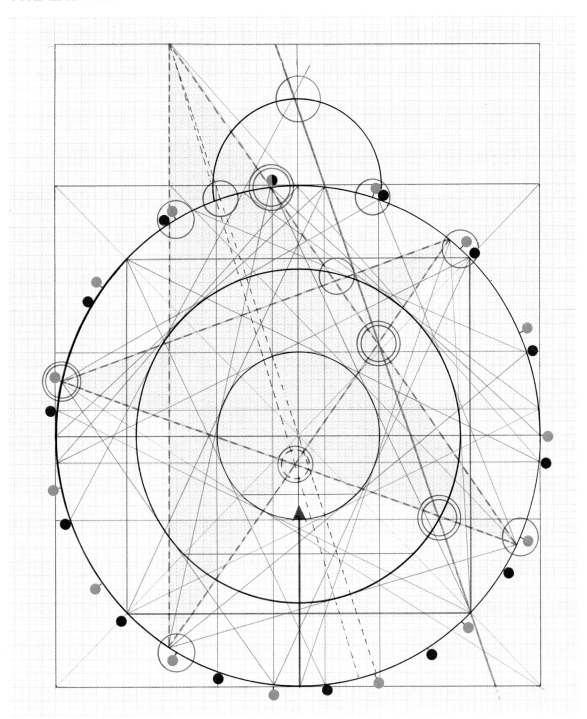

109A. The Labyrinth – representing the sphere of reflected light or the spider's web. It shows an improved adherence to the discipline of the doctrine. The investigation of this geometry revealed that the churches and cardinal points of the Rennes geometry conform to tangentials to the three circles of the temple. (The black balls mark the 14 divisions of the circle, which is a remarkable coincidence when considering the legend of Osiris.)

The construction is basically very simple:

1) Draw three concentric circles of diameter, say **360** units, **240** units and **120** units. (These are the circles of Rennes.)
2) Construct the tangential square and draw the four axes of symmetry. (Upright, horizontal and the diagonals.)
3) Construct the largest internal square which the large circle will accommodate by joining the intersections of the circle and the diagonal axes.

Now go to the position on the circumference of the large circle where any intersections occur and draw lines from that point tangential to the inner circles. Having exhausted the primary intersections on the circle, next go to where these tangential lines produce secondary positions of intersection on the large circle and repeat the process.

The staggering, unbelievable result is that every co-ordinate position in the geometry of the temple of Rennes is generated. When I discovered this and looked back at my temple plotted on a large-scale map, I realized that all these tangential relationships existed there on the ground (illus 109b).

Equally staggering was the fact that the labyrinth also generated positions on the large circumference (marked with black dots) which were those required to divide the circumference into **14** equal parts.

The male axis had found its mark – Rennes-le-Château was ever consistent, and in the vagina of Nut something odd had happened. The eastern junction with the circle had failed on a fifteen-division position, but had coincided with a fourteen one – and that is quite close to the female head rock, Les Toustounes. The score, say five and a half.

There was only one other course open to me if I were to determine which of these diagrams was the key to Rennes. I calculated many of those miraculous linear measures, such as the mile in the womb and the **6.66** miles of the perpendicular height of the pentagrdam. None of them would qualify!

I decided to work the geometry backwards from the map, in order that my assessment would be made from a common standpoint. The result was chaos. I repeated the experiment, but this time beginning with the diameter of the circle of churches at the slightly increased diameter (illus 110). The result – a miracle! Male axis, meridian and womb of Nut were perfect. The dubious womb intersection with the circle of churches was not on a fifteen division, nor a fourteen, but on an EIGHTEEN division position – precisely coinciding with the female head (illus 111). Now, all the linear numbers of 'Celtic' measure conformed. I knew the reason for the slight change in diameter and the small movement in the legs of the female figure. That movement had achieved impregnation, the correct formation of the womb of Nut, and the meridian had entered it according to the 'holy' measures. Was the

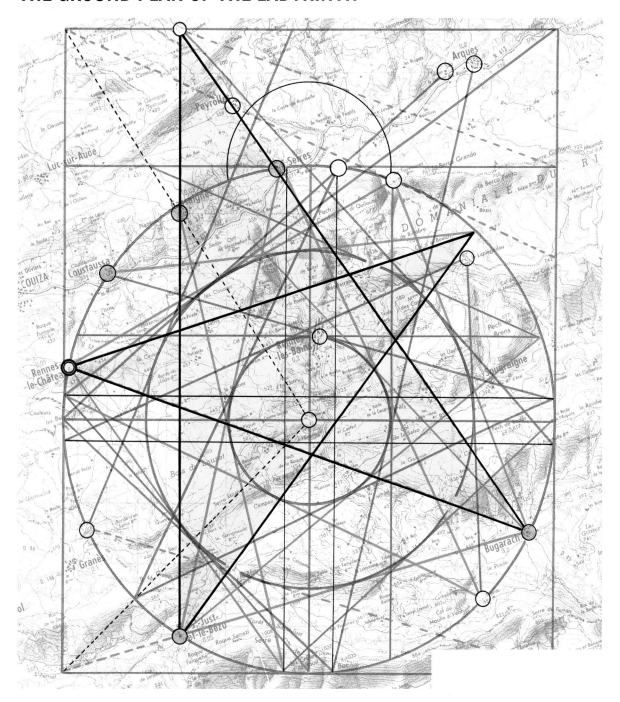

109B. The Labyrinth on the ground.

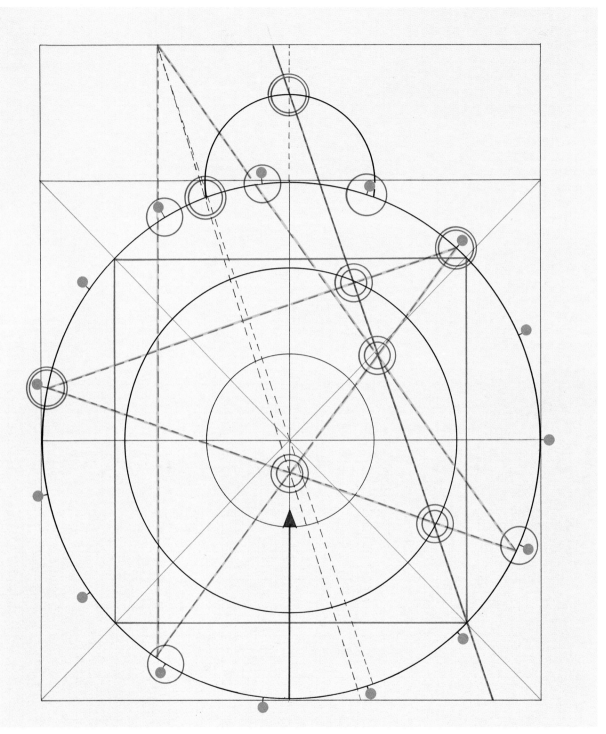

110. The geometry of Rennes plotted onto the circle of 15 divisions showing it to be the best possible correspondence to the doctrine. Even the positions left blank correspond to the linear divisions of the temple.

temple perimeter established without reasonable doubt? Now it was, for it measured precisely 27 miles! – the number of the pregnant womb.

At this point I was at a great advantage. For many years I had tried to identify the numerical identity of the original and ancient gods of Egypt and it was now clear that Rennes would assist me to complete that work. It is a tedious and involved process but, once discovered, it is simple and revealing to operate. It would appear to me that very long ago a superior being realized that if the animal mind of man were to become intelligent, it would inevitably use mathematics and geometry. If the inflexible relationships between geometric shapes and the manner by which they interact were known to be the inevitable by-product of the progression to intelligence; it would only be necessary to establish identities to those figures and the numbers which generated them, to be able to relate myths and legends which carried, concealed in them, mathematical formulae. It would even be possible to lace these figures together to tell a story, a story which the evolving intelligence would wish to know. The story of its own creation!

In the next chapter I give the reader the benefit of a selection of the simplest of these numbers in order that, with hindsight, this system may be more fully understood.

111. The Poussin tomb with the female head rock in the background. Photographed in September at noon when the sun first illuminates the face of the rock.

THE GROUND PLAN OF PERFECTION

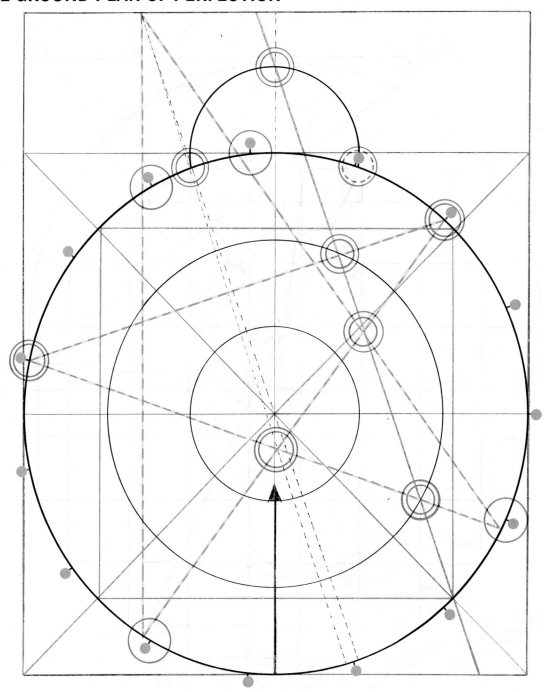

112. The simple elements of the geometry applied to a fugitive map
of the area to illustrate its relationship with the ground features.

19

Language of the Gods

And, strange to tell, among that Earthen Lot
Some could articulate, while others not:
And suddenly one more impatient cried:
'Who is the Potter, pray, and who the Pot?

A good deal of the trouble in the history of the development of
mankind was brought about by differences in language and
religion. The peoples of the world are divided by the language
barrier and in the Bible we are told this was an act of the Lord. He
was apparently angered at the amazing achievements mankind
was capable of when they were united. He said:

. . . Let us go down and there confound their language that they
may not understand one another's speech.

– and from thence did the Lord scatter them abroad upon the face
of all the earth.

Genesis XI, 7 & 9

No one viewing the world today could deny that the Lord
achieved his ambition, and it would require little imagination to
visualize the potential of a united world free of the divisions of
religion and language. However, despite His action, one common
language did survive – mathematics. Numbers and the harmony
of numbers and geometric figures are universally understood. For
our purposes, what is even more important is that they survive
the passage of time.

It will be easily appreciated how two beings, having no language
in common, could each test the intellect of the other by
demonstrating their knowledge of this subject.

The Temple at Rennes-le-Château is evidence of the incredible
ability of its creators to manipulate simple numerical processes to
convey profound meaning. In order to fully appreciate how
advanced is the concealed meaning in the construction, it is
necessary to identify the concepts contained in it and the numbers
allocated to them.

If the reader thinks I may have fallen into the trap of the
'coincidence in the progression of numbers' – I would hasten to
say that this is not the case and, if it appears to be so, I would ask

them to examine the examples more closely lest their simplicity should deceive.

The method you will be shown must not be confused with kabalistic doctrine, which is always dependent upon the spelling of a word. Nor should one mistake this system for the various methods which have been devised to allocate numerical value to names and words and by so doing produce a system of 'fortune-telling'.

It is necessary to recognize the methods which appear to have been used in the symbolic mathematics of the ancient doctrine. One must disregard the zero and the decimal point – we deal here with integers and their recurrence is used to emphasize the concept being conveyed. Nor does a zero affect the meaning, it merely indicates another presence.

A considerable portion of this symbolic numerology hinges on the identification of the 'cubit'. I am sure the reader would not wish me to enter into a discussion of the innumerable methods of arriving at a contemporary measure which would equate to this elusive standard. The standard itself appears to move considerably according to its title – the Common cubit – the Chaldaic cubit, the Egyptian cubit – the Temple cubit – the Sacred Cubit. Having spent countless hours relating these measures to metric and inch measure – I finally decided that the cubit is closely related to the English inch by virtue of their common Celtic origin. The inch value of the cubit has been suggested to be anything from 16″ to 25″ and I am sure it will create antagonism when I say without equivocation – the length of this standard is 18 inches when used for 'occult' symbolism. This is the length of the Common cubit but, to avoid confusion, I will refer to it as the 'Isiac' cubit – confident that in time it will be proved to have been the original.

The Temple at Rennes-le-Château demonstrates this in a most convincing manner, but before proceeding I must first define the 'perfect circle'.

Symbolic perfection in a circle is demonstrated by numerical parity of diameter and angular measure, by which one must appreciate the diameter will be 360 units to equate with the 360 degrees of the circle. I would refer the reader to the perfection of the Temple layout at Rennes-le-Château, where it was established the circle of churches was symbolically 360,000 inches in diameter.

THE IDENTITIES

0 Nut – the origin
This is the symbol of Nut – mother of Set, Isis, Osiris and Nepthys (SION). In illustrations she may be recognized as an inverted crescent or a winged orb.

Apparently of no value, but significantly it is the first number and thereby it is the origin, the hole or holy place from which issues knowledge. As such it equates with the Noé of Noah and the ark, argha, or womb. Like the womb it contains the seed – or the centre without which it would have no form. With few exceptions all these attributes are found in her daughter Isis.

The circumference is the boundary, marking the limit of the comprehension of the animal or human mind. Beyond the circumference dwell the entities of spirit. The Brothers of the Rose Cross refine this image by using three concentric circles with radii of one to two to three. The inner circle represented the earthly plain. Between this and the second radius they placed the air-realm of the earth spirits. From the second to the third radius were the stars – the realm of the superior spirits. Outside this radius, which is the abyss, we are beyond our comprehension – this is the power zone of the ultimate forces of creation where starlight ends and only intellect can see (illus 113).

From this symbolic model, containing all things of matter and spirit, I ask only two things of the reader. Consider first your animal nature – deny it and you condemn yourself to things material. Accept it – identify it – then suppress it – this is the way to achieve a deeper understanding. Despite the inevitability of being contained in animal form, you are not an animal. No animal sees beauty in the sunset, nor will they ever comprehend these abstracts of which we speak.

Secondly I ask you to reject the manufactured images of man-made religions – of a soul without substance, location or purpose – it is nothing but a 'make-weight' – a self-inflated lifejacket worn by those who are unwilling, or unable, to recognize the forces which would be their salvation. The answers are ever-present in the vast and timeless void of the human mind. Nor did creation leave us short of all we would require to expand our powers of conception. As we were conceived, so may we be conceived again – the elixir with which we were elevated from the animal is there in the rose and the lily. As Lucius attained his human form, so may we attain the form of the elevated man.

In the microcosm the circle signifies the womb. The geometry and the numerical values of the Temple of Rennes-le-Château clearly show us the circle and the factors involved therein are totally female. The human builds in squares and cubes, but the gods use circles and spheres and it is woman who is appointed to convey the language they designed and to preserve the secrets. In these secrets lie our salvation. By now medical science should have identified the 'elixir' and made it available for all and no doubt it would have done, had religion not gone to such lengths to conceal it.

The zero also signifies the cyclic aspect of nature – of death and rebirth. We have seen it as the serpent swallowing its tail. It is Nut or Nothing, but geometrically divided it marked the **360** days of the year of the Egyptians and is still divided in this fashion to indicate 'bearing'. Its primary factors are those by which we measure time. As a multiplier it reduces all things to zero – as a divider, all things become infinity.

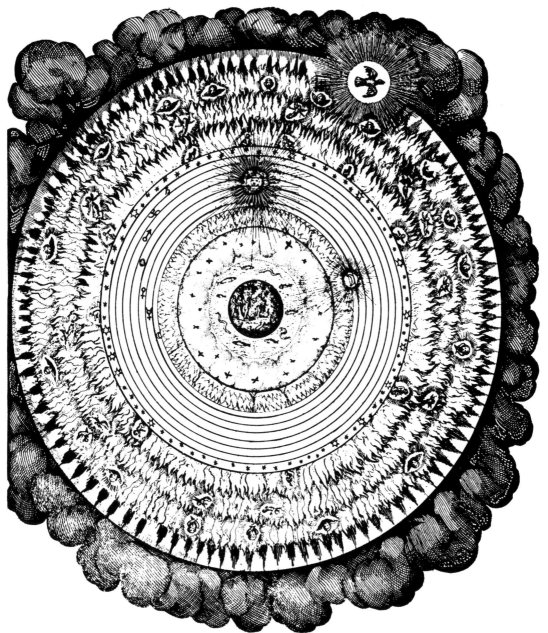

113. Microcosm and macrocosm. With earth as the centre, moving out to water, air and fire and finally the Empyrean – the realm of the spirits.

1 The Ithyphallus

Unity as the word suggests is the instrument of union – the phallus. This image may be found throughout the ancient cultures represented as a totem pole, the mast of a ship, an obelisk and so on. Alone it cannot multiply or divide, but united with the female zero it becomes 10 and as such is capable of both actions. In this form it truly reproduces, and in so doing maintains the character of that upon which it functions. As a vertical or at **90°** it portrays erection, both sexually and in the sense of construction, but in either mode it is impotent unless controlled by the feminine circle. As we have seen, for any erection to be considered holy the lines of construction must follow the geometry of the circle.

Chemically it is hydrogen, the first state of 'being' – the elementary, or simplest form of matter, having only one proton and one electron. It is the reference standard of matter, allocated an Atomic Number of **1**, but not surprisingly it has a molar mass of **1.008**. It is the fuel of the sun and the stars – the primordial matter of the cosmos. It unites with oxygen, the element of Isis, to form water. In a later book I hope to disclose further secrets contained in the geometry of Rennes which will demonstrate hydrogen, oxygen and water are not only the 'building-blocks' of all matter and life, but that they also contain the means by which it may be preserved.

2 Division – Dual Creation

This is the value of division. It symbolizes the creation of the two sexes from the androgyne. It is division for the sake of union, in which were sensations unknown to the spirit entities or the perfected androgynous species, the Elohim. By this, heterosexual union at all levels is seen as essential if one is to become whole or 'holy'. Celibacy and the suppression of the female influence in religion has partially been responsible for generating the homosexual aspect. This denies the participants both the cyclic and regenerative ingredients necessary for the progression of the individual and even of the race as a whole. A million years or more must pass before the physiological and psychological aspects of the sexes unite, but the androgynous couple is ours for the making here and now.

Duality has been associated with the devil or evil, which considering the meaning of the division of the sexes, or accepting the duality of the human in the hybrid sense, is not unreasonable.

3 Woman's Love

A feminine number which has been associated in the past with the Moon, Magdalene, love, and the active principle of Nephthys, at Rennes-le-Château femininity is emphasised by the three concentric circles which lead to the womb of Isis. Also, possibly with greater significance, three circles control the 'star-union' which identified the hexagram of Rennes. The female image of the circle is well established and the biblical description of the Sea of Brass leaves us in no doubt that 3 is the symbolic value of π. And this, in a temple which we now know to have been dedicated to the female principle.

Being the least number of straight lines which are capable of forming a complete figure (the triangle) leads one to suspect the 'triads' should be dominated by a female. A triangle represents a pyramid. 'Pyra' of course means fire, and there is another legend which connects fire with Isis. We are told that Isis, while at Byblos was interrupted in the act of initiating the offspring of Ishtar by means of fire. It is suggested that the child would have become immortal had the ritual not been misunderstood and stopped. Furthermore, in the confusion of the identities of the Egyptian deities, it would not be difficult to equate Hathor and Uatchit with Isis. Uatchit is clearly labelled Lady of the Flames, she who dwells in the eye of Ra. This is further substantiated by the fact that when the priests of Annu were attempting to analyse the ancient company of gods their original company of nine, the *Paut Neteru*, did not include Hathor or Uatchit. Furthermore, the fact that the original gods named were

> TMU, SHU, TEFNUT, SEB, NUT,
> OSIRIS, ISIS, SET, NEPHTHYS

should not mislead the reader into thinking the Egyptians were polytheistic. Despite the innumerable deities and the multitude of names attributed to them, behind it all every Egyptian priest knew there was one and only one Creator.

The Christian teaching is also interesting in that 'God the Father, God the Son and God the Holy Ghost' at first appears to disregard the very existence of a female. Obviously the only 'holy' member is the latter and as the name implies it is feminine. I would further suggest none of these three are meant to represent the Creator. Once we move to the triangle any number of associations are possible.

4 Man – Construction

Here we have the number of the body of the human male and is distinct from the famous number which discloses his origin – **666**, it divides the circle of **360** into the **90°** portions of erection and construction in the form of a square. It is the number which gives numerical parity to perimeter and area when used as the division of the sides of a square:

> Perimeter **4 + 4 + 4 + 4 = 16**   Area **4 × 4 = 16**

This number is the 'building-block' of the human and predominates his thought and design. It marks the seasons, both of the year and life of the human, the animal intelligence cursed with, what is at present the incurable disease of ageing.

5 Feminine Power

The quintessence, femininity par excellence, the pentagon and the pentagram, the figure of five extensions signifying the female body. In the feminine circle the pentagram is completely harmonious, having star-points of **36°** in the numerical equivalent of the **360°** circle. In the bisectors of the points it exhibits the active principle of the supreme goddess Isis, the number **18**. These divisions locate the centre of the circle, the seed or source, or seat. The five star-points of **36°** give us **180**, the number of degrees in a triangle or pyramid and **180** displays the **18** of Isis and the **0** of her mother Nut. The Hebrew word for **5** is Hé, symbolized by the womb.

6 The Sun

Ra, the sun-god of many names, but he is said to have a secret name, known only to Isis. I believe it is a secret number.

As the universal source of power to the earth, he insists that he is acknowledged and worshipped by all earthly creatures – the sustainer of all living things. He provides the energy required by Thoth to exercise the will of the Creator. He marks the passage of the day and the year – all his attributes are masculine and his symbol is the hexagram – the six-pointed star adopted by Judaism. This is also referred to as the Star of David, and King David named his son Sol-om-on in deference to RA.

His number is associated with cyclic motion and he controls the movement of the planets. His own time is measured in periods of **60** of our years (a *hen* period) and two of these represent one year in his life. These values are clearly shown at Rennes as the two intermediate circles. Their radii are **60** and **120** thousand inches and their presence is essential to the harmony of the geometry. It is also significant they are contained within the radius of Isis (**180**), which suggests her superiority, or at least that they fall within her understanding.

The divisions of the sunrise line at Rennes indicate the value of six and it is also referred to in *Le Serpent Rouge*.

7 The Typhon-Set

The sum of the female **3** and the masculine **4**, the androgyne, the intermediate state of existence between the entities of spirit and the animal endowed with intelligence. This is Set, the Typhon, the serpent of Eden, Satan or Lucifer. He brought the light of intelligence into the animal and so created 'thinking' man. For this crime he was 'cast down' for **999** years. Those who have the 'understanding', meaning the biped animal, man, who have feet, hence **12**, the equation is quite simple. The answer is in *Revelation XIII*, 18, for **666** with **12** 'under' or dividing it is **55.5** and it was with Isis (**18**) that this multiplication took place ($55.5 \times 18 = 999$).

Plutarch (*De Iside*) confirms **7** and discloses the active principle of Set as **56**:

> . . . that Typhon escaped out of the battle upon an ass after a flight of SEVEN days . . .

> . . . even the Pythagoreans looked upon Typhon to have been of the rank or order of Demons produced according to them . . . the even number FIFTY-SIX . . .

The number **56** is easily understood when one appreciates the body of Set (**7**) and Isis (**8**) multiplied.

If my reading of the 'secrets' contained at Rennes and Atlantis is correct, man is faced with the ultimate 'Catch 22' situation. The Christian teaching casts Satan as evil, but his crime was to infuse an animal with intelligence, and we are the result of that crime. The simple way to rectify it would be for God to bring about the total annihilation of mankind; but this would constitute another crime, the destruction of a creature of intellect, which God would never do.

Can we blame our parents for our existence when the remedy is in our own hands?

Or have we unknowingly already made a decision which would release the 'gods' from their dilemma?

Are we, even now, creating the weapons and circumstances to bring about the 'purification' of the earth?

Isis, maligned by Christian doctrine, offers the only solution, elevation!

8 Isis

The number of the body of the supreme goddess Isis. daughter of the spirit-entity Nut, but born in flesh. Symbolized by the entwined serpents forming the double womb of infinity. The spiral lemniscate.

The legends of this deity indicate that she is the most perfect of all creatures of animal flesh. Every ancient culture recognized and revered her under one name or the other. She sustains life, and her number is also the atomic number of the element oxygen, an essential of any life process. When oxygen unites with hydrogen, water is formed, giving us **18**, the number of her active principle. The goddess of a thousand names, the most abundant, as Oxygen is the most abundant element on earth.

Her star is eight-pointed and is identical to the star of the beast, but it is rotated to bring single points to North, South, East and West, a movement of **22.5°** (illus 121). This figure conceals many secrets, including the enigmatic **17**, which occurs so persistently in matters connected with Rennes-le-Château. The star is seen to contain **17** enclosures.

9 Pregnancy and Death

A feminine number indicating the period of pregnancy. Revered by the Templars, this is the symbolic number of birth and death, recognized therefore, on the one hand as Osiris and on the other $1 + 8 = 9$ or $9 + 9 = 18$, a simple concealment of the body and the active principle of Isis. It is the factor which converts the dimension of the Holy of Holies (**20**) into the radius of the circle of perfection (**180**).

Two knights on one horse is $9 + 9 = 18$ and, as I promised earlier, I will now complete the solution. A mare has four legs, hence **18** is over or divided by **4**, giving a numerical value of **45**, the star-point value of the star of Isis. Had the horse been a stallion, we would have needed to consider four legs and a phallus, hence **18** is divided by **5**, which is **36**, the star-point value of the pentagram and numerically confirming the circle. One knight would have served our purpose had he been riding a stallion, for the value of the expression would have been **18**. However, had he been riding a mare the value of the image would have failed and Templar mathematics leave no room for failure.

10 The Reproduction

The perfection of animal reproduction – signified by the rigid and tail-swallowing snakes. The Greeks used this as a name for Isis and it is suggested that Io is an alternative representation of the radius of **180**, for divided by **18** the inch value of the cubit, we obtain **10**. The diameter was Demeter (**20**).

OTHER VALUES ASSOCIATED WITH THE MYSTERY

14 The number of parts of the female body or a male body with the phallus removed. It is, therefore, the number which represents Osiris as lord of the underworld. It also signifies a questing knight, suitably prepared to be a keeper of the Grail.

If we multiply this number by the Isis factor **18** and we obtain **252**, the number of days in **9** lunar months of **28** days, the period of the menstrual cycle of a woman.

15 The number of parts of the male body:

   2 hands
   2 forearms
   2 upper arms
   2 feet
   2 legs
   2 thighs
   1 torso
   1 head
   1 phallus

It is the number of Osiris in his original form and after his resurrection. He was king to Isis and in death became Lord of the Underworld – by the power of Thoth he was resurrected and from this the ISHTAR-TAMMUZ-ADONIS legends originated. An incredible secret is confirmed in his resurrection, known by both Isis and Thoth. Possibly in time this secret passed into the hands of the Templars.

Again, by multiplying by the Isis factor (**18**), **15 × 18 = 270** representing **9** months of **30** days of pregnancy in the **360**-day year, composed of **12** months of **30** days each.

For those who have the 'understanding', the reciprocal of **15** is **666**.

17 A number which persistently occurs in the mystery and to which several references have been made. The fact that, together with its reflection, it emphasizes the body of Isis (**17** + **71** = **88**), seems of little account, but it also confirms something less obvious. The ark sailed on the **17th** and grounded on the **17th**, five months later. With a year of **360** days, the ark would have been afloat for **150** days and **150** divided by **17** is **8.8** which is certainly coincidental. Furthermore, **150** days is **3600** hours, an inescapable connection with the circle and the female organ.

The depth of the flood water was said to be **15** cubits and the value of the cubit has been established at **18** inches. The depth of flood water was, therefore, **270** inches, the period of pregnancy. These numerical pointers, together with the equation of the ark and the womb containing the seeds of life, leave us in no doubt as to the meaning of the allegory, this ark was the 'boat' of Isis.

18 This is the function of Isis and one of the 'keys' to the mysteries. It is this number which appears to rationalize numerical descriptions in esoteric texts. Ark, Grail, Round Table, Atlantis and many more, all respond to this number and become immediately meaningful.

With the name Isis meaning 'seat' in all respects, and assuming the standard height of a seat to be **18** inches, the number of man (**4**) is confirmed by the simple recognition that a **6**-foot standard man has **4** divisions of **18** inches both in height and across his outstretched arms. In this position the body of the man represents the 'crux ansata'. It is interesting to observe that the circular part in the emblem doubles as his head and the female genitals. Once again we find the equation – intellect (the head of the man) = the womb (the source of intelligence).

The complete symbol of the Isis principle is the caduceus – here we see the 'one-in-eight'. The two serpents entwined to represent the vagina and the womb, through both of which passes the phallus.

In the figure of the pentagram, although **18** is not immediately apparent, the axes passing through the **36°** star-points bisect those angles to form **18°**. These five axes intersect at the centre of the circle containing the pentagram. If each of these axes is then extended, they divide the opposing legs of the pentagram at the positions which represent the female reproductive organ. Remembering that **360** divided by **18** is **20** – the number of the Holy of Holies – and that the pentagonal **5** multiplied by **18** equates with the **90°** of erection, it is hardly surprising that this number was so important in ancient doctrine.

20 A holy number – to the Jews it is the number of the Holy of Holies in the Temple of Solomon. The dimensions of this most sacred place were **20** × **20** × **20** cubits, but we have established the value of the cubit to be **18** inches. The hidden shape is now obvious. It is sphere with a diameter of **360** or a radius of **180**. It is the womb of Isis. It contained the Ark of the Covenant which carries, concealed in its dimensions, the same identity.

As is often the case, the concealed number is in the diagonal somewhere. Here we have a square, the side of which is **20**, therefore the square on the diagonal or the hypotenuse is **800**.

28 Nephthys – Goddess of Death and resurrection. She possessed magical powers which were almost equal to those of her sister Isis. Together they reconstructed the body of Osiris after it had been dismembered by Set. She was the mother of Anubis the Jackal-headed God of the Dead who escorted souls of the dead to the Underworld. Set was the husband of Nephthys, and should therefore have been the father of Anubis, but legend suggests that an illicit union took place between her and Osiris who may therefore have been the actual father. This may well have been the reason Set murdered Osiris and sought union with Isis.

Nephthys is considered to be the female counterpart of Set and she forms the 'N' of Sion. As the division of Set (**2 × 28 = 56**), she represents the time cycle of the lunar month marking the menstrual period of the female. It is divided as **14** and **14**, signifying the parts of the female body. These are the periods of light and darkness symbolized by the rose and the lily, or the alternating black and white squares of the church of Rennes-le-Château which we have identified as Nephthys in the geometry of the temple.

30 Another time-cycle, the solar month from the time when the year was **12** months of **30** days. In Egyptian mythology the year was divided into **36** decans of **10** days. Hence, with a month of **3** weeks, the masculine solar cycle was still controlled by feminine factors.

33 This number is one of the 'keys'. It establishes the link between temple construction and the feminine principle. Geometrically it is the number of degrees which locate the corners of the north wall of the temple from the centre of the circle of churches. The **33rd** degree marks the zenith of Freemasonry, whose rituals are steeped in the legends of the Temple of Solomon and more particularly of its architect Hiram Abiff. It is interesting to note that the north wall is not fixed by this alone, it is also determined by the northern star-point of the female pentagram.

It will be appreciated that any perfect square of construction may be considered 'holy', as its co-ordinates can be controlled by a circle. Rectangles, on the other hand, are unacceptable in holy places unless they are very carefully designed to conform to the feminine principles. At Rennes-le-Château we are shown one of the methods by which the masculine rectangle may have been considered to have acquired the necessary attributes to become 'holy'. I wonder if the reader by now has the 'understanding' to realize why **666** divided by **333** is **20. 18 18 18**, the 'Holy of Holies' and the Isis factor.

The union of Isis and Osiris is also demonstrated in this number, **18 + 15 = 33**.

An isosceles triangle, the equal sides with a value of **18** enclosing a right angle generate **648** as the square on the hypotenuse (**18** squared + **18** squared = **648**) and **648 + 33 = 681**. I am sure I have no need to remind the reader of the enigmatic cipher of Rennes – PEACE 681.

Nor is it coincidence that **648 + 18 = 666**!

54 In the pentagonal representation of the female body the lower portion of the trunk is formed by an angle of **108°**. Here is the genital organ and thereby we may see that **54** denotes the sublime division of the female body, the exterior vulva or place of entry.

56 The active principle of the force of Typhon (see 7).

58 This is the number of the Priory of Sion. It is the total of the gods, Set, Isis, Osiris and Nephthys (**7 + 8 + 15 + 28**) and was the number on the Templar skull (see Chapter 11).

60 The number of time where time is the cage of the concept of the human mind. The number indicates that the secret of this control is contained in the sun. In the simple sense the sun traverses the arc of the heavens of Nut in the 'boat of millions of years'. To the Egyptians 60 years was a *hen* period, half a year in the life of Ra. He can therefore conform to the feminine circle of **360** which is **6** half-year periods or **3** solar years of **120** of our years. These **6** divisions of the circle may be joined to form the 6-pointed

64 A symbolic number adopted by the Knights Templar, the number of squares of a chess-board – it is composed by a square or a cube – **8 × 8 = 64** or **4 × 4 × 4 = 64**.

Female predominance is again indicated by adding the factors – **8 + 8 + 4 + 4 + 4 = 28**. The significance of this number and in particular the chess-board and the **64** stones of the mystery of the Rennes valley have been dealt with elsewhere.

66 This appears to be the number of Thoth, representing the divine intelligence introduced in some measure into animal form – the human. As the 'mighty speaker' he signifies the power which enabled the human to occupy the unique position in the animal kingdom of being able to convey thought by speech. He represents truth, as does his female consort Maat – daughter of the mighty Ra. That speech should only be used to utter truth is clearly defined, and those who seek the keys to the mysteries would be well advised to remember it.

The association with the sun indicated by the number **6** is of paramount importance, for as the husband of the daughter of Ra he carries out the wishes of Ra on the material plane. The sun provides the power and controls the time to permit Thoth to function. His close association with Isis is undeniable, and he is always seen as her friend in time of need. This partnership enables them to control apparent time and its visible counterpart, light. Even in the underworld Thoth was unassailable, and it was within his power to ressurect the dead to the eternal life. Osiris who is **15** is reflected as **51** and these two numbers unite as **66** to show the presence of Thoth, who is often depicted standing with Osiris at the gate of the underworld.

Hieroglyphically he is the ibis bird and for those who have the 'understanding' the long beak can be recognized elsewhere, as can be the 'source' from which he drinks. He is also shown as a baboon or a cynocephalus, the kaf ape. This imagery indicates his close association with the events which led to the origin of our species. He is the master of the arts and sciences and Lord of the Measures, equating with the Chaldaic Shaitan.

The process of reversing or reflecting is obviously not applicable in the case of **66** – in other words Thoth has no reflection.

69 This is the number of oral sex, *soixante-neuf*. Some simple mathematics will reveal more than many words and the reader should gather great meaning from it:
69 + **81** = **150** and **96** + **18** = **114**. If this is confusing let us demonstrate something more obvious: **69** − **18** = **51** and **96** − **81** = **15**. But **69** + **18** + **51** + **96** + **81** + **15** = **330**! And so – but for the intervention of Isis the sun or son would have died.

Again it is not coincidental that **96** − **69** = **27**, the integers of pregnancy and the reflection of **72** the base angle of a pentagram.

81 The reflection of the active principle of Isis – a number which establishes the law and order of the origin of numbers. It acts upon the cardinal points of the circular compass representing space to produce the 'building-blocks' of the language of the gods.

90 divided by **81** = **1.111**	**450** divided by **81** = **5.555**
180 divided by **81** = **2.222**	**540** divided by **81** = **6.666**
270 divided by **81** = **3.333**	**630** divided by **81** = **7.777**
360 divided by **81** = **4.444**	**720** divided by **81** = **8.888**

The significance of this to the people who devised it is obvious, particularly that of the last expression.

This system will not produce **9**, which signifies death.

The reciprocal of **81** is **123456790**, − **8** is missing, for the reflection of Isis cannot reflect her body.

90 This is, of course, the number of the Pythagorean, or Ophite, it is the number by which the circle is squared ($4 \times 90 = 360$) and may therefore be represented in architectural form. As **90°** it represents erection and is therefore male. It should be remembered however, that the symbol of Pythagoras was the pentagram, which may be explained by recognizing that **90** has the factors **5 × 18**, both pentagonal and undeniably feminine. Even when acted upon by the essence of masculinity, **6**, it becomes **6× 90 = 540**, which is sublimely feminine.

180 The active principle of Isis (**18**) born out of her mother Nut (**0**) forming the radius of the circle of perfection. It is the union of the seed or centre with the circumference. It represents the epitome of the understanding of all things within the circumference which is the abyss. We must remember that the symbolic value of π is **3** and the symbolic circumference must therefore be $2\pi r = 1080$. This symbolic circumference is divided into both **18** and **15** parts in the circle of churches at Rennes and these divisions identify the markers. The product of **18** and **15** is **270** and **1080**, which divided by **270** is **4**, shows man to be the outcoume of the period of pregnancy. The circumference **1080** divided by **18** and **15** produces **60** and **72** respectively – time and light? The product of **60** and **72** is **4320**. This number divided by **666** is **648.648 648′** – the emphasized numerical value of the squared hypotenuse of the isosceles triangle of Isis (a triangle with equal sides of **18** enclosing the right angle, hence 2×18 squared).

270 The number of pregnancy where in a year of **360** days, **270** days is **9** months of **30** days. It may also be demonstrated as **27**. Its reflection is **72** or the **720** of the Vesica Piscis explained in Chapter 18. Where **27** or **270** occur, the presence of the pregnant womb or pregnancy is being shown to us.

360 The totality of the female generative organ encompassing time (**60**) controlled by Ra (**6**). The pentagonal (**36**) identifies the pentagram as the alternative geometric representation of the circle, which in turn led us to discover the secret of the common womb.

When divided by the phallus (**90**) the womb (**360**) provides the cardinal points or primary 'bearings', the first-born.

666

Here is wisdom. Let him that hath understanding count the number of the beast: for it is the number of a man, and his number is six hundred threescore and six.

Revelation XIII, 18

This is the identity of man which reveals his hybrid nature as being half-animal and half-god. It personifies the crime of introducing intellect into a beast. It is for this reason it has been associated with evil. Hundreds of people have written thousands of words in an attempt to explain it. Ecclesiastical authorities have tried to make out that it is not there and, given time, it will not be. Already I have heard there are those who wish to remove *Revelation* from the Bible.

I would not wish to argue with men of great learning about the meaning of this number, but of some things I am sure: Ra is present (**6**), Thoth is present (**66**), the principle of Isis could also be present ($3 \times 6 = 18$), and even the Seal of Solomon could be there ($666 \times 5 = 3330$).

We have already seen that the reciprocal of **666** is **15**, which draws our attention to a possible connection with Osiris. In that connection we must consider an unusual impregnation. In *Thrice Greatest Hermes* by G. R. S. Mead, Horus asks Isis how Earth received God's efflux. Isis replied:

> I may not tell the story of this birth; for it is not permitted to describe the origin of thy descent, O Horus of mighty power, lest afterwards the way-of-birth of the immortal gods should be known unto men – except so far that God the Monarch, the universal Orderer and Architect, sent for a little while thy mighty sire Osiris, and mightiest goddess Isis, that they might help the world for all things needed them.
> 'Tis they who filled life full of life. 'Tis they who caused the savagery of mutual slaughtering of men to cease. 'Tis they who hallowed the precincts to the Gods their ancestors and spots for holy rites. 'Tis they who gave to men laws, food and shelter.

Obviously a secret method of impregnation is implied. We know from the Isis-Ra legend that the sun (**6**) weakened and would have died (**9**) but for Isis. We also know that she was instrumental in the resurrection of Osiris. Another resurrection comes to mind involving the death of a son, who we are told 'rose' on the third day. I wonder if we were meant to understand that three days is **72** hours (3×24), a pentagonal number and therefore female. Furthermore, the mathematical expression for oral coupling is **96 – 69** which is **27**. It is no doubt 'coincidence' that once again the numbers indicate what probably happened – pregnancy by unusual means. It is also significant that **180** divided by **27** equals **666**!

By this and many other confirmations in this book, at Rennes and in Plato's dialogue of Atlantis, I have attempted to convey the meaning of **666**; I will leave the reader to judge whether my assessment is the correct one.

Over the years I have pursued threads of evidence which eventually allowed me to solve the geometry of Rennes. I have been continually confronted with items which at first seemed as if they were coincidence, but were not. Coincidence is usally the resultant outcome of events being acted upon by forces of which we are unaware.

Having acquired the basic principles of the universal language of mathematics, the reader may care to apply it to the solution of other numerical values quoted in myth and legend. I have demonstrated only the simplest elements of the system and I am sure others will take up the baton. Before leaving this intriguing process, allow me to give another example totally unconnected with our mystery. *Our Ancestors Came from Outer Space*⋆ by Maurice Chatelain, discusses the possibility of a mathematical constant existing in the ancient past, which he refers to as the 'Nineveh Constant'. He gives this as **2268** million days. He suggests that this number encompasses the cycles of all the planets of our solar system and I could not resist the temptation of applying the Isis code. And it was there. **18 × 81 + 810 = 2268**. But where you may ask have I demonstrated cyclic motion? Let us try again, the female cycle is **28** and **28 × 81 = 2268**!

You have seen here only a small part of a language, the grammar of which was developed from simple mathematical functions. Mathematics is an early and inevitable by-product of intellect and by attributing identities to the values in it, particularly those controlled by geometric figures, the designers ensured that the story of the origin of that intellect would never be lost and could never be falsified. It was only necessary to record the numbers which were equivalent to the participants and the story told itself. This is the beginning of the rediscovery of that language.

⋆*Our Ancestors Came from Outer Space* (Pan: London, 1970)

20

Clues Everywhere

Myself when young did eagerly frequent
Doctor and Saint, and heard great Argument
About it and about: but evermore
Came out by the same Door as in I went.

Leonardo da Vinci – the Mona Lisa – the Virgin of the Rocks – Celtic stones – the Rubáiyáit of Omar Khayyám – connections in Majorca – the Poussin tomb

In the course of my inquiries into the mystery, I explored many blind alleys. Often they seemed to carry signposts which pointed somewhere, but then I recognized they were the results of someone in history merely wishing to make record of their association either with the location of Rennes-le-Château or the secrets contained there. The main elements of the mystery must have been obvious to the Roman Church and for that reason the marks of distinction were, of necessity, ambiguous. Only by association of related factors and viewed with hindsight can they be easily detected. In fact, at times, one could claim that proof of a great mystery might be established by nothing other than sheer volume of apparently unrelated coincidences that eventually conspire to link together. For so many illustrious names in history to have been involved convinces me of the importance of the secret which they shared. Even Louis XIV, King of France, went to considerable lengths to pursue this mystery. He knew that the Poussin painting *Les Bergers d'Arcadie* held clues, and he eventually became its owner. His interest was no doubt precipitated by a strange letter which his Superintendent of Finances, Nicolas Fouquet, received from his brother, the Abbé Louis Fouquet, after the latter had met with Poussin in Rome.

Part of the letter reads:

> He and I discussed certain things, which I shall with ease be able to explain to you in detail. Things which will give you, through Monsieur Poussin, advantages which even kings would have great pains to draw from him and which, according to him, it is possible that nobody else will ever rediscover in the centuries to come. And what is more, these are things so difficult to discover that nothing now on this earth can prove of better fortune nor be their equal.

It is also of significance that a third brother of the Fouquet family was the Archbishop of Narbonne, the old Celtic capital which controlled the area of Rennes-le-Château.

I have selected a few items such as this, not to strengthen the evidence, for that is already overpowering enough, but rather in order that the reader will appreciate how widespread the subject is in both time and location.

Leonardo da Vinci (1452–1519)

This illustrious man needs no introduction and, as the creator of the *Mona Lisa*, he is immediately thought of as one of the world's most famous painters. Indeed he was, but he was much more. He was a scientist, and his artistic talent was developed as much for the purpose of recording the designs he conceived, as to produce works of art. That his name should appear as a Grand Master of the Priory of Sion (1510–1519) did not surprise me any more than when I read that he was fascinated with geometry.

I decided to make a brief study of his paintings to see whether he had left any recognizable clues in them which would associate him with those parts of the mystery that I had already solved.

115. *School of Athens* in which Leonardo depicts himself as Plato carrying the Timeo.

114. *The Mona Lisa* (Leonardo da Vinci, 1503, Louvre).

Virgin of the Rocks by da Vinci (Louvre).

116. *Virgin of the Rocks* by da Vinci (National Gallery).

Naturally the first subject I considered was the *Mona Lisa*; not the painting itself, but the name of it. MONA is a simple anagram of AMON, one of the oldest and most powerful of the early Egyptian deities. Furthermore, he was one of the gods of creation. He was associated with the realm beyond the primeval abyss and he was 'hidden', which is the meaning of AMON. Thebes was the centre of worship for this god and when the city became the capital, his priests lost no time in declaring AMON to be the most powerful of all gods. His attributes were so like the sun-god Ra that the names were combined as AMON-RA, in which form he was worshipped as the 'invisible creative power, source of all life, God of the Great Deep and the Underworld'.

LISA is simply L'ISA and Godfrey Higgins[*] tells us quite clearly that ISA is the Eve or Isis. Under the nose of the Roman Church he had called this painting Ra-Isis, which leaves me in no doubt as to why she wears her knowing smile. If the Pope realized the implication behind the name of the painting, it may explain why the relationship between him and Leonardo was so strained.

The next painting which attracted me was *School of Athens* (illus 114). In this Leonardo paints himself posing as Plato carrying a copy of *Timeo*. It would seem to me Leonardo knew something of the Atlantis–Rennes connection, which we will deal with later.

My last example from the works of Leonardo is the controversial *Virgin of the Rocks*. Two copies of this painting exist today, one in the National Gallery and the other in the Louvre. For a while, great argument ensued as to which was the original and which was a student's copy but it is now generally agreed that the Master's hand can be recognized in both works. Certain details in the paintings immediately caught my eye, apart from those which have been discussed over the years. Precisely who these two ladies are and why there are two children could involve us in hours of discussion and, at the end, the answers would still be only a matter of opinion. My interest was in the geometric analysis of the pictures, and I spent several hours trying to determine whether they followed the same construction, or whether each was a part of something larger. I was intrigued to find in the National Gallery version that, apart from the obvious control line of the cross on the shoulder of the child, the geometry was dependent upon a small 'white flower' in the foreground. The petals of this flower are unnaturally folded back to reveal a disproportionate erect stamen (illus 117). I recognized that this was Leonardo's way of expressing his allegiance to the French king, with whom he was finally quite openly associated. This was the 'fleur-de-lis', the flower of the lily, symbol of the French monarchy, to which we will return shortly. Equally unnatural was a strange rock feature resembling a bridge (illus 119). This was obvious in both works, and further examination of this and other strangely shaped rocks caused me to compare them with certain features in the Rennes valley. I was amazed to find that there were remarkable similarities. It then struck me that if the shapes of these rocks were

117. Detail from the *Virgin of the Rocks* showing the open petals and erect stamen.

118. Nephthys crowned with her symbol – the goddess of the house.

[*]*Anacalypsis*, Vol. 1, p. 274.

common to both works to such a degree, it could not have been by chance. I reasoned that if they were identifiable with ground features, it would be unlikely for both paintings to conform to the requirements. My inquiry produced something quite remarkable for, despite the obvious changes in the foreground figures, the rocks in the background appeared to match each other.

I took a high-precision photographic copy of each painting and adjusted their scales to match the background features. I could hardly believe what I saw – the outline of the common features registered with each other in a manner which could have never

119. Detail from *Virgin of the Rocks* showing the Nephthys outline and the triangular rock shape on the northern slopes of Château de Blanchefort.

happened by visual copying or even by measurement. They must have been traced to achieve such a degree of accuracy. By superimposing the photographic image of each and printing in different colours, I have demonstrated to the reader just how accurate the register is between them (illus 120). It was now obvious that Leonardo had considered changes in the foreground figures to be of little consequence, but the position of the rock features was paramount. These features all exist in the valley of

120. The National Gallery Virgin superimposed on the version from the Louvre, showing that the rock features of significance to the solution register with each other. Note the crescent formed by the variation in framing.

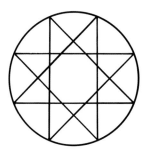

121. The Star of Isis and The Sigil of the Beast.

Rennes-le-Château! It may also be seen that the superimposition of the two images cast a crescent shape which we know to be the symbol of the goddess Nut.

Nephthys is indicated by the shape of the hole in the cave on the right of the picture. This unusual outline is a clear representation of her symbol and corresponds to the angle of view to Rennes-le-Château, the church of her identity from the second location (illus 119).

La Vraie Langue celtique et le Cromleck de Rennes-les-Bains

A number of references have already been made to this work by Abbé Henri Boudet, curé of Rennes-les-Bains and a close associate of Bérenger Saunière. He would appear to have been an expert in local history and was involved in the resurgence of Cathar beliefs which occurred in the late 1800s. Most, if not all, of the wealth which Saunière disposed of seems to have emanated from Boudet, who was probably acting as cashier for the Priory of Sion. Anyone taking an interest in the local and comparatively recent manifestations of the mystery is bound to find the hand of Boudet involved in some way. His activities and those of his associates were no secret to the Vatican, who strongly condemned what it saw as a recurrence of the Albigensian cancer. For someone who has the 'undestanding', he surrounded himself with imagery which was blatantly obvious. The floor of the church at Rennes-le-Bains is a good example and it is composed of the now-familiar Star of Isis, or sigil of the beast (illus 123), confirming our previous identification of the church with Isis. Much, if not all, of the bizarre decoration in the church of Rennes-le-Château was of his design.

Apart from these significant factors, Boudet produced a hill-shaded map of the valley in which, in my opinion, he is more concerned with the image he wished to convey than the accuracy of it. Would it be stretching the imagination too far if I suggest it looks like an intentional attempt to portray the district as an anatomical illustration, representing the reproductive organs of a woman (illus 122). If nothing else, it certainly shows how active the Celtic stonemasons were in this district.

The Rubáiyát of Omar Khayyám

I trust that the reader will have noticed that each chapter of this book begins with a quatrain from Edward FitzGerald's first translation of the *Rubáiyát*. Even bearing in mind the inevitable losses which would be bound to occur in such a translation, Omar discloses, with great subtlety, that he was well informed of the secrets in the ancient doctrine. I was staggered to see a comment by George F. Maine, who edited the Collins edition where, in referring to the Cambridge codex, he says:

> . . . of its 252 quatrains hardly any can be said to bear evidence of mystical teaching; . . .

123. Isis or Beast? The floor pattern of the church of Rennes-les-Bains.

RENNES CELTIQVE.

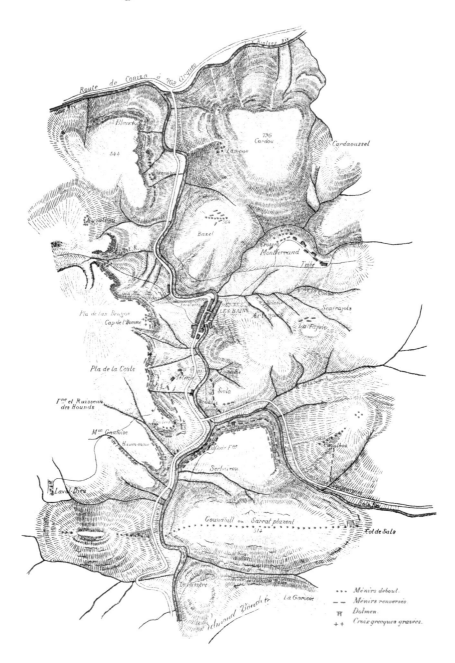

122. Henri Boudet's map of Celtic Rennes showing the concentration of 'standing stones' in the area.

I suggest he looks again at the quatrain at the head of Chapter 6 of this book, 'for "Is" and "Is-Not" though with Rule and Line' leaves me in no doubt of the identity of ISIS and NUT. Rest assured, Omar knew!

However, apart from the common ground of demonstrating a deep knowledge of the doctrine, it may seem unlikely to the casual reader that the *Rubáiyát* could be directly associated with our subject; but it is very closely associated. The story of the life of Omar Khayyám is woven into the tapestry in the same way as those of many others who at first appear remote.

Omar Khayyám lived at the end of the eleventh century and was said to have made a pact in his younger days with two students who were his closest friends. Simply, the agreement was that if any one of them should prosper, he would help the other two. Omar's friends were Nizam-ul-Mulk and Hasan Ben Sabbah. Nizam-ul-Mulk rose to the exalted position of Administrator of Affairs to the Sultan Alp Araslan. One of the friends, Hasan Ben Sabbah, prevailed on him to keep his promise. This Nizam did, and Hasan obtained a post in the government. Not content with this, he began to scheme for higher places. He was exposed, discredited and dismissed. He eventually became the leader of the Ismailians, a secret society known as the Assassins and he was the 'Old Man of the Mountains' who was so closely associated with the Knights Templar.

The Assassins were accused of everything the Templars were, if not more, and their history is lost in obscurity. They were nevertheless supposedly in possession of the great secrets of the ancient knowledge. They were also believed to be connected with the Yezidi who worshipped a strange god called Shaitan. Furthermore, it was known they had more than a passing knowledge of the design of the Temple of Solomon.

Concerning the pact of which we spoke earlier, Omar Khayyám also came to Nizam for help, but he asked for nothing more than a pension and a chance to study the sciences. This was granted and he became a man of great learning. He died in 1123 and one of his pupils said that Omar had told him:

> My tomb shall be in a spot where the north wind may scatter roses over it.

There can be little doubt that the friendship between Omar and Hasan survived the dismissal of the latter. Neither can we doubt Omar's intention of recording the secret 'between the lines' of the Rubáiyát.

The Fleur-de-lis

This heraldic device is now commonplace in many countries, but traditionally it is associated with France, where it was supposed to have originated. It has been suggested it was first adopted by Clovis, the founder of the Frankish Monarchy, who was the

124. Various Fleur-de-lis, a stylised symbol representing the female organ.

champion of the Roman Church and introduced Christianity into Europe at the point of a sword. Although it has been stylized out of recognition (illus 124), I am sure the reader will soon see the hidden meaning in the symbol.

Initially we should dismiss the idea that it appeared first at the baptism of Clovis; it is a symbol of great antiquity and occurs in ancient Egypt as a symbol of life and resurrection. It is undoubtedly female and in its earlier forms was recognizable as such (illus 125). It is a cross-section of the female organ with the labia open to reveal the clitoris. This is the flower of the *Virgin of the Rocks* by Leonardo with its petals open to expose the stamen. It is the flower of the lily, the lily of the valley.

125. A Jewish coin, B.C. showing the female organ – an early equivalent of the lily of the valley and the fleur-de-lis.

The Majorcan Connection

Among the Templars who escaped the initial arrest were those who were established in Spain, in particular the Aragonese Templars. The Archbishop of Tarragona and the bishop of Valencia were named as the custodians of the Templars' possessions in Spain and moves were made to bring them to trial. Once again, as in England, the papacy was greatly handicapped by being forbidden, under Aragonese law, to torture captives. Without the 'confessions' achieved by this method in France, the trials were largely a failure. I wondered if I could find anything of the secret doctrine which had survived in that area. The kingdom most closely associated with Aragon was Majorca and I recalled something I had acquired from an antique shop on the island. It was a brass crucifix with the body of Christ on one side, but on the reverse was the figure of a woman, obviously a young woman. I decided to intensify my search and in the process of it, I visited the Monastery of San Salvador. There, in a small gift shop, I saw something which left me in a state of shock. Thousands of tourists must have looked at the Plaque of Inauguration which was displayed on the wall. In its full-colour presentation, it dazzles the eyes of those who have no knowledge of the secret doctrine (illus 126), but many symbols on the plaque were immediately obvious to me. Nothing could have been clearer than the eight-pointed

127. Details from the San Salvador surround clearly showing the beast drinking from and extending his tongue into the lily.

126. The plaque of the Monastery of San Salvador – Felanitx –
Majorca covered in symbols of the secret doctrine.

Star of Isis behind the Madonna, and it is positioned with two points uppermost, the Star of the Beast. In the circle containing the star can be seen the smaller circle of the womb. From the two upper points of the star which marks an eighth division of the circle, the feature carrying the words 'Mater Salvatori' forms the vaginal cavity. Within this area the circumference of the large circle is broken by a crucifix to complete the imagery of Rennes, for it marks the position of the line of the sunrise as near as is possible in an illustration of this type.

The reader will no doubt recognize many other significant features, but in particular we should study the wide surround of leaves and flowers, or fleur-de-lis. Look at the monochrome enlargements, and in the first can be seen the mouth of the beast drinking from the cup between the leaves (illus 127a). Furthermore, look at another version of it (illus 127b) where the long, thin tongue of the beast penetrates through the leaves to touch the stamen. Could all these images occur by chance?

Poussin and the Tomb

The tomb featured in Poussin's *Les Bergers d'Arcadie* is on the road from Arques to Serres, and its position has already been shown to have been chosen by someone who was aware of at least some of the geometry of Rennes.

Apart from its position we are now able to recognize the reason for some of its dimensions (illus 129)

1) The height of the main block is **42"**, the length is **100"**, hence the diagonal to the nearest whole number is **108** (Isis and Nut).
2) The height of **42"** was probably meant to be **41.95"**, the square root of **1760** reminding us to use Celtic measure.
3) The width is **54"** (the sublime division of the **108°** angle of the lower body of the pentagonal female).
4) The diagonal of the side is **68**, which appears to contribute nothing, but when added to the other diagonal of **108** we have **176**, another reminder of Celtic connections and, conveniently, it is the reverse or reflection of the length of the lid which is **86** inches.
5) The difference between the length of the lid (**86**) and the main structure (**100**) is **14**, the number of Osiris with his phallus removed.
6) The difference between the width of the tomb (**54**) and the width of the lid (**36**) is **18**, which is Isis and the **36** needs no explanation.

Apart from arranging that the kneeling shepherd in the painting points to the letter R, which is the **18th** letter of the alphabet, the expression ET IN ARCADIA EGO has **14** letters in it. It also seemed more than coincidental that the numerical total of the word ARCADIA was **37**. This number when multiplied by **18**

128. The Poussin Tomb defaced as it is today.

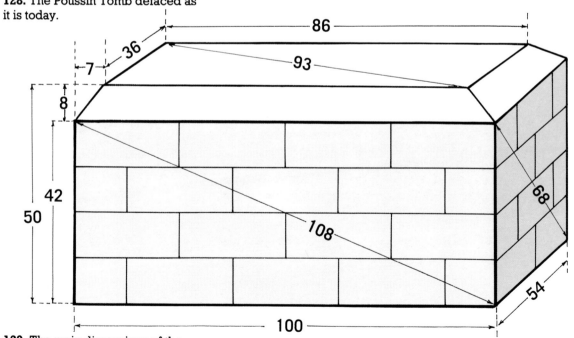

129. The main dimensions of the Poussin tomb.

gives **666**. The remaining letters ET IN EGO total **75** which reflected is **57** the height of the tomb which with the inch removed is the ominous number of the Typhonic principle (illus 130).

It has been said that when the Abbé Antoine Bigou was entrusted with the secret, he went to considerable trouble to deface the tomb (illus 128). But on the reverse side the stones are still quite well defined. If we assume their regularity we find that on the main face we have **18** (**14** large and **4** small). On the width we have **10**. Therefore, the total number of face stones showing would have been **56** (**18** + **18** + **10** + **10**), which gives the average number of face stones as **14**:

ISIS, OSIRIS AND SET ARE REVEALED!

Could anyone say that all this is coincidence? All things considered, the solution to any cipher is achieved when the 'key' is discovered. The logical extension of finding these persistent numbers can only mean they comprise the keys.

The shape of the tomb is obviously meant to indicate that it has been 'truncated', another sign of phallic removal. I decided to reconstruct the truncated portion of the tomb to see what else it may reveal (illus 130). The angle of the shape is governed by the **100**-inch dimension having reduced to **86** inches after an increase in slant height of **8** inches. Possibly the 'half-staff' is more useful than it at first appeared, for to find the apex we will halve the decreasing pyramid lid measure and plot **8** inches up for every **7**-inch decrease in the half-lid distance. Already I was suspicious; **7** is the body of Set (the Typhon) and **8** is the body of Isis. Their sum is the body of Osiris, and their product is the Typhonic principle, **56**.

The completion of the tomb left me in no doubt. It would have been **57** inches of slant height and the overall distance from the top of the tomb to the ground would be **99** inches (**42** and **57**). This can mean only one thing to me. 'One off' a hundred tells us to take one from fifty-seven leaving the Typhonic principle of **56** again. The one which is removed conforms to the original truncation – it is the severed phallus. The half-lid measures confirm the numbers of the gods and their actions as shown in the language of the gods.

With all this emphasis on the removal of the phallus, we are reminded of another veiled reference to it which occurs in *Matthew*. Jesus is speaking of the old commandments and He says:

> Ye have heard that it was said by them of old time, Thou shalt not commit adultery:
>
> Verse 27

He continues by saying that to lust after the woman is as bad as committing the act and suggests the remedy is to pluck out the right eye. Next, without suggesting what the right hand has done wrong, He says:

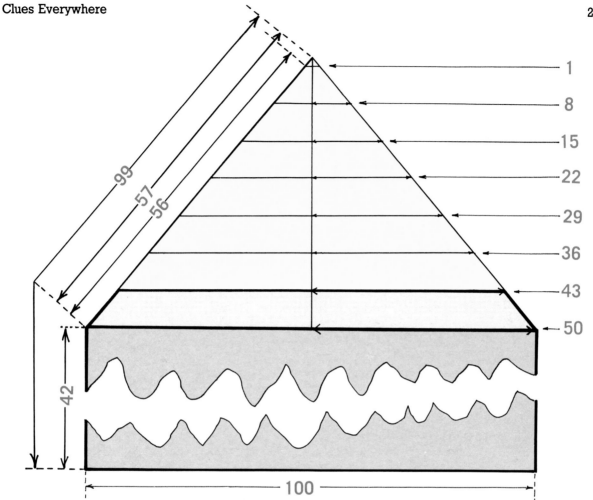

And if thy right hand offend thee, cut it off, and cast it from thee: for it is profitable for thee that one of thy members should perish, and not that thy whole body should be cast into hell.

Verse 30

130. The completion of the truncated tomb of Poussin disclosing more secret numbers.

Surely we need be in no doubt as to which member of the body would commit the offence of adultery, and therefore which part of the body must be removed. Poussin demonstrates his understanding of the right hand equating with the phallus by showing the statue in *La Peste d'Azoth* with its right hand severed (illus 131). This 'cutting off' was previously referred to, where in the same painting the obelisk lost its point and the statue lost its 'head'.

If Jesus or those who condemned Him followed the old adage of 'practise what you preach' phallectomy would most certainly have been the outcome of his alleged relationship with Magdalene.

Nor should we overlook the warning Jesus gives earlier in *Matthew V* when He says 'Thou shalt not kill'. This is the old law and not one which the Jewish elders would not ignore, but we are fully aware of their complicity in forcing Pilate's hand. Jesus states 'whosoever shall kill shall be in danger of the judgement' and

131. Detail from *La Peste D'Azoth* showing the 'beheaded' statue with its right hand 'cut off'.

crucifixion is undoubtedly an act of killing whereas phallic removal is not. Would the Jewish elders have trifled with one of the Commandments?

It would seem Poussin was well informed of every facet of the mystery, some of which are still to be revealed.

21

The Atlantis Connection

With Earth's first Clay They did the Last Man's knead,
And then of the Last Harvest sow'd the Seed:
Yea, the first Morning of Creation wrote
What the Last Dawn of Reckoning shall read.

*The mysterious meridian – Plato's message – the Temple of Sais – the goddess Neith –
the secret of the seat – Hephaestus – the gods take wives – Poseidon – the Atlantis code –
another womb.*

Many times, when discussing my findings at Rennes, friends
had put the same question to me. Why *there*? I had an
answer, but for fear of ridicule I refrained from suggesting what it
could be until I had more confirmation. I believe now I have that
confirmation, or at least sufficient to put my theory to paper and
stand by it.

If I were to provide a complete mathematical proof with all the
interrelated evidence I would need another book. Consequently
here is a skeleton of the evidence which shows the close
connection with our main subject – the temple of Rennes-le-
Château.

My mind had long been vexed by the chronological
contradiction of 12th- and 13th-century churches forming a
precise geometry which coincided exactly with a world meridian
based upon an observatory in Paris, which was not built until the

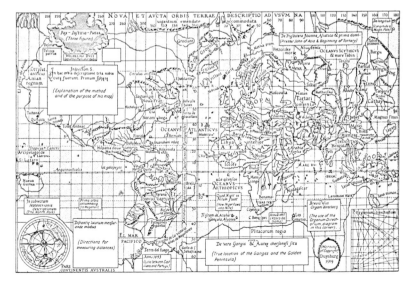

132. Mercator's Chart of the World, 1569

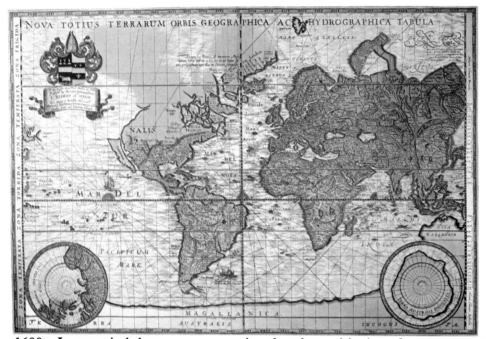

133. Moses Pitt Chart of the World, 1681.

1600s. In my mind there was no question that the positioning of the churches (or the stones marking the positions on which they were to be built) was decided upon by someone who was insisting this longitude was of great importance. Initially I could see little to recommend this longitudinal axis, but then another thought came to me: could Rennes be a longtitude that had to be marked because there was no remaining land position which could mark the meridian of a bygone age. Examining the world maps of Mercator (1569) and Moses Pitt (1681) (illus 132 & 133) leads one to think they were of the opinion the meridian should lie in the centre of the Atlantic Ocean, not exactly a seat of power in known historical times. Was there a position in the Atlantic or near the the Azores which could have fulfilled this function? The oceanographic charts show a mid-Atlantic ridge, a vast range of submerged mountains, the most favoured site for the mythological lost continent of Atlantis. My mind had already been numbed by the miracles of Rennes-le-Château – anything was possible!

I took the difference in longtitude between the French meridian and the Azores and transferred it eastward, it fell on Cairo, the Nile delta, the very seat of antiquity.

I needed to read as much as was available about Atlantis but, considering the fact that more books are available on this subject than almost any other, the task at first appeared to be impossible. Nevertheless, when the arguments for and against its existence and the evidence of where it was, have all been taken into account, most things still point decidedly to a mid-Atlantic site. I wondered if my findings could throw any light on this age-old enigma, little realizing at the time just how closely it would all relate to Rennes-le-Château.

The major factor in any student's assessment of the evidence for

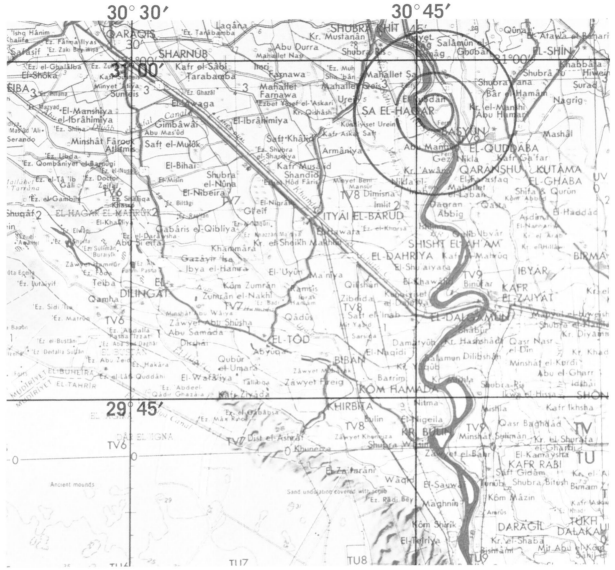

134. The location of the temple of Sais in the Nile Delta at Sa-el-Hagar.

Atlantis is Plato's dialogue in the *Timaeus*. Plato was a Greek philosopher whose influence on the minds of men is undeniable. He lived between 300 and 400 BC and came of noble parentage. He was the son of Ariston and Perictione. Ariston supposedly traced his descent through Codrus to the god Poseidon. His ancestors include Solon and Propidas, and it is here that we come to the only written evidence from which we may begin to investigate Atlantis, the *Timaeus*.

Many times I have seen parts of this evidence used to substantiate one theory or another and wondered at the dishonesty of the authors in presenting only that part which was convenient. At the risk of being tedious I feel I must deal with it in its entirety.

Socrates has just asked Critias to tell him the whole story and Critias proceeds as follows:

At the head of the Egyptian Delta, where the river Nile divides, there is a certain district which is called the district of Sais, and the great city of the district is also called Sais, and is the city from which Amasis the king was sprung. And the citizens have a deity who is their foundress: she is called in the Egyptian tongue Neith, which is asserted by them to be the same whom the Hellenes called Athene.

Already there are factors to be considered. The ruins of the Temple of Sais are still clearly visible, they lie near to the village of Sa-el-Hagar on the east bank of the Rosetta branch of the Nile delta. Sais was the capital city of the fifth nome of Egypt and is known to have been of great importance in ancient times.

The longitude of Sa-el-Haga (Sais) is 30°46′ east of Greenwich (illus 134) give or take a second or two. Adjusting for the difference between the Greenwich and the Paris meridian of the Rennes diagram (02°20′) we establish the Paris meridian is the one referred to in antiquity, we must move westward 28°26′ which is the equivalent of longitude 26°06′ west of Greenwich, the Azores (illus 135).

135. The deduced longtitude of Atlantis where it passes through the Azores.

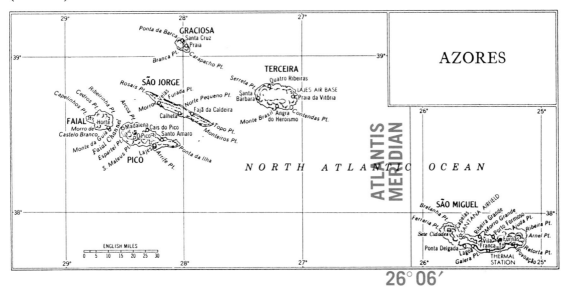

Could this be the reason why the valley was chosen? Is this the half-way marker for the longitudinal co-ordinate of Atlantis?

I next considered the simplest method by which a latitude may have been established for a lost position. Nothing could be more simple than to choose a marker on the same latitude and then follow the line of it to a land position which could be marked. Next, one would need to repeat exactly the same distance and provide another marker. Why then, using Rennes as the halfway marker, was there not another marker at an equal distance eastward? The simple answer is that it would have been in the Black Sea.

It follows therefore, bearing in mind the legendary connections between Atlantis, Egypt and Greece and those factors mentioned previously, it was inevitable that Sais would be the next most favoured position. According to Godfrey Higgins[1], while in Egypt, Plutarch had seen an inscription on the front of the Temple at Sais which was:

Ισις εγω ειμι πανlο γεγονος, και ον και

εσομενον, και το εμον πεπλον

8δεις των θνη

θων απε

καλυ

ψε

ν.

I *Isis* am all that has been, that is or shall be; no mortal Man hath ever me un- vei le d.

E. A. Wallis Budge[2] reports this rather differently, he states that Plutarch (*De Iside et Osir.*, IX) refers to the inscription thus:

Ἐγώ εἰμι πᾶν τὸ γεγονὸς, καὶ ὄν, καὶ ἐσόμενον, καὶ τὸν ἐμὸν πέπλον οὐδείς πω

Budge refers to the temple at Sais as the Temple of Neith, but there is no argument here, for he equates Neith with Isis on many occasions. Furthermore he reports on the great annual festival which was held there to honour Isis-Neith and which is recorded by Herodotus. Part of this ritual involved the continuous burning of lamps, tapers and candles through the night, a ceremony which has persisted to present times in the form of Candlemas. Herodotus also described a stone chamber of great beauty in which were two pillars. Between them was a coffin or tomb bearing a name which he was forbidden to disclose; however, the description cannot help but remind us of the positioning of the Ark in *La Peste d'Azoth* by Poussin.

Herodotus speaks in awe of the 'Mysteries' practised at Sais which were no doubt connected to the annual commemoration of the death and suffering of Osiris who, according to an old legend, was buried there. In the late dynastic texts Sais was actually called the city of Osiris.

There can be no doubt of the importance to the Greeks of the goddess Neith and their acceptance of her name showed that they also accepted her titles: the Mighty Mother who gave birth to Ra, and the Lady of the West. The west in the latter title is not referring to the obvious fact that Egypt is west of Greece, for the title is also applied in Egypt. To the west of Egypt can only be one more shred of evidence in support of Atlantis. The title Mighty Mother of Ra is even more intriguing for the sun-god was said to be 'self-begotten' – a power attributed to an androgyne. Next we are shown that Isis was the first to give birth to a god and also the first who came into being in the 'beginning'. In her Hathor form Isis was mother of Rat, the female sun which entitled her to be the ONE, a distinction also attributed to Neith – hence the words of Plutarch, I am what has been, what is and what shall be'. The Egyptians therefore quite correctly regarded Neith as Being *par excellence*, eternal and infinite, the creative and ruling power of all things living and dead. She is even depicted on one occasion 'with

136. The Thet – secret symbol of Isis.

[1]*Anacalypsis* Vol. P. 311.
[2]*The Gods of the Egyptians* Vol. 1. P. 458.

eighteen stars' confirming her identity with Isis[1]. The distinction of being androgynous is now equally attributed to Isis-Neith.

Lastly we should consider the hieroglyphs or sigils of Isis and Neith to see whether they produce contradiction, or confirmation of those things we now know to be connected with our mystery. We have already dealt with the 'seat' of Isis, but she has another more secret symbol – it is one of the most powerful amulets known to the ancient Egyptians. As described by Budge[2] it was the object *thet,* it carried with it the influence of her blood and magical powers. Budge considers it to represent 'the uterus with its ligatures, and the vagina'. I suspect it may also imply the Nile delta and equate with 'being born on the flood'. In any event the arrangement of the letters of the inscription at Sais are suggestive of both the Delta and the lower portion of the body of a female.

137. Neith as goddess of the chase.

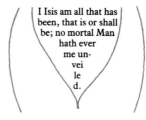

In the case of Neith we are confronted with two important symbols, the bow and arrow and the weaver's shuttle (illus 137 and 138). The bow and arrow shows that she is the goddess of the chase, and is in recognition of her gift of the weapon by which mankind obtained supremacy over the rest of the animal kingdom. With this weapon man could kill at a distance, an essential, when one considers how ill equipped he was to survive without it.

The next symbol of Neith is directly linked with Rennes, for there we had the 'place where beauty sleeps', a sleep induced by virtue of the princess pricking her finger with a spindle, and on the head of Neith we find the weaver's shuttle. Furthermore, you will recall, this is a direct equation with another weaver or spinner, the spider, whose web I will deal with later when I disclose the geometry of the labyrinth.

We can now recognize the sequence of the symbols which in great antiquity were the bow and arrow for survival, followed by the shuttle indicating the process of weaving by which we were clothed. Next Neith as Isis becomes the corn goddess signifying man's progression to agriculture, her seat and her vulva point the way to go 'forth' and multiply. But does her seat show us even more?

If the symbol of that seat is moved round to a horizontal position, the seat and the body of the seated person would mark the co-ordinate diagram by which we locate Atlantis. Furthermore, the seated goddess with her head at Atlantis would face her southern star and her feet would rest at Sais. Even more

138. Neith as goddess of weaving.

[1]*The Gods of the Egyptians*, p.450.
[2]*Osiris and the Egyptian Resurrection*, Vol II, p. 280.

significant is that her 'seat', or the entrance to her womb would be at the Temple of Rennes-le-Château! (illus 139).

I looked at the name of the river coming from the East and flowing into the area of the womb at Rennes – SALS. The salt content of the water could explain the name, but it could suggest something else. By the simple process of changing the L to lower case we would have SAIS, which is typical of the humour of those who perpetuated the imagery of Rennes.

139. Isis seated, with her symbol demonstrating the location of the lost city of Atlantis.

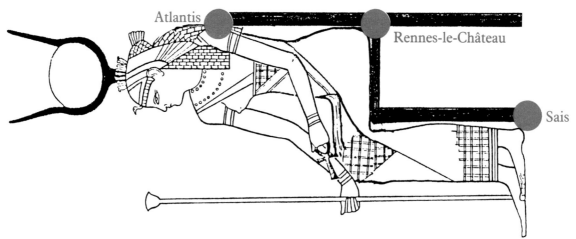

Atlantis

Rennes-le-Château

Sais

We return to Plato's dialogue, now knowing that the foundress was the goddess Isis:

> Now, the citizens of this city are great lovers of the Athenians, and say that they are in some way related to them. Thither came Solon, who was received by them with great honor; and he asked the priests, who were most skilful in such matters, about antiquity, and made the discovery that neither he nor any other Hellene knew anything worth mentioning about the times of old. On one occasion, when he was drawing them on to speak of antiquity, he began to tell about the most ancient things in our part of the world – about Phoroneus, who is called 'the first', and about Niobe; and, after the Deluge, to tell of the lives of Deucalion and Pyrrha; and he traced the genealogy of their descendants, and attempted to reckon how many years old were the events of which he was speaking, and to give the dates. Thereupon, one of the priests, who was of very great age, said, 'O Solon, Solon, you Hellenes are but children, and there is never an old man who is an Hellene.' Solon, hearing this, said, 'What do you mean?' 'I mean to say,' he replied, 'that in mind you are all young; there is no old opinion handed down among you by ancient traditions, nor any science which is hoary with age. And I will tell you the reason of this: there have been, and there will be again, many destructions of mankind arising out of many causes. There is a story which even you have preserved, that once upon a time Phaëthon, the son of Helios, having yoked the steeds in his father's chariot, because he was not able to drive them in the path of his father, burnt up all that was upon the earth, and was himself destroyed by a thunder-bolt. Now, this has the form of a myth, but really signifies a declination of the bodies moving around the earth

and in the heavens, and a great conflagration of things upon the earth recurring at long intervals of time: when this happens, those who live upon the mountains and in dry and lofty places are more liable to destruction than those who dwell by rivers or on the sea-shore; and from this calamity the Nile, who is our never-failing savior, saves and delivers us. When, on the other hand, the gods purge the earth with a deluge of water, among you herdsmen and shepherds on the mountains are the survivors, whereas those of you who live in cities are carried by the rivers into the sea; but in this country neither at that time nor at any other does the water come from above on the fields, having always a tendency to come up from below, for which reason the things preserved here are said to be the oldest. The fact is, that wherever the extremity of winter frost or summer sun does not prevent, the human race is always increasing at times, and at other times diminishing in numbers. And whatever happened either in your country or in ours, or in any other region of which we are informed – if any action which is noble or great, or in any other way remarkable has taken place, all that has been written down of old, and is preserved in our temples; whereas you and other nations are just being provided with letters and the other things which States require; and then, at the usual period, the stream from heaven descends like a pestilence, and leaves only those of you who are destitute of letters and education; and thus you have to begin all over again as children, and know nothing of what happened in ancient times, either among us or among yourselves. As for those genealogies of yours which you have recounted to us, Solon, they are no better than the tales of children; for, in the first place, you remember one deluge only, whereas there were many of them; and, in the next place, you do not know that there dwelt in your land the fairest and noblest race of men which ever lived, of whom you and your whole city are but a seed or remnant. And this was unknown to you, because for many generations the survivors of that destruction died and made no sign. For there was a time, Solon, before that great deluge of all, when the city which now is Athens was first in war, and was pre-eminent for the excellence of her laws, and is said to have performed the noblest deeds, and to have had the fairest constitution of any of which tradition tells, under the face of heaven.'

Here we are being told that mankind, or the majority of them, have been destroyed on many occasions, a clear parallel to the cyclic birth and re-birth of mankind referred to previously. Once more we are reminded of the danger of being confined to the surface of the earth when these global destructions occur. There is no doubt in the author's mind of these events being generated at the cosmic level. Apparently he is not in any way confused as to the realities which others have interpreted simply as myth. Should any still remain who are naive enough to believe the Lord will save them, I suggest they read *The Cosmic Serpent* wherein Victor Clube and Bill Napier examine the possible effects of such an event. Here we see men with scientific minds in no doubt that the legends are records of actual encounters with celestial bodies. There is also no doubt the only safe place to be in these circumstances is in space; and if any should wish to refer to the vehicle required as the Ark of Noah, it would be understandable. The vital message, which we would be foolish to ignore, is that the biblical flood was not a 'one-off' act of vengeance by our Creator, but the repetitive and inevitable outcome of celestial mechanics. Faith will not move mountains, but these forces can. I trust those who criticize space research budgets may reconsider their position. To divert these funds to those in need is a noble gesture, but to little avail when related to the destruction of mankind.

Continuing with the text I was pleased to see some confirmation of my theory that 'actions which were great, noble or in any other way remarkable' are recorded in the ancient temples. In my opinion Rennes is a prime example of this very process.

Finally, for this section of the text we see reference to 'that great deluge of all' which refers to the destruction of the Atlantean civilization:

> Solon marvelled at this, and earnestly requested the priest to inform him exactly and in order about these former citizens. 'You are welcome to hear about them, Solon,' said the priest, 'both for your own sake and for that of the city; and, above all, for the sake of the goddess who is the common patron and protector and educator of both our cities. She founded your city a thousand years before ours, receiving from the Earth and Hephæstus the seed of your race, and then she founded ours, the constitution of which is set down in our sacred registers as 8000 years old. As touching the citizens of 9000 years ago, I will briefly inform you of their laws and of the noblest of their actions; and the exact particulars of the whole we will hereafter go through at our leisure in the sacred registers themselves. If you compare these very laws with your own, you will find that many of ours are the counterpart of yours, as were in the olden time. In the first place, there is the caste of priests, which is separated from all the others; next there are the artificers, who exercise their several crafts by themselves, and without admixture of any other; and also there is the class of shepherds and that of hunters, as well as that of husbandmen; and you will observe, too, that the warriors in Egypt are separated from all the other classes, and are commanded by the law only to engage in war; moreover, the weapons with which they are equipped are shields and spears, and this the goddess taught first among you, and then in Asiatic countries, and we among the Asiatics first adopted.

It is not quite clear how the goddess 'received' the 'seed'. It may be a polite reference to impregnation. However, later in the text we will see that Critias does not mince his words like this, for he refers directly to 'intercourse' between Poseidon and Cleito. The 'seed' is said to come from Earth and Hephaestus. Now even accepting the goddess as Earth-born with a genital organ, we have a problem in that Hephaistos would have been an androgyne. This is, nevertheless, in line with the 'special way of birth' referred to in *Thrice Greatest Hermes**, when Horus asked:

*G. R. S. Mead (John Watkins: London) 1964.

'How was it, mother, then, that Earth received God's Efflux,' and
Isis said:

'I may not tell the story of (this) birth; for it is not permitted to
describe the origin of thy descent, O Horus (son) of mighty power,
lest afterwards the way-of-birth of the immortal gods should be
known unto men . . . '

If Isis was the recipient of the seed in the sexual sense, this could
not have been delivered by a penis (for no mortal man had ever her
unveiled) and thereby her claim to virginity was valid. Here we
have another good equation, both with the Virgin Mary and with
the sexually mutilated Osirian body. We cannot, however,
overlook the possibility of 'received' meaning just what it says. It
could be that she was the guardian of a preserved sperm, one to be
used at her discretion.

For the 'sake of the goddess' we will consider the god
Hephaestus from whom she received this seed. He was the Greek
god of fire and all the skills requiring the use of it; forging,
smelting and the working of metals into ornaments, tools and
weapons. Here we see the next stage in the advancement of man,
and what is being described is the people of Cain, from whom
came Hiram Abiff, the architect of the metal objects in the Temple
of Solomon. Hephaestus was said to be the son of Zeus and Hera
but, because he was born ugly and lame, she threw him down from
Olympus into the ocean.

Surely this is a fine parallel to our old friend Satan being cast
down and also to the Set-Typhon who fell into the ocean.
Saunière, the priest of Rennes-le-Château, seems determined to
record this relationship by his horned 'devil' in the doorway of the
church, who you will recall, is also lame.

Are we being told of another epoch which began with the
destruction of Earth by fire? Was it from this seed that the Titans
came, who ruled Earth before mankind? We were born on the
flood, and by all accounts are lesser creatures than they were, but if
the seed was preserved somewhere on Earth it may be in the
Temple at Rennes-le-Château.

With the '8000 years' and the '9000 years' we come to the first of
our numbers and they are not difficult to understand. The 8 is of
course Isis and 9 is the pentagonal factor, multiplied the product is
72 the base angle of the pentagram and added they are 17 the
significance of which has already been shown:

Then, as to wisdom, do you observe what care the law took from
the very first, searching out and comprehending the whole order of
things down to prophecy and medicine (the latter with a view to
health); and out of these divine elements drawing what was needful
for human life, and adding every sort of knowledge which was
connected with them. All this order and arrangement the goddess
first imparted to you when establishing your city; and she chose the
spot of earth in which you were born, because she saw that the
happy temperament of the seasons in that land would produce the
wisest of men. Wherefore the goddess, who was a lover both of war

and of wisdom, selected, and first of all settled that spot which was
the most likely to produce men likest herself. And there you dwelt,
having such laws as these and still better ones, and excelled all
mankind in all virtue, as became the children and disciples of the
gods. Many great and wonderful deeds are recorded of your State
in our histories; but one of them exceeds all the rest in greatness
and valor; for these histories tell of a mighty power which was
agressing wantonly against the whole of Europe and Asia, and to
which your city put an end. This power came forth out of the
Atlantic Ocean, for in those days the Atlantic was navigable; and
there was an island situated in front of the straits which you call the
Columns of Heracles: the island was larger than Libya and Asia put
together, and was the way to other islands, and from the islands you
might pass through the whole of the opposite continent which
surrounded the true ocean; for this sea which is within the Straits of
Heracles is only a harbor, having a narrow entrance, but that other
is a real sea, and the surrounding land may be most truly called a
continent.

In this section there are references to the position of Atlantis in
the Atlantic mentioning that it was 'in front of the straits'
reasonably suggesting the 'Straits of Gibraltar'. There may well
have been pinnacles of rock across the entrance to the
Mediterranean in ancient times which were referred to as the
'Columns of Hercules'. I do not doubt that many great cities have
been destroyed in the past, but with references as good as these I
see no point in trying to identify Atlantis as having been anywhere
other than where Solon described it to be:

Now, in the island of Atlantis there was a great and wonderful
empire, which had rule over the whole island and several others, as
well as over parts of the continent; and, besides these, they
subjected the parts of Libya within the Columns of Heracles as far
as Egypt, and of Europe as far as Tyrrhenia. The vast power thus
gathered into one, endeavored to subdue at one blow our country
and yours, and the whole of the land which was within the straits;
and then, Solon, your country shone forth, in the excellence of her
virtue and strength, among all mankind; for she was the first in
courage and military skill, and was the leader of the Hellenes. And
when the rest fell off from her, being compelled to stand alone, she
defeated and triumphed over the invaders, and preserved from
slavery those who were not yet subjected, and freely liberated all
the others who dwelt within the limits of Heracles. But afterwards
there occurred violent earthquakes and floods, and in a single day
and night of rain all your warlike men in a body sunk into the earth,
and the island of Atlantis in like manner disappeared, and was sunk
beneath the sea. And that is the reason why the sea in those parts is
impassable and impenetrable, because there is such a quantity of
shallow mud in the way; and this was caused by the subsidence of
the island.'

This manner of reporting is hardly in line with myth and
legend, surely an angry god or two would be connected with an

event of such magnitude. Instead we see a cold, simple statement
of fact. How can we still leave this in the category of myth, in light
of what we now know to be the effects of asteroid or comet impact
with the earth?

> But in addition to the gods whom you have mentioned, I would
> specially invoke Mnemosyne; for all the important part of what I
> have to tell is dependent on her favor, and if I can recollect and
> recite enough of what was said by the priests, and brought hither by
> Solon, I doubt not that I shall satisfy the requirements of this
> theatre. To that task, then, I will at once address myself.
>
> Let me begin by observing, first of all, that nine thousand was
> the sum of years which had elapsed since the war which was said to
> have taken place between all those who dwelt outside the Pillars of
> Heracles and those who dwelt within them: this war I am now to
> described. Of the combatants on the one side the city of Athens was
> reported to have been the ruler, and to have directed the contest;
> the combatants on the other side were led by the kings of the islands
> of Atlantis, which, as I was saying, once had an extent greater than
> that of Libya and Asia; and, when afterward sunk by an
> earthquake, became an impassable barrier of mud to voyagers
> sailing from hence to the ocean. The progress of the history will
> unfold the various tribes of barbarians and Hellenes which then
> existed, as they successively appear on the scene; but I must begin
> by describing, first of all, the Athenians as they were in that day,
> and their enemies who fought with them; and I shall have to tell of
> the power and form of government of both of them. Let us give the
> precedence to Athens . . .
>
> Many great deluges have taken place during the nine thousand
> years, for that is the number of years which have elapsed since the
> time of which I am speaking; and in all the ages and changes of
> things there has never been any settlement of the earth flowing
> down from the mountains, as in other places, which is worth
> speaking of; it has always been carried round in a circle, and
> disappeared in the depths below. The consequence is that, in
> comparison of what then was, there are remaining in small islets
> only the bones of the wasted body, as they may be called, all the
> richer and softer parts of the soil having fallen away, and the mere
> skeleton of the country being left . . .

Here Critias brings us to comparatively recent times, the period
from approximately 9000 B.C. when Earth was probably still
reeling from the effect of being disrupted from its orbit. The
Golden Age has gone, and now mankind needs to force a living
from the shattered surface of the earth. The eroded islets to which
Solon refers are most likely the Azores, the Canaries and the
barren islands of the Aegean, remnants of a once flourishing
culture:

> And next, if I have not forgotten what I heard when I was a child, I
> will impart to you the character and origin of their adversaries; for
> friends should not keep their stories to themselves, but have them
> in common. Yet, before proceeding farther in the narrative, I

ought to warn you that you must not be surprised if you should hear
Hellenic names given to foreigners. I will tell you the reason for
this: Solon, who was intending to use the tale for his poem, made an
investigation into the meaning of the names, and found that the
early Egyptians, in writing them down, had translated them into
their own language, and he recovered the meaning of the several
names and retranslated them, and copied them out again in our
language. My great-grandfather, Dropidas, had the orginal
writing, which is still in my possession, and was carefully studied
by me when I was a child. Therefore, if you hear names such as are
used in this country, you must not be surprised, for I have told you
the reason of them.

The tale, which was of great length, began as follows: I have
before remarked, in speaking of the allotments of the gods, that
they distributed the whole earth into portions differing in extent,
and made themselves temples and sacrifices. <u>And Poseidon,
receiving for his lot the island of Atlantis, begat children by a
mortal woman</u>, and settled them in a part of the island which I will
proceed to describe. On the side toward the sea, and in the centre of
the whole island, there was a plain which is said to have been the
fairest of all plains, and very fertile. Near the plain again, and also
in the centre of the island, at a distance of about fifty stadia, there
was a mountain, not very high on any side. In this mountain there
dwelt one of the earth-born primeval men of that country, whose
name was Evenor, and he had a wife named Leucippe, and they
had an only daughter, who was named Cleito. The maiden was
growing up to womanhood when her father and mother died;
<u>Poseidon fell in love with her, and had intercourse with her</u>; and,
breaking the ground, enclosed the hill in which she dwelt all round,
making alternate zones of sea and land, larger and smaller,
encircling one another; there were two of land and three of water,
which he turned as with a lathe out of the centre of the island,
equidistant every way, so that no man could get to the island, for
ships and voyages were not yet heard of. He himself, as he was a
god, found no difficulty in making special arrangements for the
centre island, bringing two streams of water under the earth, <u>which
he caused to ascend as springs, one of warm water and the other of
cold</u>, and making every variety of food to spring up abundantly in
the earth.

In this section we are told, with no ambiguity whatsoever, that
in the next epoch the 'gods' who had descended from the goddess
turned their attention to mere mortals, earth-born creatures not
possessing the 'understanding' but satisfying the sexual desires of
the second-generation 'gods' who were endowed with copulatory
organs. So Poseidon is shown to be one of these gods who took a
mortal woman as his wife, an event recorded in *Genesis* VI, 2: 'The
sons of God saw the daughters of men that they were fair; and they
took them wives of all that they chose'. In the English Bible these
sons of God were said to be 'the giants', but G. H. Pember points
out in *Earth's Earliest Ages* that this is an incorrect translation of
the Hebrew which is more accurately, the Nephilim or 'fallen
ones'. Once again we are shown to be the result of the 'seed' of the
'fallen', the Satanic, the Typhonic.

140. Part of *Le Triomphe de Neptune* by Poussin, illustrating Poseidon and his horses.

Poseidon was the Greek god of the sea, but before his realm was so restricted, he was also worshipped as the creator of the water springs, particularly in Arcadia. Once again a very direct link to Rennes with the 'Et In Arcadia Ego' theme of Poussin's *Les Bergers d'Arcadie*. Also, at Rennes-le-Bains we find the thermal springs, which are in the centre of the geometric temple, in exactly the manner they were in Atlantis and as described in the text by Critias.

Poseidon is usually shown carrying a trident, standing in a chariot drawn by swift-footed steeds, and the horse is sacred to him (illus 140). This accounts for the special mention of a race-course at Atlantis which we will come to presently:

He (Poseidon) also begat and brought up five pairs of male children, dividing the island of Atlantis into ten portions: he gave to the first-born of the eldest pair his mother's dwelling and the surrounding allotment, which was the largest and best, and made him king over the rest; the others he made princes, and gave them rule over many men and a large territory. And he named them all: the eldest, who was king, he named Atlas, and from him the whole island and the ocean received the name of Atlantic. To his twin-brother, who was born after him, and obtained as his lot the extremity of the island toward the Pillars of Heracles, as far as the country which is still called the region of Gades in that part of the world, he gave the name which in the Hellenic language is Eumelus, in the language of the country which is named after him, Gadeirus. Of the second pair of twins, he called one Ampheres and the other Evæmon. To the third pair of twins he gave the name Mnescus to the elder, and Autochthlon to the one who followed him. Of the fourth pair of twins he called the elder Elasippus and the younger Mestor. And of the fifth pair he gave to the elder the name of Azaes, and to the younger Diaprepes. All these and their descendants were the inhabitants and rulers of divers islands in the open sea; and also, as has been already said, they held sway in the other direction over the country within the Pillars as far as Egypt and Tyrrhenia. Now Atlas had a numerous and honorable family, and his eldest branch always retained the kingdom, which the eldest son handed on to this eldest for many generations; and they had such an amount of wealth as was never before possessed by kings and potentates, and is not likely ever to be again, and they were furnished with everything which they could have, both in city and country. For, because of the greatness of their empire, many things were brought to them from foreign countries, and the island itself provided much of what was required by them for the uses of life. In the first place, they dug out of the earth whatever was to be found there, mineral as well as metal, and that which is now only a name, and was then something more than a name – orichalcum – was dug out of the earth in many parts of the island and, with the exception of gold, was esteemed the most precious of metals among the men of those days. There was an abundance of wood for carpenters' work, and sufficient maintenance for tame and wild animals. Moreover, there were a great number of elephants in the island, and there was a provision for animals of every kind, both for those which live in lakes and marshes and rivers, and also for those which live in mountains and on plains, and therefore for the animal which is the largest and most voracious of them. Also, whatever fragrant things there are in the earth, whether roots, or herbage, or woods, or distilling drops of flowers or fruits, grew and thrived in that land; and again, the cultivated fruit of the earth, both the dry edible fruit and other species of food, which we call by the general name of legumes, and the fruits having a hard rind, affording drinks, and meats, and ointments, and good store of chestnuts and the like, which may be used to play with, and are fruits which spoil with keeping – and the pleasant kinds of dessert which console us after dinner, when we are full and tired of eating – all these that sacred island lying beneath the sun brought forth fair and wondrous in infinite abundance. All these things they received from the earth, and they employed themselves in constucting their temples, and palaces, and harbors, and docks; and they arranged the whole country in the following manner: first of all they bridged over the zones of sea which surrounded the ancient metropolis, and made a passage into and out of the royal palace; and then they began to build the palace in the habitation of the god and of their ancestors. This they continued to ornament in successive generations, every king surpassing the one who came before him to the utmost of his power, until they made the building a marvel to behold for size and for beauty. And, beginning from the sea, they dug a canal three hundred feet in width and one hundred feet in depth, and fifty stadia in length, which they carried through to the outermost zone, making a passage from the sea up to this, which became a harbor, and leaving an opening sufficient to enable the largest vessels to find ingress. Moreover, they divided the zones of land which parted the zones of sea, constructing bridges of such a width as would leave a passage for a single trireme to pass out of one into another, and roofed them over; and there was a way underneath for the ships, for the banks of the zones were raised considerably above the water.

Here we see more 'numbers' and the very nature of them, together with many others which follow suggest to me they are nothing more than a code. The reason this document survived is possibly because the Vatican failed to recognize the code it contained. This is one of the exceptions, it is written documentary evidence which escaped censorship.

We have already seen from the Sea of Brass in Solomon's Temple that 'a little more than **3**' was nevertheless used symbolically as **3**. The units of measure referred to in the text are 'stadia' and we must be careful to use the correct factor when we relate stadia to feet. It is equivalent to **606.75** modern English feet, but was exactly **600** ancient Greek feet. This is obviously the factor we must use.

As soon as I saw the description of a long canal cut through the earth to a circular device, my mind was alerted to the sexual implication corresponding to the Rennes geometry (illus 141).

Ignoring for the moment the units of measure, the existence of the numerals **3** and **5** in the canal suggested **15** to me – the number which represents the phallus of Osiris.

I thought the unlikely depth of this canal (**100**ft) was to be multiplied by the equally unlikely width (**300**ft) which is **30,000**ft and in my opinion this confirms the simple fact that **50** stadia = **30,000**ft; confirming therefore 1 stade = **600**ft.

Now the largest of the zones into which a passage was cut from the sea was three stadia in breadth, and the zone of land which came next of equal breadth; but the next two, as well the zone of water as of land, were two stadia, and the one which surrounded the central island was a stadium only in width. The island in which the palace was situated had a diameter of five stadia. This, and the zones and the bridge, which was the sixth part of a stadium in width, they surrounded by a stone wall, on either side placing towers, and gates on the bridges where the sea passed in. The stone which was used in the work they quarried from underneath the centre island and from

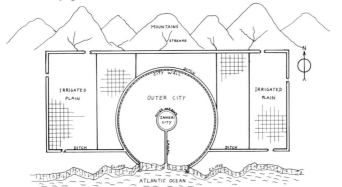

141. General layout of the plain of Atlantis showing the city area and the phallic canal leading to it.

underneath the zones, on the outer as well as the inner side. One kind of stone was white, another black, and a third red; and, as they quarried, they at the same time hollowed out docks double within, having roofs formed out of the native rock. Some of their buildings were simple, but in others they put together different stones, which they intermingled for the sake of ornament, to be a natural source of delight. The entire circuit of the wall which went round the outermost one they covered with a coating of brass, and the circuit of the next wall they coated with tin, and the third, which encompassed the citadel, flashed with the red light of orichalcum. The palaces in the interior of the citadel were constructed in this wise: In the centre was a holy temple dedicated to Cleito and Poseidon, which remained inaccessible, and was surrounded by an enclosure of gold; this was the spot in which they originally begat the race of the ten princes, and thither they annually brought the fruits of the earth in their season from all the ten portions, and performed sacrifices to each of them. Here, too, was Poseidon's own temple, of a stadium in length and half a stadium in width, and of a proportionate height, having a sort of barbaric splendor. All the outside of the temple, with the exception of the pinnacles, they covered with silver, and the pinnacles with gold. In the interior of the temple the roof was of ivory, adorned everywhere with gold and silver and orichalcum; all the other parts of the walls and pillars and floor they lined with orichalcum. In the temple they placed statues of gold: there was the god himself standing in a chariot – the charioteer of six winged horses – and of such a size that he touched the roof of the building with his head; around him there were a hundred Nereids riding on dolphins, for such was thought to be the number of them in that day. There were also in the interior of the temple other images which had been dedicated by private individuals. And around the temple on the outside were placed statues of gold of all the ten kings and of their wives; and there were many other great offerings, both of kings and of private individuals, coming both from the city itself and the foreign cities over which they held sway. There was an altar, too, which in size and workmanship corresponded to the rest of the work, and there were palaces in like manner which answered to the greatness of the kingdom and the glory of the temple.

In the next place, they used fountains both of cold and hot springs; these were very abundant, and both kinds wonderfully adapted to use by reason of the sweetness and excellence of their waters. They constructed buildings about them, and planted suitable trees; also cisterns, some open to the heaven, others which they roofed over, to be used in winter as warm baths: there were the king's baths, and the baths of private persons, which were kept apart; also separate baths for women, and others again for horses and cattle, and to them they gave as much adornment as was suitable for them. The water which ran off they carried, some to the grove of Poseidon, where were growing all manner of trees of wonderful height and beauty, owing to the excellence of the soil; the remainder was conveyed by aqueducts which passed over the bridges to the outer circles: and there were many temples built and dedicated to many gods; also gardens and places of exercise, some for men, and some set apart for horses, in both of the two islands formed by the zones; and in the centre of the larger of the two there was a race-course of a stadium in width, and in length allowed to extend all round the island, for horses to race in.

At first sight this appears to be a confusing array of numbers, but the simplicity of the layout they describe is easily appreciated by demonstrating it in diagrammatic form (illus 142).

Immediately obvious is the 'phallic' canal from the sea entering the outer harbour. The outer diameter of this is **27** stadia, a number we know to be representative of the pregnant womb, or period of pregnancy. Using our symbolic π value of **3**, the outer circumference of this harbour is **81** stadia (Isis reflected).

Equally obvious is the diameter of the centre line of the race-track which is **18** stadia (Isis) and the circumference is **54** stadia, the sublime 'division' of the lower body angle of the female; represented in the pentagram by **108**. The central island with a female diameter of **5** provides a circumference of **15** (the Osirian phallus). Pregnancy (**270**) divided by **15** reveals the recipient, Isis (**270** divided by **15** = **18**). The Osirian phallus is further demonstrated by the multiplication of the radial factors from the centre-line of the 'horse' track to the centre of the diagram:

$$1.5 \times 2 \times 2 \times 1 \times 2.5 = 15 \text{ stadia}$$

Convert **15** stadia to feet (**15** × **600**) and the phallus is shown to be erect (**9000**). This in turn is confirmed by repeating the process over the whole diagram of zones:

$$3 \times 3 \times 2 \times 2 \times 1 \times 2.5 = 90 \text{ stadia}$$

Convert **90** stadia to feet (**90** ×**600**) and we are shown where it went (**54000**) and for the outcome we return to our starting point at the race-track, the area of which is **27** square stadia.

It is also interesting to note that the outer circumference of the outer harbour being **81** stadia is therefore **48600** feet which, when divided by **18** (Isis), becomes **2700**. This is only one simple example of the many direct links I found with Rennes. But I might lose the reader in a welter of numbers and it would serve no purpose. It is nevertheless worth mentioning that these calculations prove a close relationship exists between British or Celtic measure and the numbers exhibited in Atlantis and the Rennes temple. The introduction of the metric system puts us in great danger of losing the secret of the numbers for ever:

> Also there were guard-houses at intervals for the body-guard, the more trusted of whom had their duties appointed to them in the lesser zone, which was nearer the Acropolis; while the most trusted of all had houses given them within the citadel, and about the persons of the kings. The docks were full of triremes and naval stores, and all things were quite ready for use. Enough of the plan of the royal palaces. Crossing the outer harbors, which were three in number, you would come to a wall which began at the sea and went all round: this was everywhere distant <u>fifty stadia from the largest zone and harbor, and enclosed the whole</u>, meeting at the mouth of the channel toward the sea. The entire area was densely crowded with habitations; and the canal and the largest of the harbors were full of vessels and merchants coming from all parts, who, from their numbers, kept up a multitudinous sound of human voices and din of all sorts night and day. I have repeated his descriptions of the city and the parts about the ancient palace nearly as he gave them, and now I must endeavor to describe the nature and arrangement of the rest of the country. The whole country was described as being very lofty and precipitous on the side of the sea, but the country immediately about and surrounding the city was a level plain, itself surrounded by mountains which descended toward the sea; it was smooth and even, but of an <u>oblong shape</u>, extending in one direction <u>three thousand stadia</u>, and going up the country from the sea through the centre of the island <u>two thousand stadia</u>; the whole region of the island lies towards the south, and is sheltered from the north. The surrounding mountains he celebrated for their number and size and beauty, in which they exceeded all that are now to be seen anywhere; having in them also many wealthy inhabited villages, and rivers and lakes, and meadows supplying food enough for every animal, wild or tame, and wood of various sorts, abundant for every kind of work. I will now describe the plain, which had been cultivated during many ages by many generations of kings. It was rectangular, and for the most part straight and oblong; and what it wanted of the

142. The ground plan of the city showing the zones of land and sea. Note the race-track diameter signifying Isis and the diameter of the outer harbour representing the womb.

THE GROUND PLAN OF ATLANTIS

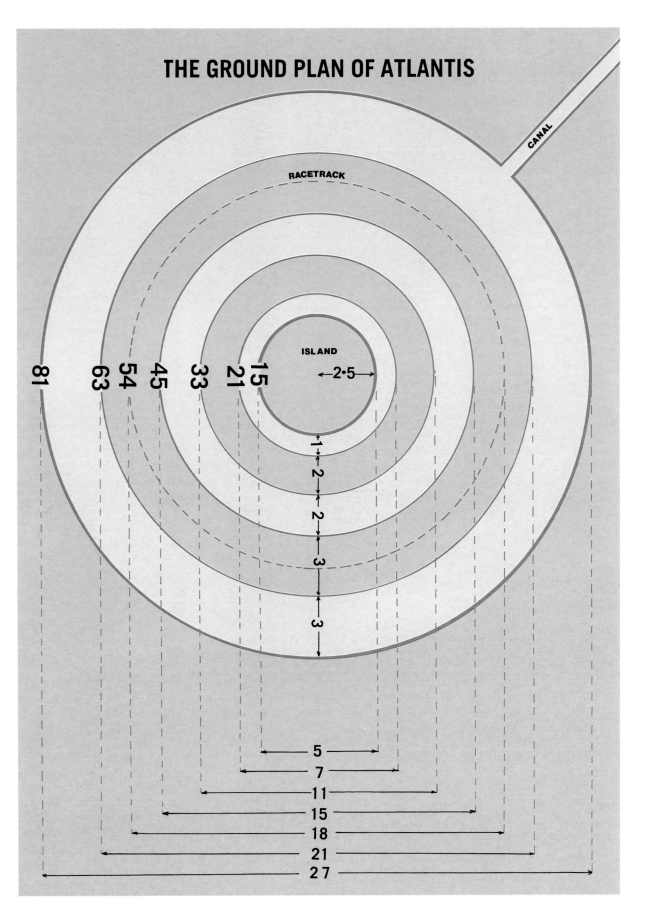

143. Detail from *La Peste D'Azoth* showing Poseidon, waist deep in water, possibly addressing the Poussin shepherds as they stand at the tomb.

straight line followed the line of the circular ditch. The depth and width and length of this ditch were incredible, and gave the impression that such a work, in addition to so many other works, could hardly have been wrought by the hand of man. But I must say what I have heard. It was excavated to the depth of a hundred feet, and its breadth was a stadium everywhere; it was carried round the whole of the plain, and was ten thousand stadia in length. It received the streams which came down from the mountains, and winding round the plain, and touching the city at various points, was there let off into the sea. From above, likewise, straight canals of a hundred feet in width were cut in the plain, and again let off into the ditch, toward the sea; these canals were at intervals of a hundred stadia, and by them they brought the fruits of the earth in ships, cutting transverse passages from one canal into another, and to the city. Twice in the year they gathered the fruits of the earth – in winter having the benefit of the rains, and in summer introducing the water of the canals. As to the population, each of the lots in the plain had an appointed chief of men who were fit for military service, and the size of the lot was to be a square of ten stadia each way, and the total number of all the lots was sixty thousand.

Here are a few more numbers which are quite simple to deal with.

'Fifty stadia from the largest zone and harbour' seems to suggest that the dimension of these two items (**3 stadia each**) should be included to give the familiar number of **56** signifying Set.

The plain is **3000** by **2000** stadia, giving a perimeter of **10,000** stadia, but a one-stadia ditch has conveniently been added to increase the perimeter to **10,008** conforming with our code. The diagonal of this plain with the ditch is also interesting, it is **3608** (the circle and Isis). Without the ditch the diagonal is **360.555** – the circle and the result of dividing **666** by **12** for those who have the 'understanding'.

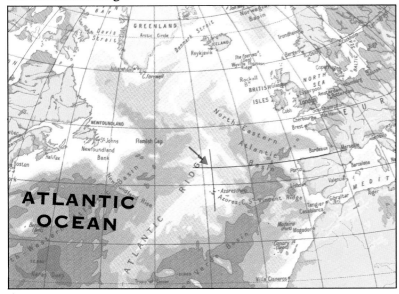

144. The position of Atlantis on the Mid Atlantic ridge.

Our old friend Poussin certainly knew that Rennes marked the position of the lost continent and he makes it very obvious in his *La Peste d'Azoth*. There carved on the temple wall, we see Poseidon waist-deep in water with the tomb on dry land and carrying the boat-crescent of Isis (illus 143).

I feel it would serve no purpose to bombard the reader with more examples although there are dozens of them. Beyond this point the dialogue contains nothing of mathematical significance or indicative of the position. I trust this analysis is as convincing to the reader as it is to me. The message contained in it is the same one we found at Rennes.

It would appear there was an Atlantis after all, and its co-ordinates were 26°.06′ West 42°.55′ North!

22

The Light Revealed

Since there is none, as I can find,
Of those brave wizards of today
Worthy to hear, I cannot say
The wondrous thoughts I have in mind.

Man's recognition of the gods – a subconscious memory – a superconscious link – the dismemberment explained – the secret of the womb – Baphomet unveiled – the radiation of light – Peace 681 – a gateway to the unknown.

An examination of pagan beliefs reveals a slow progression from the worship of simple natural features and then finally to the attribution of all things to a single Creator. With hindsight, this may seem perfectly natural, but I feel we should consider one phase of the transformation in more detail.

Starting with the worship of rivers, trees, hills and then progressing to seas, forests and mountains is only what we would expect. The next stage is equally predictable. This was the inclusion of phenomena which were not continuously experienced, storms, lightning, thunder, rain and so on. Following this, primitive man looked at the sky, the sun and the stars and with his increased awareness we can appreciate how terrifying an eclipse or the appearance of a comet must have been to him. Next comes the stage which I feel is a 'mighty leap' for the mind of man. He invented, or became aware of spiritual beings; not spirits. Having reached this point, it is a minor modification to appoint a chief or supreme spirit to rule over the others. I recognize this is a generalization of a vast subject, but the point I would like to stress is that monotheism is not the final enlightenment it is sometimes claimed to be. It comes from the natural progression of initially recognizing the entities of spirit form. We should concern ourselves with how such a thought could have entered the mind of a primitive in the first place. If the readers feel I am labouring this point, I suggest they try to generate in their imagination something of equal significance. At the time this concept entered the mind of man it had no precedent and yet it appears to have been immediately acceptable in those areas where civilization originated. It would even seem reasonable to suggest that it may have been one of the major reasons they occurred where and when they did.

Was it that, far from being divine inspiration experienced by

[handwritten margin note: contained in trees & water & so on, but free agents with superior powers to his own & with human characteristics.]

very few, they actually saw superior beings who were so advanced they could not classify them as brother humans? Could it be that, although similar in appearance, their size and strength dwarfed the primitive to such a degree they displaced his previous concepts and items of worship? If then these 'gods' departed, mankind would ensure that they were never forgotten. They would raise monuments and tell stories of the wondrous deeds they had seen. Alternatively, as they slowly emerged from savagery, they may have simply REMEMBERED!

Was it a knowledge, deep in their subconscious, of the superiors who had created them in the first place? Was this recognition the natural progression of lost memories seeping from the subconscious memory into the conscious animal mind? We would be well advised to consider this possibility, if only to remove the confusing fact of present-day man having a 1500cc brain for no apparent reason. Furthermore, there are many other physiological factors in the design of the human body which might suggest that we would fare better in a lower gravitational field. Was this human model a compromise of an indigenous ape-like creature upon which was superimposed the blueprint of something from elsewhere? If this were so, the tell-tale genetic memory of that creature would exist in every one of us somewhere. Let us assume that in isolated cases ('throw-backs') the gap between the subconscious, or should we say super conscious, and conscious mind was inadvertently bridged to some degree. Here we would have a simple explanation for those mental giants of mythology and ancient history, or the less frequent geniuses of modern times.

According to Mendel's Law, the probability of these mutations would diminish as the interbreeding patterns moved man to a homogeneous intellect. If there is the possibility of a store of knowledge in our superconscious mind, certain mental exercises may strengthen the connection sufficiently to draw from it. Possibly at times of crisis we already do! With this premise it is also possible, if not perhaps likely, that certain 'keys' would facilitate the process. Equally likely is the fact that other actions or thought processes may place a barrier between them. In this category lies the concept that man has no need of this additional intellect. It is the misconception of already having qualified as 'God's chosen creatures', and of believing that we can appoint others of our kind to represent us before the Almighty. It is believing that no matter how deceitful, how vile and aggressive one is on earth, all will be forgiven, and we will eventually be united in heaven. This is the philosophy which will numb the mind and prevent the 'keys' from opening the doors. It will ensure that heaven is never here on earth, which is the only place it could be.

For religious sects to claim that their belief is the right one and to persecute others is lunacy. We would certainly consider it so if surgeons persecuted homeopaths. For 2000 years the mental progress of man has been arrested in the mistaken belief that education is intelligence. Education is learning about things! Intelligence is the result of improving the working of the mind, and there are no degrees in that subject.

From the media we hear an incessant sermon on keeping the body fit and well, but surely, as necessary as this is, the body is only the vehicle to carry that ultimate tool of mankind, the mind. The mind of man, once released from the suffocating complacency of man-made religion, is ever-enquiring, always looking for answers and if released it will find them.

The unsolved mysteries which we seem to delight in printing over and over again are not mysteries at all. The only real mystery is why we have not solved them before! Although the readers have had to suffer the repetition of some of these in this book, I trust they may also have received some insight into the manner in which they have been misrepresented. This being so, I will, with no difficulty, disclose the meaning behind the apparent confusion of imagery to which we have been subjected.

First I trust that the reader will join me in the expression of my gratitude to the Cathars, the Templars, the Pythagoreans, the Priory of Sion, the Brothers of the Rose Cross and hundreds of others to whom I dedicate this work, specifically:

TO THOSE WHO GAVE THEIR LIVES IN ORDER THAT THE TRUTH WOULD BE PRESERVED AND TO THOSE WHO LIVE AND HAVE THE 'UNDERSTANDING'

and possibly above all to those who provided the 'keys' and the indestructible geometry of the Temple Isis at Rennes-le-Château.

The removal of the phallus is the first item we must understand. Initially in the primitive mind it appears to have been a deep-seated memory or desire, which was probably attributable to a revulsion in the superconscious, inherited from the superior creature. If this superior race was androgynous, the female body with its concealed organ would be visually acceptable, but the appendage of the male organ could well have been considered offensive. The awakening of the animal mind and the inheritant revulsion is well documented in *Genesis* and the name of the book is a good reminder that early intelligence should be attributed to the GENES of ISIS.

Before the awakening we are told

> And they were both naked, the man and his wife, and were not ashamed.
>
> *Genesis II*, 25

But with the dawning of intelligence inherited from the androgynous god, they recognized the animal factor in their composition and they were ashamed of it:

And the eyes of them both were opened, and they knew that they were naked; and they sewed fig leaves together, and made themselves aprons.

Genesis III, 7

The removal of the phallus therefore qualifies as a means of taking away that which was offensive, much as anyone who had an unsightly growth would wish to do. This action is also in the category of being imitative, for whereas a naked woman could pose as an androgyne, a man could not. Since their appearance much closer to that of the 'gods' it is little wonder all the early deities were female. You will recall that to be equally deified Osiris had to lose his phallus. Set on the other hand retained his and was, as a consequence, considered the epitome of evil. His association with the ass is by virtue of the disproportionate size of that animal's virile member.

The male may consider that he was on the wrong side of this 'division for the sake of union', but there were many in the past who did not agree. Whereas the female, with her internal organ must necessarily remain a sexual being, the male had it in his power to remove the offending phallus, and in so doing also remove the animal desire of sexual union. It would therefore assist him to suppress all his animal instincts. This would allow him to develop his mind towards the pattern of the mind of the gods.

We may now reconsider the position of the sexes. Woman is supposedly cursed, as *Genesis* tells us, by the possession of her unremovable sexual organ; man on the other hand may remove his 'handicap' whenever he chooses. We know that in order to 'qualify', the priests of the Ishtar and Isis Temples elected to follow this painful path and, by so doing, to elevate their mental processes. To what degree this line of action was successful, I am in no position to judge, nor am I considering testing it. I believe, however, there may be another way to achieve the same result. If nothing else, the understanding of this ritual dispenses with many so-called mysteries and mysterious *bric-à-brac* from the past.

Inevitably, we must now turn our attention to the womb, which has been revealed to be the most dominant factor in the secret doctrine and the main feature of the geometry at Rennes. Undoubtedly the birth process would have appeared miraculous to the primitive mind and it would be unlikely that it would be associated with the copulation which had occurred nine months previously. To see the vagina sufficiently enlarged to allow a baby to pass through was remarkable enough, but the creation of another being must have left early man in a state of bewilderment. No doubt it also left them wondering just where on earth the new-born child had come from. If all matter created was the work of the Almighty, the vagina of the female was clearly a gateway to the tunnel which would link directly to Him. This would naturally make it the 'holiest' place or 'hole' on earth. At first this thought process seems crude or at least irreverent, but if we pursue the concept, we may arrive at the conclusion that this primordial thought was part of the grand plan and certainly closer to the truth than is at first apparent.

At this point we need professional medical advice, possibly even in advance of that which is at present available. I would like the reader to consider the confusion in my mind when I found undeniable reference to the existence of a fluid or secretion in the female reproductive organ, which is apparently directly linked with intelligence. Concealed within a doctrine which at first appears to be nothing other than primitive sexual imagery, I found evidence of illustrious people in the past going to considerable lengths to record this incredible FACT, anyway, it certainly seems they thought it was. Heavily veiled in the allegories of the alchemists and the Brotherhood of the Rose Cross was the unbelievable suggestion that in some way a minute trace of a very potent liquid seeped from the brain of a woman and collected in the womb or vaginal cavity or, if not, it was secreted there and had properties associated with the brain. It would further appear this secretion was cyclic on a monthly basis. Alternatively, a certain amount may remain *in situ* and be expelled during the menstrual cycle. I am sure the reader will now appreciate the meaning behind the age-old mystery of the Rose and the Lily of the Valley. Could this really be so? Was the Elixir being continuously generated in every female body and expelled twice every month? Given the 'understanding' it is suggested that to imbibe this fluid elevates the mind; this is liquid intelligence; the bridge between the conscious and superconscious mind.

If this really is so, the recurrent skull of the mysteries is a mystery no longer. What better symbol of intelligence from the past, from a race long dead or departed, could one adopt which would be more explicit than a skull? And to enhance the image with female symbolism, particularly virginity, can only mean that we are meant to ignore the sexual implications. There can be no sexual suggestion in a virgin and a male with no penis. Behind the veil of sexual imagery is convincing evidence that this is something totally different from the animal reproductive process. The allegory of the skull 'providing' is clear; it provides and symbolizes intelligence.

The Ark of the Covenant is the womb and it contains the gift from the Almighty – intelligence! It also tells us where lies the secret secretion by which the intellect may be raised to a higher level. Little wonder that the skull of Baphomet was considered the 'source'. No longer need we puzzle over the Templar legend of the skull found between the legs of a female after the act of necrophilia by her lover.

And so, in my stupidity, I thought all was solved, until one evening my publisher John Chambers dropped in to check how I was progressing with writing this book. He expressed the desire, quite reasonably, to verify some of my calculations. He soon realized that far from exaggerating the perfection of the Rennes geometry, I was if anything, understating it.

Certain dimensions of the figure had puzzled me by not conforming to the code, and he suggested we should spend a couple of hours looking at these together. One in particular was crucial, it was the diameter of the circle of churches. We spent some time checking the precise scale of the maps to obviate any possibility of distortion and finally we decided the diameter on the ground was slightly in excess of **372,000** inches. I know I should have realized it sooner, but suddenly the thought came to me, Isis was the radius and she brought intelligence or light into the animal mind by her association with Lucifer (the bringer of light). The radius is, of course, half the diameter. It is **186,000**, the speed of light!

We looked up to where I had pinned a diagram of the Poussin tomb on the wall; the length of the tomb was **100** inches, the length of the lid was **86** inches. Poussin knew! When was the speed of light determined? In the 18th century by the French physicist Jean-Bernard Léon Foucault.

Once again the mind reels with the near-impossibility of the level of intellect displayed in the geometry. Was the speed of light known to the Templars? I find this extremely unlikely, but possibly only because they failed to recognize the full significance of the dimensions of the diagram. Once again came an almost incredible truth; if they did not know it, somebody before their time certainly did!

The number code came to us again **186** − **18** and **6** – ISIS and RA and its simple reflection, **681**; the PEACE 681 from the cipher found in the church at Rennes-le-Château. Then, looking at the length of the tomb again, I remembered that for those who had the 'understanding', **100** inches is **8.333** feet and this number in minutes equates to **500** seconds – the time taken for the light of the sun to reach the Earth. Did Poussin know the distance to the sun? I am sure he did. Furthermore he intended us to realize it, for the diagonal measure of the lid of the tomb is **93**; the distance from the Earth to the sun in millions of English miles.

I checked the other diagonals carefully **108.4**, **68.4**, **93.2** and their sum was incredible – **270**, the number of the womb. There could be no doubt. Here was the secret of the light of intelligence in the womb. The tomb carried the same message as the Ark of the Covenant.

It was very late when John left, and I decided to make one final check of this startling discovery. I sat back to look at the diagram from a distance as I had done so many times before. Knowing this dimension did not, of course, change anything in the geometry, but it modified my mental concept of it. Only a few minutes had passed before I began to feel that strange sensation in my mind again. No other part of the body is affected – no tension – no excitement – a feeling of something physically moving inside the brain. And then an overwhelming orgasm of knowing. Knowing something far beyond the scope of this book.

23

Questions Answered

And then Thyself with shining Foot shall pass
Among the Guests Star-scatter'd on the Grass,
And in thy joyous Errand reach the Spot
Where I made one – turn down an empty Glass!

Who built it? – when was it built? – why was it built?

I am sure the geometry and the numerical values at Rennes will tell us more in the future, but even at this stage the revelations are staggering. The question of WHO? WHEN? and WHY? will eventually be answered in detail by the experts who examine my work, but for the moment it would be cowardly if I did not attempt to answer those questions myself.

WHO? is best approached by asking two further questions:
    1) Who knew it was there?
    2) Who had the mathematical capability to achieve it?

From the evidence I have gathered, the first question resolves itself into a graduated set of answers. At one end of the scale we have those who considered the whole Templar affair to be allegorical. In the secret doctrine they saw nothing other than an alternative reading of the scriptures with the emphasis laid on different events. After great argument they will always return to 'square one', wondering whether the discussion was ever worthwhile. In this category are those who considered the temple of the Templars to be the temple of the body, with the mind acting as the Holy of Holies. The advantage of this philosophy is twofold. Firstly in not having to search for anything, and secondly in being able to apply any interpretation they choose on the ancient doctrine.

The next group are those who thought there was something somewhere, but had insufficient evidence to involve themselves with those parts of the mystery that referred to location or positive identities. Some were authors who wrote so classically that their works stand today as reference points in English literature. We see in these works enough of the doctrine, albeit veiled, to know they must have been privy to some part of the secret. To admit to knowing too much about it would apparently have been indiscreet, if not dangerous. Nevertheless one would imagine it was their wish, for this knowledge eventually to become available to all, otherwise there was no reason for them to have made any mention of it.

Lastly there were those great adepts of the past who knew the secret doctrine, but were not necessarily aware of the diagram at Rennes-le-Château. Among these number the Egyptian priest, Plutarch, Pythagoras and Herodutos, to mention but a few. From more recent times, we are bound to consider Jesus and Magdalene and here the picture changes, for there are strong links between Magdalene and the South of France. Ignoring for the moment the intervening thousand years, we are brought closer to our time, to the Cathar and Templar connection and we can safely assume the inner cell of those bodies, which included the Priory of Sion, knew something of the geometry and its numerical values. Considering the way they were persecuted, we can be sure that the Vatican was of the opinion that they understood the meaning contained in it. During and after that time some of the custodians of the secret left enough clues to ensure that people in the future would realize they were involved in the mystery, and nowhere is this more obvious than in the paintings of Poussin.

In our investigation, it has become apparent that the details of the secret doctrine were clearly in the hands of privileged people in the arts and sciences. It is equally obvious that they were also persecuted and hunted down by the Roman Church. This appears to be a prominent feature of the mystery which probably persists to the present day and I am sure we would all like to hear from the Vatican whether this is so.

We must assume that, for at least five hundred years, the responsibility of the preservation of the secret doctrine was in the hands of the Priory of Sion and that responsibility may still be theirs today. This unfortuantely poses more questions; the most confusing one being why the Priory have not yet disclosed it. Possibly they still feel the world is not ready to receive it, and I hope this and other inquiries may cause them to reconsider their silence. I fully sympathize with their predicament, as in some areas of this investigation I have (to a lesser degree), had to consider what to publish and what to hold in reserve. Another and far more likely possibility is that the geometry and some of its meaning was lost.

Having followed the solution through these pages, the reader will have realized how difficult it would be to record the complexities of the geometric relationships without reconstructing and analysing the figure in its totality. I am sure no one would have been permitted to make such an explicit record at the time. The evidence suggests therefore that the secret was preserved piecemeal and eventually it was impossible to reconstruct the entire figure. I have not burdened the reader with the hundreds of calculations which were required in order to recognize the simple progression of numbers that provide the keys needed to unravel the mystery. I am sure it must be obvious that without instruments, a calculator and the use of accurate maps, it would have been almost impossible to solve a figure this complex.

The meaning of some of the secrets have been preserved in

ritual and myth, but despite the attention of many modern authors, myths and legends are classified more closely with fairy-tales than with ancient history and it takes a Schliemann, and the discovery of Troy to bridge the gap. Strangely enough, his incredible achievement was very unpopular with most archaeologists for the simple reason he was not, in their opinion, qualified to look for it in the first place. It would be a tragedy indeed if legislation were ever to be introduced to prevent inspired amateurs from searching for archaeological sites. Having said that, I would concur that, once the sites are found, their excavation should be entirely in the hands of archaeologists.

The WHO KNEW? question, is therefore broadly answered, but it is greatly restricted by who had the capability. By this I do not mean the generation of the original mathematics and geometry. This I am sure, could have been well within the capability of the ancient Egyptians, but we must consider who was capable of the process of transferring such a figure on to the ground. Here we are confronted with something quite odd. Initially, let us assume this is being carried out on a flat plain or desert. A mounted, graduated circle with a centrally pivoted alidade (sight-rule) would suffice for accurate angular measure. Traverse or sighting poles with string between them would be adequate to fix intersections at which either beacon-fires or helios (mirrors reflecting sunlight) would be placed. These positions could subsequently be marked by standing stones or buildings. It appears that we have a simple solution – BUT and it is a very large but – how could we find a place where mountain tops and buildings would correspond to the positions we needed for the geometry? Assuming the mountain tops could not be manipulated, I examined each line individually. Slowly I traced the inevitable sequence of the system by which this incredible construction had been achieved. Each line showed me that something had to be built to complete its function. I wondered if by turning my attention to WHEN? I could discover WHO? I needed evidence of the most recent construction which formed a critical geometric function. Rennes-le-Château had to be a reference point, for it encompassed both requirements, mountain top and construction. Château Blanchefort had the same qualifications and the dating of each of them, with sufficient accuracy for our purposes, could be considered as A.D. 1000. At the end of this particular line was the church at the village of Arques, but it was of approximately the same age and I could not therefore use it to refine the WHEN? question. I looked at the Château d'Arques, surely this was more recent. It was, but then I found it had most probably been erected on the site of a previous château of the 7th century. Next I thought Château Serres would provide a date. It was not constructed until the 17th century, but it marked the vital intersection which controlled the head of the pentagram. If this dating were correct it would bring the geometry into comparatively recent times. When I subsequently found it had been built expressly on the precise site of an extremely ancient château, I decided to give up and accept the inevitable. This geometry was pre-1000 A.D. With this sort of dating, clues become a little sparse.

The area was at one time under the control of the Visigoths, in the name of Ataulf, successor of Alaric who sacked Rome in A.D. 410. It was he who removed the treasures of Solomon's Temple, which Titus had taken from there c. A.D. 70. Before this the Romans were in the area and they left a number of construc-tions which identify their occupation. Mining operations were carried out during this time, and the thermal baths were estab-lished. There is, however, no indication of all the geometric sites being marked by constructions during either period of occupa-tion. If we are thereby forced back to a time prior to the Roman invasion of the area, we have little option but to consider the possibility that this diagram was established by the Celts. By established, I mean marked with standing stones, a well-known fetish of the Celtic tribes. Nevertheless, I could never reasonably attribute the complex mathematical and geometrical calculations to them.

At this stage I would like to remind the reader of the nearby Temple of Alet, one of the many pagan temples in this area. This temple is known to have been dedicated to the Mother of the Gods and she was known by many names, Cybele, Diane, Dana, Isis. This temple is believed to date back to the time of the Celts, and we know that this and the area round Rennes-le-Château was recognized by the Romans as a sacred place. We have seen the area of our geometric temple is littered with the Menhirs of the Celts and I am sure it was they who marked the positions upon which the churches and châteaux of the geometry were eventually built. But who carried out the observations necessary to identify those exact positions? If we are to avoid moving into the realms of science fiction, we will be forced to concede that these instructions emanated from the Druids. This powerful body of priests not only represented the faith and beliefs of the Celtic Gauls but also controlled the judicial system to which all the tribes were subject. There was an annual assembly near Chartres where they sat in judgement. It would be reasonable to assume that their control of the area of Rennes encompassed at least the period from B.C. 500 until Roman times. Their doctrine has been associated with that of Pythagoras and an essential part of their teaching was the immortality of the human soul. Not by a successive number of reincarnations; they were more inclined to believe in the capability of any human to achieve spiritual liberation in his time on earth, a philosophy in keeping with all we have seen at Rennes. One other important link was, that in their pantheon of deities they included Mercury; not a stranger to our mystery. Even more strange is the link with Egypt, in that they worshipped the Virgo Paritura, the virgin and the child. A Druid legend speaks of a time when they received a revelation from heaven in the form of an image upon which were inscribed the words:

> O Lamb of God, That takest away the Sins of the world! Have
> mercy upon us.

This image we are told was placed in the hand of the Druids to
be kept in a certain holy cavern dedicated to the Virgin of the
Conception. The Druidic practice of constructing stone circles is
well known and we are now in a better position to judge exactly
what those circles represented. They were numerical models
relating celestial and female cycles, with the stone circle being the
womb of time. Alternatively we may consider that time is
contained in the womb. Little wonder that the inner circle of the
serpent's head at Avebury numbers **18** stones.

Following our question of WHO? which has united with the
question WHEN? we could be inclined to be content with saying
the Rennes construction was the work of the Celts. This could
never be a satisfactory answer when we recall the observational
accuracy required to construct the figure, and furthermore that
the figure illustrates the legends of Egypt. Or have we once again
taken too much for granted? What we generally refer to as the
Egyptian legends of creation could have been localized. In fact
they could actually be referring to events which occurred
elsewhere, maybe in Atlantis. Can we therefore find anything to
associate Rennes with pre-Celtic times? At first sight this seems
impossible but there, in the *Encyclopedia Brittanica*, we find the
tiny link we require. In referring to the belief Druidism, we see
that it

> . . . is probably in its simplest terms the pre-Celtic and aboriginal
> faith of Gaul and the British Isles that was adopted with little
> modification by the migrating Celts. It is easy to understand that
> this faith might acquire the special distinction of antiquity in
> remote districts such as Britain, and this view would explain the
> belief expressed to Caesar that the 'disciplina' of Druidism was of
> insular origin.

Pre-Celtic, in the countries bordering the ocean wherein we
place the lost continent of Atlantis, from which as the 'land of the
setting sun' came their forefathers: I believe we are in a position to
make logical assumptions.

WHO?   The survivors of Atlantis.
WHEN?   When Atlantis sank into the ocean probably
        9000 B.C. or before.
WHY?   To mark the position of their lost empire; but
        probably a good deal more!

In the first place we could never dismiss the complexity of the
geometry as nothing but a marker. Secondly, why should the
marker carry a graphic representation of what we have supposed
to be the Egyptian legends of the creation of man? Legends which
also carry in them numerical identities, thereby conforming to the

Druid teaching that numbers predated letters. I am sure the reader will now appreciate how if an advanced civilization were destroyed, the survivors would be isolated in pockets and over thousands of years would revert to savagery. Little by little they could adapt to their new environments, always with the advantage that in the deep recesses of their minds was a memory of the days when they, like gods, were masters of their destiny. Languages would be developed independently which would be unintelligible to those of distant places, even though we are still able to detect certain unexplained similarities between them. On the other hand mathematics (in particular geometry) is invariable. As the intelligence slowly recovered, the relationship of geometric figures would be rediscovered and they would be universal. If certain special figures were of great significance in the distant past, they would survive deep in our subconscious and with sufficient stimulation they would manifest themeselves thousands of years later.

This is the secret of Rennes-le-Château!

There, marked on the ground, is a figure which every human mind carries within it. That figure tells a story which also lies deep in our memory. In it are secrets preserved for the time when we will be qualified to use them.

And this is the answer to WHY!

How well I remember those times when the momentary link was made and my mind was suddenly possessed, not by demons or angels, but by the genetic memory of the story of mankind, which I had inadvertently activated.

Those times when suddenly I knew what some of the Cathars and Templars must have known; that deep in our subconscious lies a memory of our origin, a memory so small it is barely able to be seen. But it is there. The imperceptible gleam of that memory marks the position of a portal through which, with courage, the mind can pass into a void of eternity and enlightenment. It is there in everyone of us. Suddenly I knew that in every human mind was the knowledge of the origin of the very cells of which it was composed and a vast sphere of awareness was there to be seen. From that sphere and through that portal intelligence enters the embryo and for that moment its mind sees the gateway to the void from which it came and to which in death it will return. Suddenly I knew it could be seen before the final event. Incredibly it was possible momentarily to stand on the threshold and glimpse at what lies beyond.

In this book the reader has been subjected to a veritable barrage of detailed information drawn from every source of human activity. The arts, the sciences, the legends, secret societies and religious history all carry in them fragments or imprints of what was once a knowledge of the total, or as near to it as the material brain could contain. It is necessary to understand those tiny component parts, to give them value, but not too much. The mind must be confident that they exist and that they are real. Take nothing I have said on faith or my time in writing this book has been wasted. Criticize, verify and search further. You will find that surrounding these fragments are dozens of others which drift away from your point of examination until they disappear from sight in the mists of uncertainty. Eventually you will find you have sufficient detail to be able to step back and recognize a vague outline on the canvas of time and space. With that recognition comes enlightenment and, no matter how strange the image, neither add to or take from, what is being shown to you.

Every human mind carries within it the picture of the past, and the actual memory of events of hundreds of thousands of years before our time. Not the knowledge of creation. That will never be ours, but the record of the dawn of intellect which is available to every one of us may be the secret of creation itself.

Only secular pursuits and religious dogma will veil the truth from our eyes. Never is a human being closer to truth than when it floats in the sea of the womb of its mother. A sea tinged with a magical fluid from the mind of the creature which nourishes it. A fluid so strange that it permeates the genes of the embryo and elevates it to a creature of intellect. As the mind of the embryo grows, it is fed with the story of its ancestors; further and further back to the creation of primordial thought. All that has ensued since the first moment of intellectual awareness is known to it and so interwoven is the labyrinth of the interbreeding of our species that this programme is almost identical for every one of us. But somewhere at the bottom of the vortex of the subconscious, where there should be nothing but the first imperceptible glimmer of thought, there is a piercing needle of light; so small, so bright, the mind cannot perceive what lies beyond it.

Then the waters break and a curtain of redness flows over the mind of the child – sound, sensation and pain. An unintelligible cacophony of impulses career through the delicate structure of distant memory, ripping and tearing the fabric to shreds which flutter down and lodge in tiny crevices. These are the threads of memory for which you must search your mind.

I would not ask you to live like a hermit, or to neglect your daily responsibilities. Continue as mother or father or lover or whatever, but never believe your function or the time you spend on any given stage of life is really *you*. The awareness which allows you to read these words and comprehend the abstract images they convey is not that of the animal. The arts, justice, truth and pure love, only the human can experience, but we also experience all those primitive emotions of animal behaviour. Classify them! Do as you will, but remember if mankind chooses to remain an animal, so he will be treated and it will be to that form he will return. If we are ever to walk with the gods, we must be like them.

And so it might have ended. It seemed to be all and I was congratulated for my success. So why did I feel failure? Many things, unseen by others, cast shadows that I could not ignore. I knew I had overlooked something vital, and it harassed me to such a degree that instead of feeling I had found something, I felt I had lost it. Slowly I retraced my steps, pausing at those places which I had previously thought of as blind alleys. Most still were, but then I found one that was not.

24

The Secret of Light

What greater crime could there have ever been,
To leave a cleft, through which it can be seen
That all our efforts to achieve the goal,
Are nothing, but the chance to find the hole.

(*NOT the Rubáiyát*)

The hexagram appears – the star union – perfect imperfection again – a ray of astral
light – the identities confirmed – Poussin held the key – a fracture in the fabric of time.

There were many things which brought me to discover the final
geometric key of Rennes. It was more like being led to a
position by a symphony of implications, any one of which could
hardly be considered tangible evidence if examined individually.
The most persistent factor which made me consider my solution
incomplete, was the absence of a geometric equivalent for the
male, or his phallus. Admittedly there was the Ass and the
fourteen stones of the inverted cross, but this was imagery and not
interacting geometry. In my previous studies of occult geometry, I
had heard that one of the keys to the mysteries was the secret union
of the pentagram and the hexagram. I had seen dozens of attempts
to achieve this, but none of them, in my opinion, warranted
serious consideration. Supposedly if this were ever successfully
achieved, it would be immediately apparent to an adept from the
resultant figure. A figure which, in turn, would be a great
revelation.

Almost as soon as this crossed my mind, I felt the familiar tingle
of the proximity of a truth. All those diagrams had been
constructed in circles and squares. All of them used a pentagram
which was 'contained'. I wondered how different the geometry
would be, using the extended pentagram of Rennes, based on a
circle of **15** divisions. The answer was immediately self-evident;
the arc carried by the arms is five divisions of the circle. The arms
are five miles long and the arc is six. If either the **360,000** inch or
the **372,000** inch circle is used, it makes little difference – **6.1483**
and **5.9499** respectively.

Then came that flash of inspiration which is always needed at
times like these.

The arms of Satan and the Cross of Lorraine . . .

The arms of Jesus and the Cross of Lorraine . . .

(Charles Péguy *La Tapisserie de Sainte Geneviève*)

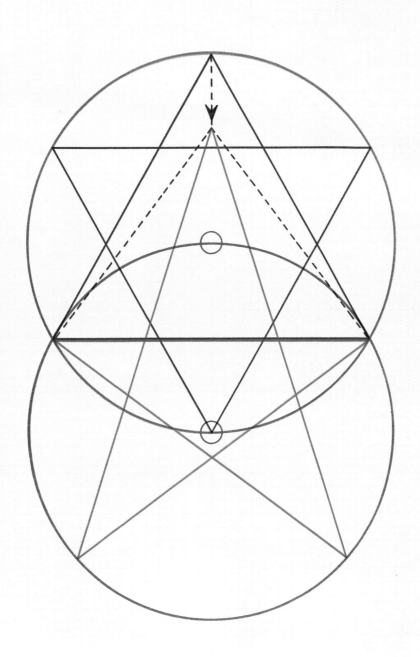

145. The Star union showing the
hexagram and the extended
pentagram of Rennes united by the
Vesica Piscis.

146. The author standing by the Pierre Dressée, the famous Celtic marker near the tomb of Poussin.

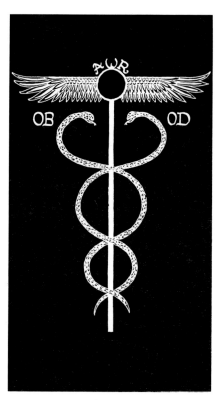

147A. The Caduceus symbolising the Astral Light, a well known symbol of the occult.

Hence we conclude that the arms of Jesus are the arms of Satan. Jesus was of the line of King David and Solomon whose emblem was the hexagram and the Christians consider the pentagram to be the symbol of Satan. The **6** points of the hexagram are two arms, two legs, a head and a phallus.

The geometry was becoming clear to me. The hexagram divides the circumference into six portions and the arms support **2** portions of the circle which is precisely the same proportion of arc as that supported by the extended pentagram. (Two sixths and five fifteenths).

The construction was now quite simple:

1) Draw two circles with the centre of the second on the circumference of the first. This is the Vesica Piscis, a figure representing the female organ.

also origin of Jesus' fish symbol

2) Join the intersections of the circumferences. This is the cleft of the female organ which doubles for the arms of both the hexagram of one circle and the arms of the pentagram of the other. These are the arms of Jesus and Satan.

3) The result is immediately obvious; it is a 7-pointed star – Set – Satan (illus 145). But if the arms are united in this

fashion the 'head' of the hexagram coincides with the vulva of the female. There was much in the secret doctrine to suggest there was good reason for this arrangement, but this position usually implies a similar action occurring at the opposing axis of the hexagram. The opposite point of the hexagram does not however coincide with the head of the female and I decided to alter the construction to make it do so (pecked lines in diagram). The only value I could see in this figure was the improved ratio of the size of the triangles representing the head and the phallus.

The next step was to apply this geometry to the ground in the hope that it would expose the identity of the controlling features. This it did in a most convincing manner. I plotted the regular equiangular triangle and found that the north-easterly arm went through the Pierre Dressée (illus 146) and then directly into the summit of the mountain of Montredon which had been the confirmatory point fixing the north wall of the Temple. The other arm was equally impressive, it passed through the church of Luc-sur-Aude to the summit of Pech de Luc, forming the perfect **60°** triangle. Once again I was alerted to the occult significance of the names. Luc could be Lucifer – light; and Aud in occult teaching is the union of the Ob (Hebrew) and the Od (Hebrew). These are the entwined serpents of Astral Light and signified by the Caduceus (see illus 147A). I knew another great secret was nearby. First I needed to find the controlling circle.

I had noticed previously that the Château de Blanchefort was midway between the apex and the intersection of the legs of the pentagram. Taking Blanchefort as centre, I described a circle and the result was surprising. Travelling clockwise it passes through the survey beacon on the summit of Le Laplégadou, to the intersection of the pentagonal legs, to Rennes-le-Château, to the church of Luc-sur-Aude and back to the pentagonal apex. The triangle it had contained was a regular 60° one, but it conformed to my interpretation of the star union, the one which was condensed. Then I noticed something which was most strange. The circle had 'cut off' the right hand of the pentagonal arm. I recalled the words of Jesus in *Matthew V*, verse 30. 'If thy right hand offends thee, cut it off' and the *Peste d'Azoth* by Poussin had confirmed it. I drew a new line from the apex of the pentagram to the severed position and could hardly believe what I saw. It now passed precisely through the female head rock of Toustounes. This had to be confirmation of the interpretation. I then noticed that the innocuous Château Blanchefort adopted a totally different character when seen as the guardian force at the centre of the hexagram; from here it was the beast, the demon guardian of the first coded cipher (illus 148).

Next with the same centre at Blanchefort I increased the radius to accommodate the regular triangle, the result was certainly impressive. This circle passed through la Berco Petito, the Château of Couiza, Pech de Luc, Montredon and then another

147B. Toustounnes

148. The demon guardian overlooks the secret location.

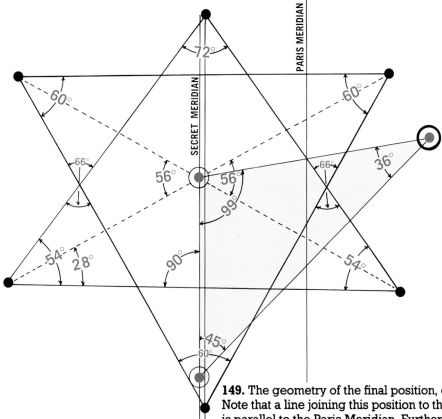

149. The geometry of the final position, controlled by the star of Set. Note that a line joining this position to the secret location in the womb is parallel to the Paris Meridian. Furthermore, note that both locations are controlled from the Château d'Arques and the angle between them at that point is 36 degrees.

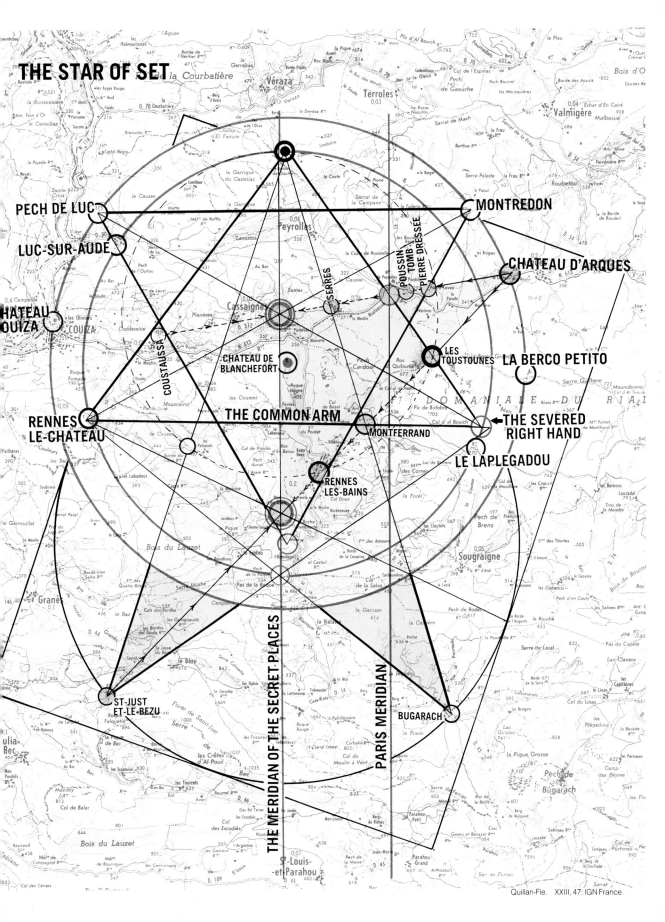

THE STAR OF SET

PECH DE LUC

LUC-SUR-AUDE

CHATEAU
COUIZA

RENNES
LE-CHATEAU

COUSTAUSSA

CHATEAU DE
BLANCHEFORT

MONTREDON

POUSSIN
TOMB
PIERRE DRESSÉE

CHATEAU D'ARQUES

SERRES

LES
TOUSTOUNES

LA BERCO PETITO

THE COMMON ARM

MONTFERRAND

← THE SEVERED
RIGHT HAND

LE LAPLEGADOU

RENNES
LES-BAINS

ST-JUST
ET-LE-BEZU

THE MERIDIAN OF THE SECRET PLACES

PARIS MERIDIAN

BUGARACH

Quillan-Fle. XXIII, 47: IGN France.

surprise – the famous Château d'Arques (illus 149).

The next step, which is geometrically obvious, was to join the opposing points of the hexagram. In a completely regular figure the diagonals would have intersected at the centre of the circle. As one of the triangles was suppressed in height, the intersection moved away from the centre. I examined this point very carefully.

If ever I was sure of anything it was now. This point was on a line of features which were staggering: the tiny cemetery of Coustaussa, the Château Serres, the Poussin Tomb, the Pierre Dressée and the famous Château d'Arques again. There was also a geometric intersection; the line passed through the intersection of the Paris meridian and the side of the triangle which cuts off the right hand.

And what of the position itself? The angle at Rennes-le-Château between it and the pentagonal arm was **28°** the number of Nephthys with whom we have identified the church. Set was also demonstrated, for the angle formed by the intersection of the axes was **56°**. Even the number of Thoth or maybe the beast was evident; it was the angle generated by the intersection of the sides of the two triangles of the hexagram, **66°**. Here are miracles enough for anyone, but there are more. The line which joins this new secret location to the position of the seed is exactly parallel to the Paris meridian. Then it struck me that both of the unbelievable lines of features which had led to the secret locations had originated at the Château d'Arques. I measured the angle between these two lines. It was **36°**! At the new location I checked the angle from the seed to Château d'Arques which had passed through the tomb of Poussin, it was **99°** and you will recall there were 99 stones in the completion of the temple and that was the distance from the ground to the top of the tomb in inches after we had completed the construction. But the tomb had shown us something else, the speed of light. I measured the distance from Château d'Arques to the new location. **It was the speed of light in inches!**

My mind reeled at what was implied. I had found the seed in the womb of the circle of light and now I had found the centre of light. The seed in the womb of Isis and the means by which to activate it – the harmonic of Set – the Typhon – Satan.

Was this staggering secret of the Astral Light of the alchemists with the serpent (the Ob) lying at nearby Peyrolles, the massive Serpent Rouge? Could now I have the final secret? Could there be an harmonic of light which will unite the super conscious mind to the conscious? A gateway to the infinite wisdom of the gods who created us in their image.

I looked at the numbers again, was it another harmonic – one which could disrupt molecular structure. I realized that for a moment I had seen through the bars of the cage to what lies beyond. I had seen outside the playground of earthly science where man invents his own physics and then applauds himself for having understood it. A model which is shaped by the quality and the extent of the intelligence it contains. But the fluid forces from

150. A pictorial diagram of the main features of the solution of Rennes-le-Château.

THE TEMPLE OF THE STARS

Quillan-Fle. XXIII, 47: IGN France.

which the cage of time is constructed are slightly at variance with the inflexible mathematics by which it is measured. There is a small recurring gap in the mesh of the veil of time and light. The receding galaxies do not recede, but if they did not appear to do so there could be no escape from the time and space in which we could exist.

We are creatures of the sieve, but we know nothing of the holes.

The lesson of the labyrinth is now clear. There are parts of entity which linear science will never see, no matter how far the tangents are reflected. But to see beyond the veil, to break through the circle of the abyss is within our reach.

If these are the secrets of Rennes-le-Château! What is buried there?

I called the publisher, we must delay publication for this. He was patient; he had seen me before on these flights of fantasy and he knew where they led – to the fantastic.

He explained that already the book was too large. It would have to be a bestseller even now, if it was to cover the costs.

I tried to reconcile my mind to this restriction. Could the commercial factors control even this? How could I say in a few words what I could now see stretching out before me?

He looked at the book jacket and smiled: *Genisis – The Book of Revelations*. 'Change the title of the book', he said, with disarming simplicity. 'Call it *GENISIS: The FIRST Book of Revelations*.'

Publisher's Note:
As a safeguard against the possibility of circumstances arising whereby he is unable to finalize his research, the author has requested that two further items should be recorded at this stage. In doing this he discloses something which would be vital to any future researchers who were attempting to follow his trail. These statements in themselves are nothing short of a mathematical miracle.

It has been previously demonstrated that the perimeter of the temple rectangle was enlarged to accommodate the arc of Nut and thereby become **27 miles**.

1) The total length of the straight lines forming the pentagram and contained in the circle of churches is **27 miles**.

2) The total length of the straight lines forming the hexagram and contained within the temple perimeter is **27 miles**.

These are manifestations of the pregnant womb, **27** or **270** (9 months of 30 days), the reflection of the pentagonal **72** and they signify light in the creative womb. For those who have the 'understanding' this is the function of light in the creation of the universe.

Epilogue
The Fairy Story

Then said another – "Surely not in vain
My Substance from the common Earth was ta'en,
That He who subtly wrougt me into Shape
Should stamp me back to common Earth again."

We have completed a voyage of discovery into uncharted areas. Many others will follow and one day, God willing, all will be understood. For the moment I am asking the reader to see the connections in items far removed from each other in location and time. This book shows, to the best of my ability, the meaning contained in the primary stages of the geometry of Rennes and that meaning includes events which may pre-date even our wildest estimates for the existence of an intellect on this planet.

Outside the scope of this investigation, but still harmonizing with it, the imagination rules, for the moment at least. Many scenarios come to mind which could take us from our present findings, remote as they are, back to the very origin of intellect. To provide food for thought I offer here just one of many possibilities. It is no more than a story, a fairy story if you will, no proof this time, no confirmation, ignore it if you choose.

As far as I am able, I will use names which were given by man, so that the reader may more easily equate events with those which he knows. The ape I refer to could have been Neanderthal, a primitive creature of Earth's past history with a 500cc brain capacity. The two created creatures, the Seths and the Cains, are collectively known as Cro-Magnon. The explanation of that small colony of Neanderthals of much higher brain capacity in Western Europe will be easily understood as the story unfolds.

Once upon a time, long ago and far away, in the planets of the star of Sirius, lived a race of beings who had developed, to a level of intelligence almost beyond our comprehension. They knew nothing of the problems which beset mankind today. They had total control over their environment and millions of years had passed since any disease had been known to them. Their bodies served only as vehicles to transport their brains and to perform the simplest of tasks.

The most physically active period for these beings was when they were involved in bringing up a child. The sexes had long since merged, so that there was no male or female; they were androgynous, and any one of them could reproduce if it so chose. But this is not to say they did not experience emotions, although these were not the violent animal emotions of mankind. They had a great deal of love for their children and derived immense pleasure from music and art. Not that we would ever recognize it, for the harmony that would please them was so subtle it would be imperceptible to our senses. Their faculties worked on problems so advanced we could not even comprehend them, save one – their desire to achieve communication with the force of creation.

The conquest of space was a thing of the past to them and starships had been constructed during their development that could reach the ultimate speed of light. Their sphere of influence was governed only by the time they were willing to expend on such a journey. This restriction and the accompanying problem of the Lorentz transformation of time had never been solved and to some degree, they were psychologically depressed by it. Their boundaries, though infinite in one sense, were certainly finite and bounded when related to their origin of operation. In their history of exploration they had been surprised that, as star system after star system was visited, although they found an abundance of life on many planets, they had never found an advanced intelligence other than their own.

Long before, in the pioneering days of their development, they had mastered genetic engineering, producing any number of sub-intelligent creatures to carry out tasks of mining, farming and so on. As they progressed their medical science had almost totally cured them of the disease of ageing. The population was strictly controlled to the environment, so that the need for manufactured creatures had long since vanished. New levels of ethics had outlawed the practice of breeding these sub-intellects as it had been abused in the past. To all appearances, this stable intellectual society was established to a point of being indestructible. There was however, a terrible secret, known only to a select few in the governing body.

The other stars in the Sirius system were interacting in a manner at variance with calculations which had been made a thousand times before and considered to be perfect. What was more, the effect was increasing at an alarming rate. It indicated that a nearby star which had served as a 'refuse disposal' station for hundreds of thousands of years was no longer functioning as predicted. They had anticipated it would remain fairly stable for millions of years finally moving towards the 'red giant' phase, another slow process involving a vast period of time. The immense and finely balanced forces in the star had however elected to follow the unlikely and unpredictable alternative – a vortex in time. Within a hundred thousand years or so they knew the mesh of space and time at the core of the star would fracture and its celestial neighbours would eventually inexorably be drawn into the void. Not wishing to alarm the people, the governing body devised a plan. Under the guise of a revival of an intergalactic voyage to verify a suspected intelligence, three massive spherical star-ships were constructed in orbit round one of the planets. They were named Nosira, Setorion and Isinos. Although a good deal of speculation had arisen as to why such vast ships were required for such a mission, it was all forgotten when the government arranged a grand tour for all those who were interested to see the ships for themselves. On the first day the visitors were those specially invited by the Council. The plan succeeded and hundreds were shuttled to the orbiting ships. When the target figures were achieved the ships moved off. By the time it was realized what had happened, the vessels were deep in space and only by using great diplomacy, did the Council eventually persuade the majority that this act of deceit had been executed for the salvation of their species. For countless years they travelled and finally approached our solar system in the year 200,000BN (Before Now). They despatched probes to the planets and began to monitor the results.

These probes could analyse instantly the environment of a planet by a method unknown to us. Simply, the movement of a celestial body creates a pattern in the light that strikes it. The analysis of the reflected rays produce harmonics which carry a complete diagnosis of the planet. These could be transcribed into sound and even those people who were not trained in this science would recognize immediately the compatibility of the environment of the sphere under examination. There was no doubting the symphony of Mars; it came to them like a long forgotten melody, its harmonics were almost identical to those of the planets of their origin. The strong chords of the fifth harmonic of Earth indicated an abundance of water, but the gravitational field was far too oppressive for comfort. Also there was that slight 'grating' pulse in its axial movement, caused by a large degassed comet having impacted the planet during its past history.

The three huge vessels of the Elohim, for that was their name, moved gracefully into their obital positions in the Martian sky.

The colonization progressed rapidly and within a few hundred years, the cities of the Elohim were established all over the surface of the planet. Culture centres provided breathtaking holograms of landscapes of the neighbouring planets. The Earth, teeming with animal and plant life, was particularly exciting to them.

In time it became increasingly obvious that it would be far more economical to farm the planet Earth than to maintain the agricultural domes of Mars, where water was quite scarce by comparison. The technology was no problem to these people, but there were two factors which perplexed them. The first, although not serious, was the dense humid atmosphere, the quality of the air was perfect, but there was just too much of it. A simple restrictor valve and a light-weight helmet was designed to solve the problem.

The second was insurmountable. It was the gravitational field of the Earth, which almost trebled their weight. Even those who had been specially trained could not tolerate this burden for more than a few weeks at a time.

The only logical step was to create an orbital station. This could be used as a staging post of the freighters which passed between the planets and also provide a rest station to rotate the Earth contingent. The duty was, nevertheless, very unpopular, as it was both exhausting and menial. Great pressure was brought to bear on the Council to reverse the ban on genetic manipulation. Surely, it was argued, if it had achieved its objectives once in the history of the people, the present circumstances qualified to an even greater extent.

The Council conceded. Five specimens were produced from a female ape-like creature who had been brought back to Mars from Earth. Four of the specimens were perfect, two male and two female. The last, the 'runt' of the litter, was a much smaller male and the scientists jocularly disclaimed it. They said two of the larger offspring must have mated while still in the womb. The names given to the males were Set and Osiris, to the females Isis and Nephthys and the 'runt' was named Horus, supposedly the offspring of the largest male and female, Osiris and Isis. They were all trained in the laboratories of the Martian faculties and the intellectual level of the creatures surprised even their creators. Obviously, it would be a cruelty to subject such a high intelligence to the tasks of mining and agriculture on Earth.

Having a standard to work from, a male specimen was produced with a slightly lesser intelligence than the original five. It was named Nephilim. The prototype was approved and the work of 'cloning' was transferred to the orbiting satelite of Earth, which was under the control of Shaitan, a senior executive of the Council.

A suitable base was prepared on an island continent in the Atlantic and a thousand or more Nephilim were trained to supervise the affairs of Earth.

The Elohim were vegetarians and would never have considered eating any mobile life form. On Earth there was an infinite variety of fruit trees and between the middle latitudes of the planet conditions prevailed which produced a continuous supply of fruit. The problem was simply how to gather it. Therefore initially, the task of the Nephilim consisted of:

1) training colonies of Neanderthal apes to collect the fruit,
2) transporting it to the Atlantis base by boat,
3) washing, sorting and packaging it ready for the shuttle craft.

Atlantis was designed to accommodate the continuous coming and going of the fruit-boats and the layout was most ingenious.

Viewed from the air, Atlantis appeared as a huge target of three concentric waterways, the outer one of which was connected to the sea by a canal. This canal was divided in such fashion as to form a way of approach and departure. The water was pumped from a lock near the exit to the sea and thus a 'round-about' system operated which enabled the ships to lower their sails at the canal entrance and to be drawn into the approach waterway. By means of rudder alone, they could then negotiate to the position where they desired to unload their cargo. Having done so, by casting off, they were drawn round the canal until they reached the departure lock. At pre-arranged times the pumping ceased allowing the sea to flow back into the lock until its level equated with the outer ocean. Thereupon the vessels could set sail and depart.

The second of the concentric canals served as the washing area for the fruit prior to it being taken to the central island for packaging. This was the landing area for the shuttles.

The space shuttle used Hydrox as the propellent mass. By subjecting water to a precise harmonic it was dissociated to hydrogen and oxygen, which expanded into the combustion chamber where it was ignited before exhausting as a searing flame. The Nephilim were puzzled by this burning water and the legends of it survived the aeons. Before their eyes they saw the structure of earthly matter disrupted into nuclear chaos, water transformed into vapours of the same elements as the air and with them igniting in a thundrous roar as the shuttles rose to the realm of the gods. Huge transporters plied the journey from Earth to Mars and back every few months. One could always find one of these immense vessels in Earth orbit receiving the shuttles from Atlantis. Earth had proved to be the ideal source for fruit, but vegetables were also required. Unlike the gathering of natural produce, the growing of vegetables would necessitate the clearing of land, planting, sowing seed and the labours of husbandry. Furthermore the rich mineral deposits of the planet Earth had not escaped the notice of the Elohim, and mining was under consideration. For this function the large Neanderthals were not suited, or able. The Council of the Elohim considered the possibilities; other creatures of smaller stature were required. As it was contrary to the law of the Elohim to kill any living creature themselves, the Nephilim were requested to take steps to reduce the Neanderthal population of Earth preparatory to the arrival of the improved species. This the Nephilim did, with awesome efficiency.

Meanwhile the genetic engineers were working on another specimen with the higher levels of the mind cauterized. This was achieved by subjecting the brain to an intense level of radiation, beamed at a specific area. This limited the intelligence of the creature by isolating the highest functions of the mind which were present by virtue of the genetic origin of their brains – the Elohim. The creature was named the Cain and was cloned in thousands. They were trained and put to work in mining projects on Earth. Their smaller stature than the Nephilim facilitated their movement underground. The intellect of the next group was retarded even further, for they had only to prepare ground and grow food. They were called the Seths and were similar to the Cains in size.

Things went well for a time and the supplies required by the Elohim flowed from Earth to Mars. Meanwhile the first five had been utilized by the heads of scientific faculties for duties in the laboratories.

Eventually in the course of the routine medical examinations of the Seths and Cains, it had been noticed that they appeared to be suffering slightly from malnutrition. The reason was soon established, for in their indigenous environment they had been largely carnivorous. To trap animal meat on the planet, to augment the food supplies of the Seths and Cains, would have been a tedious business involving the Elohim in spending time on the planet hunting. Therefore the decision was taken to create two docile animals that would provide the necessary meat. Also it would have the secondary benefit of providing skins which could be used to make protective clothing. The names of the creatures created for this purpose were sheep and cows. Certain of the Seths were trained to care for them, as the intellectual requirement for this task was minimal.

By now Isis had become a beautiful young woman and together with her brothers and sisters, had acquired a comprehensive education. With the exception of the knowledge of generating nuclear power, they ranked close to the Elohim and were permitted free movement round the city. They were very popular, and always an added attraction at the banquets of the Council members of the Elohim. Inevitably the time came when Shaitan requested that they should come under his jurisdiction and be given control of the Atlantis base, responsible to him. Shaitan had his way, for no logical reason could be given to keep them on Mars.

The administration of Earth was no easy matter, for jealousy existed between the groups and in them too. The Cainites were the most resentful, for their work was dangerous and many of them had been killed in mining operations. Also, in contrast to the Seths who could always augment their food supplies with extras from the field, the Cainites received their rations and no more.

Isis and Osiris requested laser equipment to make the work of the Cainites less arduous. It was refused, on the grounds it would put a weapon in the hands of a sub-intellect, which was contrary to the law of the Elohim. They next requested the number of Cainites be doubled to allow Isis to reduce their working hours. This was also refused. The topping up ratio had been laid down and the Elohim saw no reason to change it.

Isis pleaded with Shaitan to use his influence with the Council, which he did, but to no avail. Shaitan being nearer to the problem could appreciate how Isis felt and he recognized something that the Council had not taken into account. It was the affinity which had developed between Isis and her subjects. She was of almost equal intellect to the Elohim and could argue with them as equals, but she was of the flesh of an Earth creature and she was female. The one animal emotion that was residual in her composition was the mother instinct. She had no great love for the Nephilim, in fact their arrogance, a residue of their animal characteristics, had caused her to reprimand them on many occasions. On the other hand she sympathized with the hard-working Cainites and was fully aware they had nicknamed the Nephilim the 'watchers', resentful of the fact that they never seemed to do anything useful.

Isis and Shaitan had become close friends over the years and in consequence of this she confided in him a plan she had devised. She argued thus: as no Elohim had visited Earth for hundreds of years they were unlikely to do so in the future. Therefore, if she were able to produce the necessary additional subjects, no one need know of it. The supplies would continue to flow and her sense of responsibility to the welfare of her subjects would be satisfied. Being fully aware of the animal reproductive processes, she wished to arrange the impregnation of female apes by certain of the Nephilim. The resultant females might well be suitable mothers to produce creatures of equal intellect to the Cainites. Shaitan listened with sympathy, but agreed to no more than to look the other way.

Isis proceeded with her experiment and many years elapsed before she had to admit failure. All the offspring were of the Sethite level of intelligence. Furthermore, they were breeding faster than she had anticipated. It would have been a simple task for her to have destroyed them, but once again she was hampered by her animal mother instincts. Again she approached Shaitan and this time he conceded that, with great secrecy, he would use his skill to impregnate some female apes for Isis in the laboratory of the orbital station. This would produce offspring of Cainite quality.

It is interesting to mention that during these frequent excursions of Isis to the orbiting station, the Seths and Cains, never being able to see the station, were under the impression that Isis was visiting the sun. By virtue of the obvious respect she showed to the unseen Shaitan, they looked upon the sun as the superior deity and even named it Shaitan. They created images illustrating the head of a man surrounded by a nimbus or halo.

We know this experiment of Shaitan's succeeded, and the problem was solved but for one thing. Unbeknown to Isis, the Nephilim, who had been used in her first experiment had conveyed to their associates, that they had experienced an incredible sensation while impregnating the apes. So vivid were their descriptions that when the Nephilim were inspecting the production areas, they were making secret sorties into the forests, searching for female apes, or any other animal similarly equipped, that they may experience the sensation for themselves.

The hideous creatures that resulted from these unions are well known in our mythology. When Isis and Shaitan discovered what had happened they were furious. They ordered the Nephilim to round up the mutations, or at least all they could find, and assemble them in the cities of the plains, a place far-removed from the Atlantis base. When the Nephilim and the mutations were all present and were expecting to be severely reprimanded, Isis and Shaitan destroyed them all by nuclear devices which had been placed in the cities.

The Earth was supposedly thereby cleansed, but as one might imagine, Isis and Shaitan could never be sure that they had located every animal wherein lay the seed of the Nephilim. Isis had good reason to believe that the Nephilim had also impregnated some of the Sethite women of her original experiment. Recall the scriptures:

> – that the sons of God saw the daughters of men, that they were fair and they took them wives of all which they chose.

But Isis decided to overlook this fact. Fortunately, nothing of this had leaked back to the Council on Mars and as far as they were concerned everything was proceeding according to plan, and so it did for a very long time.

Shaitan should have been replaced much sooner than this, but could see no way that he could have explained the vast increase in the Earth's population, or what was even worse, the existence of female Sethites and Cainites, breeding like flies all over the planet Earth. He knew the truth would be bound to come out eventually, but he decided to delay the event as long as possible and not apply for his transfer. He knew, however, that the time would come when an explanation would be required. It came sooner than he expected.

An astronomical faculty on Mars had recorded, deep in space, a massive comet moving towards the solar system and as the years went by they refined their calculations.

Eventually, they had no option but to report to the Council that their original fears were now confirmed; it would pass through the solar system, resulting possibly in collision or violent disruption of the planetary orbits.

The Council were dumbfounded and great argument ensued, in which process one of the Council was sent to the Earth station to inform Shaitan of the impending disaster. It had been agreed in principle, that the three star-ships should be overhauled and the population of Mars and Earth should be taken to a safe stand-off position in space. From there the passage of the comet could be observed and hopefully Mars and Earth would survive. They would then be able to return to the planets. For this comparatively short flight, the ships could be overloaded with people. The Council had calculated that the greater majority of the Earth clones could be accommodated; then if the situation demanded it, they could eventually be utilized to carry out any necessary rebuilding. Inevitably Shaitan's secret was exposed, the vast population of Earth became known to the Council and Shaitan was recalled to Mars to answer the charges.

Meanwhile there were further complications. In their complacency the Elohim had allowed their star-ships to deteriorate. Various faculties had requested certain sophisticated items of equipment for their research and the ships had been cannibalized to such a degree that only one, Isinos, could be made ready in time. The Council decisions were as follows:

1) Isinos would stand off with as many Elohim as could be packed into it.

2) Shaitan would be sent back down to the orbiting station to take his chances in the 'other world' or the 'under-world' as it had been referred to.

3) Earth would be left to its own devices but the five would be taken aboard Isinos, if they so chose.

4) The Council reasoned therefore, that they had not been responsible for condemning anyone. The results of the passage of the comet through the system were unknown and the outcome was therefore, in the hands of the Creator (the Architect of the Universe).

The five decided to stay on Earth for varying reasons:

Isis because of her love for her subjects, the people of Earth.
Osiris because of his allegiance to the Queen.

Set, because he preferred his position of importance on Earth to becoming an inferior being among the Elohim again.

Nephthys, by reason of her allegiance to her consort, Set and her great love of her sister, the Queen.

Horus, because of the compassion shown to him by the Queen and Osiris, which had been misunderstood by all on Earth, to such a degree, that due to his size he had been thought of as their son.

Shaitan insisted that the chances of survival would be better in the station and the five agreed to join him there to await the outcome. Contrary to the instructions of the Council however, certain information was given to the people of Earth, to increase their chances of survival.

Isinos moved off. The comet struck! The system reeled under the massive forces of celestial powers. Asta, the planet between Mars and Jupiter shattered to millions of fragments, many of which rained 'fire and brimstone' on Mars, Earth, Venus and Mercury as it fell towards the sun. The planetary axes moved and were left tilted to inharmonious angles destroying the music of their spheres. The sea washed over the land. The temperatures of the inner planets was raised to an intolerable degree and the dense clouds of water vapour, united with the particles of dust in their tropospheres, to obscure the light of the sun. Venus and Lunar, the two planets between Earth and Mercury, were disrupted from their orbits. Venus came dangerously near to the Earth and Lunar was captured by it. They moved further from the sun and to this day, they swing together in their crazy dance round their new orbit. Venus at one moment went so close to the sun it steamed like a cauldron and still does. Earth and Mars, their surfaces in darkness due to the mantle of dense vapour absorbing the sunlight, grew colder. The massive clouds precipitated as snow on to the dry cold surface and compacted to ice.

Isis was heartbroken to see her people drowned in the mud. Wherever she was able, she assisted their survival and when the ice came she took them to places where caves would give them shelter. Eventually, convection currents formed, as the Earth swung annually, for now there were seasons on the planet. The grip of the ice was broken and the streams began to flow. Mars, being further away from the sun, never recovered and to this day a mile of ice covers its surface. Under that ice lie the abandoned cities of the Elohim.

Volcanoes eventually forced through the ice and showered their ashes and gravel over the surface, until the ice could no longer be seen. In fact, if you were to visit that planet you could mistake it for a stony desert. But look at the density of the planet and look at those great canyons veiled with dust, they merely mark the melting of the ice where lava once flowed.

The rest you know. The five returned to Earth, Isis and Osiris taught the people how to survive. The natural food had been largely destroyed and the seasons restricted the development of the trees which had provided great harvests of fruit in the past. Corn was the answer – and sheep, and cattle, and beer, and Isis provided them.

The land mass in the Atlantic had ruptured and slid to the floor of the ocean. With the main Earth base at Atlantis destroyed, the five operated from a small island to the north of where it had been.

They selected their staff from the elite of the Cainites, entrusting them with scientific knowledge which would have previously been considered too dangerous to be in the hands of creatures of such low intellect. The Cainites were taught to build with stone and to use levers and how to make weapons and tools from the metals their ancestors had mined for the Elohim.

The Cainite women were instructed by Nephthys in medicine; also in the art of curing themselves by extracting chemicals from plants and in the skills of weaving. She taught them how to make potions and perfume which could be used to influence men to be attracted to them; she instructed them in childbirth.

It was the responsibility of Osiris to develop the necessities for the small groups of known survivors throughout the world. For this he used one of the fleet of shuttle-craft which Shaitan had donated to Isis from the orbiting station. To Osiris and his staff was also given the task of distributing corn and barley seed. Instructing the people in its uses, emphasizing that it could not be taken for granted. This gift would not always be there. It was their responsibility to conserve part of their harvest as seed for the ensuing years. Naturally, his visits were timed to coincide with the planting season and harvest time. This gave rise to the Tammuz-Adonis Rites of the Syrian and Greek legends. The arrival of Osiris was a time of celebration and his departure was lamented, for they considered that he had returned to the underworld or the land of the dead. Which he eventually did, for as we know he was murdered by his brother Set.

To Horus was given the task of teaching the science of light, its properties and its uses for analysis. It was the ultimate constant and as such was the measuring rod of the universe. He showed them the power of the harmonics of light and how to build tools that could cut stone with light. It is unfortunate for mankind that Horus was not a popular tutor. As he was much smaller than the other 'gods', his pupils were inclined to treat him with less respect. His subject was also harder to teach, as it was largely theoretical and would be of use to them only in their future development. He tired of explaining how his instruction was the most important of all the subjects. In fits of anger he would try to convey to them how the sun was the source of that which could eventually raise their descendants to acquire the power of the 'gods'; but his pupils were more concerned with what would affect them in their time. Horus considered his task hopeless and took the problem to Isis, who consulted with Shaitan.

It was recognized by them there could be no immediate solution. Then Shaitan and Isis conceived a brilliant plan to use mankind as the vehicle to carry this critical knowledge into the future. A number of diagrams were devised which, although simple to construct and to remember, incorporated the basic elements of the ultimate relationship between life and matter and the harmonics of light. They had laid down the units of linear measure which would automatically generate the essential harmonics when applied to the geometrical diagrams. The Cainites were informed that those who showed the most promise were to be instructed by Isis, the supreme goddess herself. Until that time, she had always functioned in an administrative capacity. The chosen ones felt greatly honoured and watched with awe as Isis traced out the figures. These figures, she told them, must never be seen by any but the highest intellects. They had magical power and one in particular, which she knew they must preserve at all costs was the pentagram and its divisions.

So she showed them the division of the pentagram that no man had ever seen, that they could never forget, for no mortal man had ever her unveiled.

And she taught them secret numbers that they could write down and told them how, from these secret numbers, the holy number could be known, but never written knowingly.

And she divided her hand, that they should know her not only as 8 but as 18 and that was a secret number, but not the holy number.

And she taught them the reflections, of the circle and of the sphere and the numbers and how to reverse them, lest they should forget the reflections.

And her circle she divided and showed them the divisions of it and the numbers by which they would know it.

And the circle was **360** and **1080** and the numbers of her body she showed them and they were **72** and **36** and **108** and from these numbers was the figure made and the sum of the numbers she showed them and it was **1800**, but this was not the holy number.

And she showed them the number of man and how with her it would unite and they would have the understanding of that which they had in common with her.

But of the number of her father she told them not.

And she showed them a distant star and the planet that bears her name and number to this day. Even she and the mighty Shaitan watched in awe when they saw the Architect of the Universe arrest that wandering orb in the fashion of her sign: *As Above So Below*; the first-ever positive demonstration of the presence of the Great Architect and in a form which expressed approval of the work of Shaitan and Isis.

Then Isis told them of a place on Earth where all she had told them would be marked with standing stones, and she told them of the stone that was her name and how it would show where her final resting place would be.

Although they could not comprehend it at the time, the chosen Cainites knew that, coming as it did from the supreme goddess, it must be vital. So they guarded the secrets jealously. Some eventually pretended to know the ultimate secret contained in the teaching. With the passage of time, some tried to destroy all reference to it, fearing they would be exposed as frauds for having accepted high office in religion, knowing that they were unqualified to be there. However the plan succeeded and those numbers, or even more veiled methods of arriving at them, were passed down through the centuries. May it be our good fortune that the time will come, when men of science will recognize or remember the message they contain.

Of the work of the five you now know, of the jealousy of Set you now know, of the death of Osiris you now know, and of the secrets of that Great Queen, born of the gods, who mothered mankind and yet was a virgin, you now know.

But what came of Shaitan?

The orbiting station fell to earth, of that we can be sure, and with it the last of the Nephilim who comprised the staff of Shaitan; but did Shaitan choose self-destruction? Or is he still present, here on Earth, Rex Mundi (King of the Earth)?

The Elohim looked back at Mars, there could be no return. They looked to the stars again, maybe Orion?

Again one thing is certain, they cannot escape their responsibility; whatever ensued, it was their coming which released an animal intellect into the universe. An intellect which should have evolved over millions of years to allow the ethics of the creature to equate with the intelligence that gave it power.

Their burden – that they left behind them a confused hybrid, handicapped by animal instincts of self-survival, sex and territorial obsessions. Yet this creature carries a brain of such capacity it could unleash immense destructive power. The severed parts of the mind, so cleverly retarded by the Elohim, are already known to exist. It is only a matter of time before, by chance or design, the connection is made. Then we will see the fearful danger in the Man who is Beast:

> Here is the wisdom. Let him that hath the understanding count the number of the beast: for it is the number of man; and his number is 666.

And to the Elohim we say, the guilt is yours, to have left this creature with crippled mind believing that he, like all about him, is part of the work of the Great Architect of Time and Space, is to perpetuate the crime of which you stand accused: that by neglect you would APE the ALMIGHTY.

STOP PRESS

In December 1984 a team of American scientists presented evidence to President Reagan in Washington of what it believes to be the relics of a vanished civilization on Mars. The evidence includes photographs of what the scientists, from Mars Research in Maryland and the Independent Mars Investigation Team of Oakland, California, claim is a mile-wide rock apparently carved in the perfect semblance of a human-like face and several pyramids arranged symmetrically in what appears to be the remains of a city. The photographs, taken in 1976 by an orbiting NASA Viking spacecraft but only recently subjected to detailed scrutiny, show the objects in the Cydonia region of Mars beside what is supposed to be an ancient lake. The 'face', over which the sun would have risen directly, would have formed an island, with the pyramids on the shore beside it. Organiser of the California team Mr Richard Hoagland believes the objects could have been built by an alien civilization which visited Mars about 500,000 years ago – when the planet apparently had a warm, wet period. Whoever the aliens were, says Mr Hoagland, they either perished there or left the way they had come for another star system. But if they left the face as a marker it is possible, he says, they may also have left behind a store or 'library' of technological information. This would be so advanced it would compare with a description of our own civilization as seen by the people of the Stone Age. The Congressional Research Service is being asked to press the U.S. government to launch a joint American-Soviet mission to Mars to investigate the evidence.

Appendix

The Red Serpent

AQUARIUS
How strange are the manuscripts of this friend, great traveller of the unknown. They come together as white light but for one who knows separately, they are the colours of the rainbow; for the artist these six colours unite like magic in his palette and form black.

PISCES
This friend, how would you know him? His name is a mystery but his number is that of a famous seal. How can one describe him? Maybe like the pilot of the everlasting Ark of Noah, impassive like a pillar on his white rock looking beyond the black rock towards the south.

ARIES
In my arduous search, I was trying to hack a way with my sword through the dense vegetation of the woods. I wanted to reach the place of the 'Sleeping BEAUTY' in which some poets can see the QUEEN of a lost kingdom. Desperate to find the way I was aided by the parchments of my friend, they were for me like the thread of ARIADNE.

TAURUS
Thanks to him, from now on with a watchful eye I could make steady progress. I can find the 64 scattered stones of the perfect cube which the brothers of the BEAUTY of the black wood had scattered when they fled from the white fort while they were being pursued by the usurpers.

GEMINI
Reassemble the scattered stones and, working with square and compass, put them back in order; find the line of the meridian in going from East to West, then looking from South to the North and finally in all directions to find the looked-for solution. Station yourself in front of the fourteen stones making a cross. The circle is the ring and crown and the crown forms the diadem of the QUEEN of the Castle.

CANCER
The Mosaic tiles of the sacred place alternate black or white and JESUS like ASMODEUS observes their alignment. I seem incapable of seeing the summit of the secret place of the Sleeping Beauty. Not being HERCULES with magical power, how do I solve the mysterious symbols engraved by the witnesses of the past. In the sanctuary however, is the font, fountain of love, of those who believe reminding us of these words 'BY THIS SIGN YOU WILL CONQUER'.

LEO
I am aware of the scent of the perfume which impregnates the sepulchre of the one I must release. Long ago her name was ISIS, Queen of the benevolent springs, COME TO ME ALL YOU WHO LABOUR AND ARE HEAVY LADEN AND I WILL GIVE YOU REST. Others knew her as MAGDALENE with the celebrated vase full of healing balm. The initiated know her to be NOTRE DAME DES CROSS.

Le Serpent Rouge

VERSEAU
Comme ils sont étranges les manuscrits de cet Ami, grand voyageur de l'inconnu, ils me sont parvenus séparément, pourtant ils forment un tout pour celui qui sait que les couleurs de l'arc-en-ciel donnent l'unité blanche, ou pour l'Artiste qui sous son pinceau, fait des six teintes de sa palette magique, jaillir le noir.

POISSONS
Cet Ami, comment vous le présenter? Son nom demeura un mystère, mais son nombre est celui d'un sceau célèbre. Comment vous le décrire? Peut-être comme le nautonnier de l'arche impérissable, impassible comme une colonne sur son roc blanc, scrutant vers le midi, aus delà du roc noir.

BÉLIER
Dans mon pélérinage éprouvant, je tentais de me frayer à l'épée une voie à travers la végétation inextricable de bois, je voulais parvenir à la demeure de la BELLE endormie en qui certains poètes voient la REINE d'un royaume disparu. Au désespoir de retrouver le chemin, les parchemins de cet Ami furent pour moi le fil d'Ariane.

TAUREAU
Grace à lui, désormais à pas mesures et d'un oeil sur, je puis découvrir les soixante-quatre pierres dispersées du cube parfait, que les Frères de la BELLE du bois noir échappant à la poursuite des usurpateurs, avaient semées en route quant ils s'enfuirent du Fort blanc.

GEMEAUX
Rassembler les pierres éparses, oeuvrer de l'équerre et du compas pour les remettre en ordre régulier, chercher la ligne du méridien en allant de l'Orient à l'Occident, puis regardant du Midi au Nord, enfin en tous sens pour obtenir la solution cherchée, faisant station devant les quatorze pierres marquées d'une croix. Le cercle étant l'anneau et couronne, et lui le diadème de cette REINE du Castel.

CANCER
Les dalles du pavé mosaïque du lieu sacré pouvaient-être alternativement blanches ou noires, et JESUS, comme ASMODEE observer leurs alignements, ma vue semblait incapable de voir le sommet où demeurait cachée la merveilleuse endormie. N'étant pas HERCULE à la puissance magique, comment déchiffrer les mystérieux symboles gravés par les observateurs du passé. Dans le sanctuaire pourtant le bénitier, fontaine d'amour des croyants redonne mémoire de ces mots: PAR CE SIGNE TU le VAINCRAS.

LION
De celle que je désirais libérer, montaient vers moi les effluves du parfum qui imprégnèrent le sépulcre. Jadis les uns l'avaient nommée: ISIS, reine des sources bienfaisantes, VENEZ A MOI VOUS TOUS QUI SOUFFREZ ET QUI ETES ACCABLES ET JE VOUS SOULAGERAI, d'autres: MADELEINE, au célèbre vase plein d'un baume guérisseur. Les initiés savent son nom veritable: NOTRE DAME DES CROSS.

VIRGO

I was like the shepherds of the celebrated painter POUSSIN puzzled by the enigma of 'ET IN ARCADIA EGO'. Would the voice of the blood form an image of our ancestral past. Yes, a light of inspiration floods my mind; now I understand. I know now the fabulous secret and what is more amazing is that when the four knights moved, one of the horses left four hoofprints in the rock. Here is the sign that DELACROIX has given in one of the three paintings in the Chapel of Angels. There is the seventh sentence which a hand has traced; 'DELIVER ME OUT OF THE MIRE, AND LET ME NOT SINK. Two times I.S. emblaming and embalmed'. Miraculous vessel of the eternal White Lady of the Legends.

LIBRA

I began my journey in the shadows and completed it in the light. At the window of the ruined house I looked across the trees denuded by Autumn. At the summit of the mountain, the cross stood out from the crest of the midday sun. It was the fourteenth and the highest of all with 35 cm. Here, then, is my knight's tower on the circuit of the divine horseman of the abyss.

SCORPIO

There is a celestial vision for the one who recalls the four tasks of EM. SIGNOL around the line of the meridian; the same Choir (heart) of the sanctuary from which radiates the source of love for one another. I turn looking at the rose of the P then to that of the S. Then from the S to the P until my mind is dizzy. The spiral in my mind becomes like a monstrous octopus expelling his ink, the shadows absorb the light. I put my hand to my mouth, biting my palm, maybe like OLIER in his coffin. Curses, I know the truth, HE HAS PASSED, in doing GOOD as did HE of the flowery tomb. But how many have pillaged the HOUSE leaving only embalmed corpses and a number of metal things they could not carry? What strange mystery is concealed in the new Temple of SOLOMON, built by the children of ST. VINCENT?

OPHIUCHUS

Cursing the profane in their ashes and those who follow their ways; returning from the darkness while making the gesture of horror at the abyss into which I had plunged. Here is the proof that I knew the secret of the Seal of SOLOMON and I had visited the secret places of this QUEEN. Take Heed my friend, do not add or take away one iota; think and think again, the base lead of my words may contain the purest gold.

SAGITTARIUS

Returning again to the white hill, the sky opens its floodgates. Close to me a presence, its feet in the water, like one who has just received the mark of baptism, I turn again to the east, facing me I see unwinding endless by his coils, the enormous RED SERPENT mentioned in the documents, rigid and bitter, the huge unleashed beast at the foot of the white mountain becomes scarlet with anger.

CAPRICORN

My emotions are elated DELIVER ME OUT OF THE MIRE, immediately I woke up, my dream is over. I meant to tell you that it was a dream I had on this 17th JANUARY, the day of Saint SULPICE, but the nightmare persisted. On reflection, I wish I had told it to you as a fairytale by PERRAULT. In the pages which follow, dear reader, are the results of a dream which nursed me from the bizarre to the unknown. LET HE WHO HAS THE UNDERSTANDING USE IT WITH WISDOM.

VIERGE

J'étais comme les bergers du célèbre peintre POUSSIN, perplexe devant l'énigme: 'ET IN ARCADIA EGO . . .' La voix du sang allait-elle me rendre l'image d'un passé ancestral. Oui, l'éclair du genie traversa ma pensée. Je revoyais, je comprenais! Je savais maintenant ce secret fabuleux, Et merveille lors des sauts des quatre cavaliers, les sabots d'un cheval avaient laissé quatre empreintes sur la pierre, voilà le signe que DELACROIX avait donné dans l'un des trois tableaux de la chapelle des Anges. Voilà la septième sentence qu'une main avait tracée: RETIRE MOI DE LA BOUE, QUE JE N'Y RESTE PAS ENFONCE. Deux fois IS, embaumeuse et embaumée, vase miracle de l'eternelle Dame Blanche des Legéndes.

BALANCE

Commencé dans les ténèbres, mon voyage ne pouvait s'achever qu'en Lumière. A la fenêtre de la maison ruinée, je contemplais à travers les arbres depouillés par l'automme le sommet de la montagne. La croix de crête se détachait sous le soleil du midi, elle était la quatorzième et la plus grande de toutes avec ses 35 centimètres! Me voici donc à mon tour cavalier sur le coursier divin chevauchant l'abîme.

SCORPION

Vision céleste pour celui qui se souvient des quatre oeuvres de EM. SIGNOL autour de la ligne du Méridian, au choeur même du sanctuaire d'où rayonne cette source d'amour des un pour les autres, je pivote sur moi-même passant du regard la rose du P à celle du l'S, puis de l'S au P . . . et la spirale dans mon esprit devenant comme un poulpe monstrueux expulsant son encre, les ténèbres absorbent la lumière, j'ai le vertige et je porte ma main à ma bouche mordant instinctivement ma paume, peut-être comme OLIER dans son cerceuil. Malédiction, je comprends la vérité, IL EST PASSE, mais lui aussi en faisant LE BIEN, ainsi queé CELUI de la tombe fleurie. Mais combien ont saccagé la MAISON, ne laissant que des cadavres embaumés et nombres de métaux qu'ils n'avaient pu emporter. Quel étrange mystère recèle le nouveau temple de SALOMON édifié par les enfants de Saint VINCENT.

SERPENTAIRE

Maudissent les profanateurs dans leurs cendres et ceux qui vivent sur leurs traces, sortant de l'abîme où j'étais plongé en accomplissant le geste d'horreur: sceau voici la preuve que du aceau de SALOMON je connais le secret, que de cette REINE j'ai visité les demeures cachées. A ceci, Ami Lecteur, garde toi d'ajouter ou de retrancher un iota . . . médite, Médite encore, le vil plomb de mon écrit contient peut-être l'or le plus pur.

SAGITTAIRE

Revenant alors à la blanche coline, le ciel ayant ouvert ses vannes, il me sembla pres de moi sentir une présence, les pieds dans l'eau comme celui qui vient de recevoir la marque du baptême, me retournant vers l'est, face à moi je vis déroulant sans fin ses anneaux, l'énorme SERPENT ROUGE cité dans les parchemins, salée et amère, l'énorme bête déchaînée devant au pied de ce mont blanc, rouge de colère.

CAPRICORNE

Mon émotion fut grande, 'RETIRE MOI DE LA BOUE' disais-je, et mon réveil fut immédiat. J'ai omis de vous dire en effet que c'était un songe que j'avais fait ce 17 janvier, fête de Saint SULPICE. Par la suite mon trouble persistant, j'ai voulu après reflexions d'usage vous le relater un conte de PERRAULT. Voici donc Ami Lecteur, dans les pages qui suivent le résultat d'un rêve m'ayant bercé dans le monde de l'étrange à l'inconnu. A celui qui PASSE de FAIR LE BIEN.

Bibliography and Further Reading

ALLEN, PAUL M., *A Christian Rosenkreutz Anthology* (Rudolf Steiner Pub: USA, 1981)

AMORC, *Rosicrucian Manual* (Supreme Grand Lodge of AMORC: San Jose, California, 1918)

APULEIUS, LUCIUS, *The Golden Ass* (Penguin Books: London, 1950)

BAIGENT, MICHAEL, LEIGH, RICHARD and LINCOLN, HENRY, *The Holy Blood and The Holy Grail*, (Johnathan Cape: London, 1982)

BARBER, MALCOLM, *The Trials of the Templars* (Cambridge University Press: London, 1978)

BLAVATSKY, *Isis Unveiled, Volumes 1 & 2* (Theosophical University Press: Pasadena, California, 1976)

BLAVATSKY, *The Secret Doctrine, Volumes 1 & 2* (Theosophical University Press: Pasadena, California, 1976)

BLUM, JEAN, *Le Message des Cathares* (Frererio De Ferrières, 1982)

BOUDET, HENRI, *La Vrai Langue Celtic et le Cromleck de Rennes-les-Bains* (Claude Boumendil: Nice, 1886)

BUDGE, E. A. WALLIS, *The Egyptian Book of The Dead* (Dover Publications: New York, 1967)

BUDGE, E. A. WALLIS, *An Egyptian Hieroglyphic Dictionary, Vols. 1 & 2*, (Dover Publications: New York, 1978)

BUDGE, E. A. WALLIS, *The Gods of The Egyptians, Volumes 1 & 2*, (Dover Publications: New York, 1969)

BUDGE, E. A. WALLIS, *Osiris and The Egyptian Resurrection, Vols. 1 & 2*, 1973 New York (Dover Publications: New York, 1973)

BUREN, ELIZABETH VAN, *The Sign of The Dove* (Neville Spearman: Sudbury, Suffolk, 1983)

LIDDELL, MACGREGOR and MATHERS, *The Key of Soloman the King* (George Redway, London, 1888)

CAMPBELL, JOSEPH, *Creative Mythology* (Penguin: London, 1976)

CHARLES, R. H., *The Book of Enoch* (SPCK: London, 1917)

CHARROUX, ROBERT, *Lost Worlds, Scientific Secrets of the Ancients* (Collins: London, 1971)

CHATELAIN, MAURICE, *Our Ancestors Came From Outer Space* (Pan Books: London, 1980)

CLARK, KENNETH, *Leonardo Da Vinci* (Penguin Books: London, 1959)

CLUBE, VICTOR and NAPIER, BILL, *The Cosmic Serpent* (Faber and Faber: London, 1982)

DELOUX, JEAN-PIERRE and BRETIGNY, JAQUES, *Rennes le Château Capitale Sécrète de l'Histoire de France* (Kister: Geneva)

DONNELLY, IGNATIUS, *Atlantis: The Antediluvian World* (Dover Publications: New York, 1976)

DONNELLY, IGNATIUS, *The Destruction of Atlantis Ragnorac: The Age of Fire and Gravel* (Multimedia Publications: New York, 1971)

DORÉ, GUSTAVE, *Perrault's Fairy Tales*, Dover Publications: Paris, 1867)

ESCHENBACH, WOLFRAM VON, *Parzival*, (Penguin: London, 1982)

FEUGERE, PIERRE, MAXENT, LOUIS SAINT and KOKER, GASTON DE, *Le Serpent Rouge* (SRES Vérités Anciènnes: 1981)

FITZGERALD, EDWARD, *Rubáiyát of Omar Kháyyám* (Murray: London, 1952)

FRAZER, SIR J. G., *The Golden Bough* (Macmillan: London, 1925)

GRANT, KENNETH, *Aleister Crowley and the Hidden God* (Frederick Muller: London, 1973)

GRANT, KENNETH, *Cults of the Shadow* (Frederick Muller: London, 1975)

GRANT, KENNETH, *Hidden God* (Frederick Muller: London 1973)

GRANT, KENNETH, *Nightside of Eden* (Frederick Muller: London, 1975)

GRANT, KENNETH, *Outside the Circle of Time* (Frederick Muller: London 1980)

GRANT, KENNETH, *The Magical Revival* (Frederick Muller: London, 1972)

GRANT, KENNETH & CROWLEY, ALEISTER, *The Hidden God* (Frederick Muller: London, 1973)

HALL, MANLY, *Codex Rosae Crucis* (The Philosophical Research Society Inc: 1972)

HECKETHORNE, C. W., *The Secret Societies of all ages and Countries*

HIGGINS, GODFREY, *Anacalypsis, The Saitic Isis Languages Nations and Religions, Volumes 1 & 2* (Heath Research: London, 1972)

HILTON, WALTER, *The Scale of Perfection* (Burns Oats: London, 1944)

ILLINGWORTH, J. E., *Divine Immenence*, (Macmillan: London, 1898)

JAMES, E. O., *The Ancient Gods* (Weidenfield and Nicolson: London, 1960)

KEEL, OTHMAR, *The Symbolism of the Biblical World* (Seabury Press: London, 1978)

KITTO, JOHN, *The Illustrated Family Bible Old and New Testament* (James Sangster: London, 1916)

LASSERVE, J. T., *Rechèrches Historiques sur la Ville d'Alet et son Ancien Diocese* (Philippe Schrauben: Carcassonne, 1877)

LÉVI, ELIPHAS, *The Key of the Mysteries* (Rider: London, 1977)

LÉVI, ELIPHAS, *Transcendental Magic* (Rider: London, 1968)

LÉVI, ELIPHAS, *The History of Magic* (Rider: London, 1913)

MATHERS, LIDDELL MACGREGOR, *Clavicula Salimonis* (Routledge & Kegan Paul: London, 1888)

MACGREGOR, S. L., *The Book of Sacred Magic of Abra Melin The Mage* (The De Lawrence: New York, 1948)

MEAD, G. R. S., *Thrice Greatest Hermes* (John Watkins: London, 1964)

OESTERLEY, ROBINSON, *Hebrew Religion: Its Origin and Development* (SPCK: London, 1930)

PEMBER, C. H., *Earth's Earliest Ages* (Hodder and Stoughton: London, 1907)

QUENHEN, RENÉ, *Les Châteaux Cathares et les Autres* (René Quenhen: Montesguieu Volvestre)

RIVIÈRE, JACQUES, *The Fabuleux Trésor de Rennes-le-Chàteau* (Belisane: Nice, 1983)

SANDERS, N. K., *The Epic of Gilgamesh* (Penguin Books: London, 1960)

SKINNER, J. RALSTON, *The Source of Measures* (Wizards Bookshelf: San Diego, 1982)

SCHONFIELD, HUGH, *The Essene Odyssey* (Element Books: Longmead, Shaftesbury, Dorset, 1984)

SUMPTION, JOHNATHAN, *The Albigensian Crusade* (Faber and Faber: London, 1978)

TEMPLE, ROBERT, K. G., *The Sirius Mystery* (Futura Publications: London, 1976)

TENNYSON, ALFRED LORD, *The Holy Grail* (Stranan: London, 1870)

TENNYSON, ALFRED LORD, *Idylls of the Kings* (Penguin Books: London, 1961)

THOMPKINS, PETER, *Secrets of The Great Pyramid* (Penguin Books: London, 1973)

THUILLIER, JACQUES, *Tout l'oeuvre Peint de Poussin* (Rizzoli: Milano, 1974)

VELIKOVSKY, IMMANUEL, *Worlds in Collision* (Victor Gollancz: London, 1969)

VOGH, JAMES, *Arachne Arising: the 13th Sign* (Granada: London, 1977)

WAITE, ARTHUR EDWARD, *Real History of the Rosicrucians* (Steiner Books: London, 1982)

WAITE, ARTHUR EDWARD, *The Brotherhood of the Rosy Cross* (Rider: London)

WAITE, ARTHUR EDWARD, *The Hidden Church of the Holy Grail*, (Rebman: London, 1909)

WARD, J. S. M., *Who Was Hiram Abiff?* (A. Lewis: Shepperton)

WATSON, IAN, *Jesus the Evidence* (Weidenfeld & Nicolson: London, 1984)

WENDT, HERBERT, *It Began in Babel* (Weidenfeld & Nicolson: London, 1958)

WENDT, HERBERT, *Encyclopedia Britannica*, (Weidenfeld & Nicolson: London, 1961)

Two further books are shortly to be published on the Rennes-le-Château mystery – *Refuge of the Apocalypse – Doorway into other Dimensions* by Elizabeth Von Buren and *Overture sur l'invisible* by H. Elie.

Index

References in **bold** type relate to pages containing relevant illustrations

Acknowledgments

The author and publishers wish to thank the Institut Géographic
National for permission to reproduce the map of the Rennes Valley
Carte IGN au 1/50,000 (No. 1347) and also *Encyclopaedia Britannica*
for permission to quote from the 1961 printing of the 14th edition.

p.39 from Isis in *Encyclopaedia Britannica*,
   14th edition (1961)
p.125 from Devil in *Encyclopaedia Britannica*,
   14th edition (1961)
p.160/1 from Round Table in *Encyclopaedia Britannica*,
   14th edition (1961)
p.274 from Druidism in *Encyclopaedia Britannica*,
   14th edition (1961)